The Prefigurative Imagination of John Keats

The Prefigurative Imagination of John Keats

A Study of the Beauty-Truth Identification and Its Implications

By

NEWELL F. FORD

ARCHON BOOKS
HAMDEN, CONNECTICUT
1966

Originally published 1951
STANFORD UNIVERSITY PUBLICATIONS
UNIVERSITY SERIES
LANGUAGE AND LITERATURE, VOL. IX, NO. 2

Reprinted 1966 with permission
in an unaltered and unabridged edition

Library of Congress Catalog Card Number: 66-15387
Printed in the United States of America

PREFACE

Keats's "prefigurative imagination" is not to be understood as the totality of his imagination, but as one strain in his imagination, one current in its flow which, during certain rapturous moments, caused him to identify "beauty" with "truth."

"Take every man hys turn, as for hys tyme." In this book I take my turn in unraveling the meaning of Keats's celebrated identification of "beauty" and "truth." Unraveling is the primary purpose; the secondary purpose is to reinterpret many of the poems in the light of the findings. The justification of another attempt to explain Keats's enigma is, I believe, the use of a method not previously applied to the problem. Clerklike, I began simply by making a concordance of every occurrence of the word "truth" in Keats's writings. Starting with no preconceptions, I hoped to learn whether Keats had left any clues as to his meaning, whether this meaning was traditional and "Platonic" or perhaps private and personal. Did his famous equation contain no more than an "emotive" meaning (I. A. Richards' solution) ; was it, perhaps, "an uneducated conclusion, albeit pardonable in one so young" (Quiller-Couch) ?

Once the concordance was assembled, the study of contexts, and contexts of contexts, began. Gradually meanings emerged, and it was soon clear that Keats was not always faithful to the accepted usage of words (as had long been known with respect to his use of "philosophy" and "abstract"). It became necessary to add other words to the list, such as "essence" and "essential," "empyreal," "ethereal," "spiritual," "sensations," "abstract" (no complete listing was available), "speculation," "imagination," "fancy." A concordance for all occurrences of these words in Keats's prose (his letters, essays, and marginalia) is included in the Appendix of this book. As for the verse, the invaluable Concordance of D. L. Baldwin, L. B. Broughton, and their collaborators was happily at hand. One or two supplements to their listings are here included.

Word meanings affect poem meanings. The result is that orthodox views have not always been confirmed, especially on *Endymion,* and to some extent also on the "Ode to a Nightingale," the "Ode on a Grecian Urn," "Lamia," and the "Bright star" sonnet. The final chapter reports that Keats sometimes nurtured a relativistic view of truth—despite the fact that the Absolute was widely worshiped in his day. Could it be shown that he read Plato or, having read, understood or "took" to him, the story might be different. Having missed Plato, and also a university training, Keats was left to grow up on the English poets. Hence his imagination and his vocabulary were molded by what he called "eternal poetry" rather than by logic or philosophical inquiry. He habitually thought in images, both in prose and in verse, and seems to have had little inclination for abstract ideas. Images, especially when vivid and blissful, sometimes replaced reality for him, but the statements that accompanied these images were less metaphysical than naïve. For this reason Shelley's resplendent tribute is slightly inappropriate: Keats "beacons from the abode where the Eternal are," but we are more likely to find him in the Poets' Elysium than in Plato's heaven.

That Keats was gifted with something more than a vivid sensorium it would be foolish to deny. Though his poems do not always persuade us of this fact, his letters give ample and dramatic testimony. And in such poems as the two versions of "Hyperion," "To J. H. Reynolds, Esq.," and even the early "Sleep and Poetry," he was as soberly reflective as in his most serious and meditative letters. The story of his remarkable mental growth, of his suffering, meditation, sobriety, and sanity has been ably told in more than one book. I therefore take this for granted, devoting myself to the inspection of his uses of "truth," particularly in relation to "beauty." Since the beauty-truth identification represents the more naïve side of Keats's mind, this procedure makes for disproportion so far as space is concerned; six of the eight chapters are devoted to the "truth" identified with "beauty," and to the bearing of this on the poems; only one chapter is given to the "truth" not so identified. There are several reasons for this disproportion: (1) The elucidation of the "truth" identified with "beauty" (here called prefigurative truth) is a fairly complex matter, and the consequences of the elucidation lead out in several directions when applied to the interpretation of poems. (2) Measured by duration, the prefigurative moments ("eternal moments") in Keats's life would not add up to a very imposing figure, but measured by intensity and value they are quite as important as his nonecstatic and soberly reflective existence. (3) Keats's notion of prefigurative truth is closely allied to his absorbing interest in sleep and dreams, and illuminates his ultimately violent condemnation of "the dreamer tribe." (4) His conception is really a personal version of a paradisal yearning as old as the history of the race, a yearning frequently converted into belief, or something approaching belief, by romantic writers, as a kind of corollary of the new faith in imagination. (5) To a considerable degree Keats's mental evolution is emblemed in his gradual movement from certitude to skepticism with respect to his celebrated beauty-truth proposition. (6) The final chapter, like the concluding portion of chapter vii, tends to set the balance straight, for in his non-prefigurative usages of "truth" Keats reveals himself as a penetrating thinker, an acute judge of life and art—sane, healthy, sublunar, no victim of romantic illusion.

If this is kept in mind, the necessary emphasis in this study on the naïve element in Keats's thinking—what he called his "young minded" phase—will not be construed as an attempt to diminish his stature as a poet. In the same way, the revealing of the strong amorous strain in his opulently sensuous imagination should not disparage or devaluate but humanize him. For his well-rounded, wholesome normality we can well be thankful. If he was more an impassioned lover than a philosophical idealist, need we therefore be troubled? He loved beauty in all its forms with a passion akin to religion. There is nothing gross in this, despite the fact that his love, when a mythic or real woman was its object, may not seem disembodied enough for some tastes. He was but twenty-one years of age, an apprentice, when he wrote *Endymion,* twenty-three when he wrote the great Odes. He was in his grave at an age when Shakespeare had not yet written *Venus and Adonis.* Yet "he is with Shakespeare."

I wish to acknowledge my indebtedness to the many scholars who by their industry, patience, and critical discernment have gradually built up our present conception of Keats. Without their help I might have wandered aimlessly. To name them all would require a bibliography of writings on and editions of Keats (cf. the up-to-date bibliography by J. R. McGillivray, 1949), but I wish particularly to confess my debt to the scrupulous editions and discerning commentaries of H. Buxton Forman, Maurice Buxton Forman, Ernest de Sélincourt, and H. W. Garrod; and to the indispensable biographical and critical works of Sidney Colvin, Amy Lowell, Clarence Dewitt Thorpe, J. Middleton Murry, H. W. Garrod, Robert Bridges, A. C. Bradley, and Claude Lee Finney. Where I mention these, or other, names in the text, however, I should not be understood to be weighing the value of their contributions; for my references to previous studies are made for a quite different reason: simply to show at what points my conclusions diverge from standard interpretations.

I take this opportunity to thank the persons who have assisted me by reading my manuscript and offering helpful criticism: Professors Myron F. Brightfield, Gordon McKenzie, Arthur G. Brodeur, and Samuel C. Chew. My deepest debt is owed to Professor Richard F. Jones, who has given me constant support and encouragement, and to Professor Benjamin P. Kurtz, who has been my guide and mainstay from the beginning. I might never have tracked down Keats's usage of "essence" if Professor Kurtz had not sent me on the quest.

NEWELL F. FORD

STANFORD UNIVERSITY
STANFORD, CALIFORNIA
February 1951

CONTENTS

I. TWO KINDS OF TRUTH

"Beauty" and "truth," as they existed for Keats, have been like water to many scholarly sieves. But their fascination, heritage of all the post-Platonic centuries, is not the less for this. Like Donne's falling star, they may be fated forever to elude the grasp; yet every new adventurer hopes to discover the mysterious law of marriage by which Keats, priestlike, made "beauty" and "truth" one flesh.

The "law" herein discovered, or seemingly discovered, might be called the "prefigurative veracity" of the imagination. It was stumbled upon by a more or less lexicographic method: the collation of all occurrences of "truth" in Keats's writings, the study of their contexts, and the fixing, wherever possible, of the principal categories. Through this process, but avoiding the detours and false starts, this book now proposes to lead the reader, in the belief that the accumulation of evidence should precede the establishment of conclusions. He may feel at times like the wildered Endymion, wandering benighted under earth and sea, but from these dark regions he will ultimately ascend, not perhaps to mystic heavens where light shines changeless and eternal, but at least to the daylight where human beings, and poets among them, commonly spend their lives.

It may be said in anticipation that two main categories of meaning will reveal themselves in Keats's usage of the word "truth." Of these two categories, here labeled "prefigurative" and "non-prefigurative,"[1] the latter can be found more frequently in Keats's writings, and in some respects is more characteristic of his thought. Yet it has received slight attention from critics, who have been more readily attracted by the beauty-truth identification (herein called "prefigurative" truth). Why these labels have been chosen will presently become clear.

Since the non-prefigurative usage of "truth" offers comparatively few difficulties of definition, whereas the beauty-truth identification has perplexed students as long as they have been aware of the problem,[2] the non-

---

[1] Though "non-prefigurative" is not a very specific label, it conveniently covers the various comparative and evaluative judgments which Keats called "truths." To classify these truths as "relativistic" (a term that conveys Keats's own estimate of their verity) was tempting, but a few exceptions make the label inappropriate.

[2] Since 1880, that is, when Matthew Arnold attempted, not very clarifyingly, a paraphrase: " . . . to see things in their beauty is to see things in their truth, and Keats knew it." See "John Keats," *Essays in Criticism*, Second Series (London: Macmillan and Company, 1898), p. 116; the essay had originally appeared as the introduction to selections from Keats's poetry in Ward's English Poets, 1880.

prefigurative sense of the word will be reserved for the final chapter. In the meantime it will be necessary to examine the beauty-truth identification in considerable detail. The reward for such painstakingness will, it is hoped, be more than an accurate definition of a baffling usage. For this definition leads to an understanding of the close relation between rapture and optimistic credence in Keats's poems. His capacity for fervor was perhaps greater than has been suspected; in any event, it was "the elevation of the moment" that produced his celebrated identification of "beauty" and "truth" and that will illuminate not a few passages in his poems.

The most familiar among Keats's usages of "truth" is, of course, the "Beauty is truth, truth beauty . . ." of the "Ode on a Grecian Urn." Yet probably nothing that Keats wrote has been so variously understood. There is one other statement of the identity of "beauty" and "truth" in his writings, viz., in Letter 31,[3] and two further statements, in Letters 32 and 98,[4] bring the words into close association. Partly because identification of words so famous in lineage is itself spectacular, critics have frequently assumed that here is, as A. C. Bradley wrote, "the central article of the faith of Keats."[5]

Whether or not the "central article" of Keats's faith is here formulated, or whether indeed he had a single faith, the four statements suggest a salient category in his usage of "truth." A question must be asked immediately, however. Does this category include all four of the statements in which "beauty" and "truth" are either equated or associated? Is an identification the same as a coupling? Obviously, it would be unwise to begin with such an assumption, and even unwise to conclude that the two statements of identification have the same meaning. The "Ode" was written in 1819, Letter 31 in 1817. The letter was a prose statement, essentially reflective; the "Ode" was an act of intuitive creation. Perhaps their purport is the same or similar; if so, this can be demonstrated inductively, not deductively. We ought to begin with the fact that the "Ode" had not, while the letter had, been written in 1817. The prime question then becomes: What did Keats mean when he set down the enigmatic formula of the letter: "What the imagination seizes as beauty must be truth . . ."?

In this letter, addressed to his friend Benjamin Bailey, he generously

---

[3] "What the imagination seizes as beauty must be truth . . ."—Letter 31, p. 67. The reference here, and all references to the letters hereafter, assume the edition of M. B. Forman, *The Letters of John Keats* (New York: Oxford University Press, 1935). A later edition of the letters, dated 1947, conforms in pagination to the 1935 edition, except that the order of Letters 1 and 2 is reversed, and four new, brief letters are printed as addenda, on pp. 530–32.

[4] Letter 32, p. 71; Letter 98, p. 259.

[5] "Keats and 'Philosophy,'" *A Miscellany* (London: Macmillan and Company, 1929), p. 189.

amplified the formula, rewording it several times and citing specific examples from his own and from Milton's poetry. Consequently this letter, together with *Paradise Lost* and *Endymion* (as will be shortly evident), comprise the context of the equation; these we must study if we hope to seize Keats's meaning.

As might be supposed, virtually every critic has made some attempt to explain the letter. No one, however, has given the entire letter a close and continuous scrutiny (in published form, at least), no one has paraphrased more than a few of its phrases and sentences, and few have sought to explain Keats's words simply and untechnically, preserving the fervid but naïve spirit in which they appear to have been written.

The writer of this letter was a young man, just twenty-two, and still "young minded" as he called himself later.[6] He had not studied at a university, was unfamiliar with philosophical writings, and had only recently escaped from a restrictive apprenticeship in medicine. Exulting in his freedom, he had thrown himself excitedly into the poetic life, reading Spenser and Milton and Shakespeare with excited fervor, impatient to create and to enjoy. And now, on November 22, 1817, when he wrote the letter to Bailey, he had reached the mid-point of the last book of *Endymion*, his first poetic undertaking of any magnitude; he had not always been certain that he could carry it through, but now he was almost at the end. He had a right to be glad, a right to rejoice in his dedication to poetry.

Something like this is the spirit and tone of Letter 31. Every word is charged with excitement and ardor, written, one would think, almost in the same mood as poetry is created. In fact, he is "mounted on the wings of the imagination so high," as he suddenly realizes at one point in the letter, that he feels it needful to check his excitement and to proceed with more caution. Let us not look too eagerly, then, for the recondite; such youthful fervor may be naïve rather than philosophical. Now for the text itself:

O I wish I was as certain of the end of all your troubles as that of your momentary start about the authenticity of the imagination. I am certain of nothing but of the holiness of the heart's affections and the truth of imagination—What the imagination seizes as beauty must be truth—whether it existed before or not—for I have the same idea of all our passions as of love they are all in their sublime, creative of essential beauty. In a word, you may know my favorite speculation by my first book and the little song I sent in my last[7]—which is a representation from the fancy of the probable mode of operating

---

[6] In December 1818, more than a year after Letter 31 had been written. See Letter 98, p. 259.

[7] "My first book" is Book I of *Endymion*, and "the little song" is the lyric "O Sorrow," copied into Keats's previous letter to Bailey (Letter 28, p. 62), and appearing as the Indian maid's lament in *Endymion*, Book IV, ll. 146 ff. (hereafter cited as IV, 146 ff.) References to the poems, here and hereafter, assume the edition by H. W. Garrod (Oxford: The Clarendon Press, 1939).

in these matters. The imagination may be compared to Adam's dream—he awoke and found it truth. . . . However it may be, O for a life of sensations rather than of thoughts! It is 'a vision in the form of youth' a shadow of reality to come . . . Adam's dream will do here and seems to be a conviction that imagination and its empyreal reflection is the same as human life and its spiritual repetition . . .[8]

This is not the whole of Keats's explanation. But in these few sentences there are enough problems to occupy us for some time.

Perhaps the first thing to notice is that the poet's bold proposition is linked with, indeed predicated on, "the holiness of the heart's affections." Of not less importance is the label which he uses for his proposition once he has given it its initial and positive statement: "my favorite speculation," he calls it, as if he were not quite sure of its truth. And a little later he adds, in a sentence omitted from the above quotation: "[this speculation] has come as auxiliary to another favorite speculation of mine." Remembering this, and sensing also the wishfulness in the *"must be* truth" of the original statement, we need not too hastily assume that Keats has here given expression to an inalterable creed or "philosophy."

Like a good instructor, he directs Bailey to two specific illustrations of his equation (both in *Endymion*), and to an analogy or prototype, Adam's dream in *Paradise Lost*. Actually, as we shall soon see, Adam's dream is as much an illustration as an analogy, except in the sense that Milton's imagination, not Keats's, created it. Let us turn to Adam's dream; it will help us, though not without some intervening difficulty, to determine what part of "my first book" (almost one thousand lines long) Keats had in mind. The dream is found in Book VIII of the epic (ll. 449 ff.), where Adam is overcome with sleep in the midst of a colloquy with God, a colloquy in which he had requested some alleviation of his solitude. While he sleeps he dreams; the dream is a true wish-fulfillment, depicting the creation of a "lovely fair" female form. When he awakes, to his amazement he finds the dream to be true: Eve stands by his side in the flesh, exactly as he saw her in the dream. Suffused with amorous bliss, straightway he leads her "to the nuptial bower."

Had Adam paused to characterize his dream with respect to the function it performed, he might have called it, as Keats did in Letter 31, "a shadow of reality to come." It served as a veracious foreshowing or prefiguration of substantial existence. In the same way, Keats seems to be saying, the imagination functions when it creates "truth" out of "beauty."

It should be noticed in passing that Adam's dream is a love-dream, and

---

[8] Letter 31, pp. 67–68. Keats's idiosyncrasies in capitalization and his misspellings are so irregular and capricious as to have no discernible significance. They are not retained in the passage quoted. Unless otherwise specified, the same can be assumed for subsequent quotations from the letters.

that not only was Keats's proposition linked with "the holiness of the heart's affections," but when he referred in his second sentence to "all our passions . . . in their sublime," he mentioned only one of these—love. It was clearly uppermost in his mind. The importance of love in Keats's equation of "beauty" with "truth" will be dealt with later. At this point it is sufficient to notice that both Adam's dream and *Endymion* are concerned with the same human experience, and that Keats was therefore consistent in drawing his illustrations from these sources.

Since two of his illustrations are drawn from his own poem, the next step is to study the designated passages. But here two difficulties arise: (1) The song "O Sorrow" does not, on first scrutiny at least, show much resemblance to Adam's dream or to Book I of *Endymion*; and (2) a letter of later date, written by Keats to his publisher, appears to mark out a specific passage in Book I as an example of his beauty-truth, even though this passage appears to show no resemblance to Adam's dream. The consideration of "O Sorrow" will therefore be delayed (see chapter iv) until we can know more exactly what Keats meant by the beauty-truth in his first book. Did he, we must ask, really mean that *all* of Book I illustrated his conception (as he seems to say in Letter 31), or did he mean that a single passage embodied it (as he seems to say in the letter to his publisher)?

In the letter to his publisher he offered an emendation of the lines beginning:

> Behold
> Wherein lies happiness Peona? fold—

The emendation reads:

> Wherein lies happiness? In that which becks
> Our ready minds to fellowship divine;
> A fellowship with essence, . . .

In explanation of the alteration Keats wrote:

The whole thing must I think have appeared to you, who are a consecutive man, as a thing almost of mere words—but I assure you that when I wrote it it was a regular stepping of the imagination towards a truth. . . . It set before me at once the gradations of happiness even like a pleasure thermometer . . .[9]

On the strength of this letter, it has sometimes been assumed that Keats referred on both occasions (Letter 31 and Letter 42) to the cardinal passage beginning, "Wherein lies happiness? . . ." (*Endymion*, I, 777 ff.—emended version). We shall presently see why it is misleading to delimit Keats's

---

[9] Letter 42, pp. 90–91.

illustration of his beauty-truth in this way. Nevertheless the letter to the publisher proves that the poet regarded at least one passage in Book I as "*a truth*" intuited by the imagination, and accordingly this passage demands our attention. We need to know what resemblance, if any, it shows to Adam's dream.

Familiar to every student of Keats, the passage on "the gradations of happiness" consists of a simple hedonistic hierarchy or "pleasure thermometer," as the poet called it. Four[10] gradations or levels are designated: the pleasure derived from a rose leaf (and possibly other beauties of the natural world), the pleasure produced by music and its associations, and the pleasures of friendship and of love. The criterion is evidently the degree of pleasure in any category, love being "the chief intensity."

There is, however, a source of perplexity in the passage that we have not touched upon and that we scarcely dare to pass over—namely, the troublesome phrase, "fellowship with essence." Critical opinion has repeatedly accepted this phrase and the passage built around it as a "clue" and "key" to the meaning and plan of Keats's entire poem.[11] Taking "essence" in its transcendental sense, numerous critics have interpreted Keats's "pleasure thermometer" as an idealistic or specifically neo-Platonic hierarchy, and accordingly have read the entire poem as an allegory of the poet-soul in quest of transcendental Beauty.[12] It would take us too far afield at this point to show why these "mystic" interpretations are inappropriate. Elsewhere I have presented the evidence in its entirety.[13] Suffice it here to say that Keats was almost unquestionably using the word "essence" as a synonym for "a thing of beauty" or "shape of beauty" (I, 1, 12), examples of which he enu-

---

[10] There is a slight ambiguity in Keats's reference to the highest level (cf. the reference of "these" in I, 800), but if he had a fifth level in mind, he forgot all about it in his fervent panegyric of love (the fourth and "tip-top" level). The panegyric monopolizes the next fifty lines and more.

[11] It would be hard to find evidence showing that Keats shared this view of the passage, or even if he did, that the "mazy error" of his poem, written with confessed lack of plan over a period of six to eight months, very precisely follows the scheme propounded in the passage.

[12] Among the critics committed to this view (allowing, of course, for minor variations) may be mentioned Sidney Colvin, Ernest de Sélincourt, Robert Bridges (with certain reservations), H. I'A. Fausset, John Middleton Murry, Clarence D. Thorpe, Ernest Bernbaum, and Claude Lee Finney, the latter of whom brought the neo-Platonic interpretation to a categoric climax in 1936. The recent book by Werner Beyer (*Keats and the Daemon King*, [New York: Oxford University Press, 1947]) insists even more emphatically on the transcendental message.

[13] For the full presentation of evidence, and citations from "transcendental" interpretations, see Newell F. Ford, "The Meaning of 'Fellowship with Essence' in *Endymion*," *PMLA*, LXII (December 1947), 1061–76.

merated: the sun, the moon, trees old and young, daffodils and their green world, clear rills, musk-rose blooms, imagined elysiums for the mighty dead, lovely tales, the passion poesy (I, 1–29); rose leaves, music's kiss, old songs and prophesyings, lullabies, friendship, and love (I, 782–801). Without presenting the full body of evidence, we have only to compare 11. 25–26:

> Nor do we merely *feel these essences*
> For one short hour;

where "these essences" refers unequivocally to the "things" or "shapes" of beauty enumerated in 11. 1–24, with 1. 795:

> *Feel* we *these things?* . . .

where "these things" refers unmistakably to rose leaves and the various manifestations of music.

On the strength of these revealing parallels, augmented by a complete collation of Keats's usages of "essence," and by a comparison of the emended version of his passage with the draft ("blending pleasurable" was converted into "fellowship with essence"), we can conclude that "fellowship with essence" signified to Keats no wedding of finite mind with Infinite Being, but a kind of imaginative "empathy" with individual, particular, concrete "things of beauty."[14] "Essence" was a loose name for entities attractive to the aesthetic sense, entities both of the objective world and of the imagination. If Keats had written "An *essense* of beauty is a joy for ever," or "fellowship with essen*ces*," his meaning would not have been missed.

If we return now to the passage thus summarily elucidated, and read it in the light of the later statement, that "it was a regular stepping of the imagination towards a truth," we can see that some progress has been made. For if Keats chose to call his "pleasure thermometer" "a truth," he can scarcely have been referring to some transcendental or mystic illumination. He was simply labelling his gradational description of aesthetic pleasure as a "truth" of his experience or his conjecture—a value judgment, in short. And perhaps he was intentionally limiting its temporal applicability, or playing the part of caution, when he inserted the qualification: "*when I wrote it* it was . . . a truth."

---

[14] "Empathy" will not impress all readers as a satisfactory description of the "self-destroying" "sort of oneness" and "blending pleasurable" which Keats was describing. I use the term because I know of no other single-word label more appropriate, and because there are many indications in Keats's writings of his interest in, and of his further attempts to describe, this experience of imaginative fusion. The subject is treated more fully in my article, "Keats, Empathy, and 'The Poetical Character,'" *Studies in Philology*, XLV (July 1948), 477–90. See also Richard H. Fogle, "Empathic Imagery in Keats and Shelley," *PMLA*, LXI (March 1946), 163–91.

Taken by itself, the description of this "truth" in Letter 42 presents no difficulties; it is only when Letter 31 and Letter 42 are read together that uncertainty enters. We have seen that Adam's dream was regarded by Keats as the prototype of the "truth" of Letter 31, and that Book I of *Endymion* was cited by Keats as an illustration of such truth from his own poetry. Obviously, the imaginative "truth" referred to in Letter 42 is part of Book I of *Endymion*, yet it is, as we now perceive, a statement of value. Between Adam's dream and this value judgment there seems to be no similarity whatsoever, except that they are both apprehended by the imagination. Did Keats mean that truth came to him *qua* images, in vision as it were, flashing upon his mind wordlessly, later to be transmuted to words? If this was his meaning there still remain two serious difficulties, one of temporal reference and one of extensional reference. Adam's dream is a prevision with a future reference, whereas the "pleasure thermometer" is a statement (or vision?) with a present reference. The one is a visual glimpse of future, *extensional* reality; the other is an intuitive judgment of *value*.[15]

Perhaps it is too much to expect that a poet, especially a "young minded" poet, should have been aware of these differences. He was not a logician, and the distinction between subjective value and extensional substance may never have occurred to him, or if it did, may not have seemed important. Hence it is scarcely possible to decide whether Keats supposed he was speaking of one and the same "truth" in both Letter 31 and Letter 42.

Whether or not he was aware of the distinction, however, there is good evidence that the two species of "truth" were closely connected in his mind. Thus far overlooked by commentators, this evidence reveals why Adam's dream was so important in the poet's theory of the imagination, and why he associated this dream with the "pleasure thermometer." First of all, as between Adam's dream and Keats's "pleasure thermometer," there is a partial parallelism of phrase and idea. Keats's two highest values, friendship and love, are anticipated by Adam's desire, solitary as he is, for:

Collateral love and dearest amity. (VIII, 426)

Almost immediately after Adam's voicing of his desire, God supplies the prefigurative dream of the creation of Eve. When Adam awakes he beholds Eve in the flesh: she embodies the love and amity which Adam needs, and thenceforth supplies it so fulfillingly that, like Endymion, Adam speaks a fervent panegyric of passionate love, calling it not "the chief intensity" (Keats's

---

[15] Literally, of course, it is true that the creation of Eve and the dream-reflection of this were simultaneous. But the real function of the dream was to foreshow happiness, and it is in this foreshowing or prefiguration that Keats was mainly interested, as will presently appear.

phrase) but "the sum of earthly bliss" (VIII, 522). And as in Keats's "pleasure thermometer," Adam compares his superior bliss with sundry delights on lower levels ("taste, sight, smell, herbs, fruits, and flowers, / Walks, and the melody of birds"—VIII, 527–28). Though Adam does not pause to discriminate the lower levels one from another, it is clear that he also has constructed a pleasure thermometer.

Now Adam's pleasure thermometer derived directly from his love-dream: the dream promised bliss, the bliss was forthwith experienced, and the experience revealed a scale of values. This scale, when put into words, was equivalent to a value judgment. In short, the judgment was a kind of *ex post facto* corroboration and defense of the prefigurative dream. In *Endymion*, significantly, the same situation is to be found. Two hundred lines prior to the announcement of the pleasure thermometer, Endymion described an erotic dream of his own that bears a marked resemblance to Adam's dream. While sleeping, he had a vision of the stars, seeming himself to soar through the air in an "airy trance" (I, 585). Though Adam remained on the earth, Keats's words parallel Milton's description of Adam during his dream, for Adam was "abstract as in a trance" (VIII, 462). While Endymion was soaring aloft in his airy trance, his "dazzled soul" beheld a "passionately bright" moon, from which descended a golden-haired female,

> With such a paradise of lips and eyes (I, 618)

that he embraced and kissed her in an unrestrained sexual ecstasy. Then, to his indescribable sadness, the dream dissolved and left him with only the memory of love's bliss. The memory is so vivid, however, and the recollected bliss so intense, that Endymion is convinced of the veracity of his dream. And rightly so, as the progress of the poem gradually makes clear.

When he later meets his sister Peona, Endymion relates to her the story of his dream. She responds in the manner of Pertelote to Chaunticleer (though less scornfully), reading him a lecture on the vanity of dreams. Momentarily he assents to her judgment, but at once resists this skepticism and earnestly defends the veracity of his dream:

> "Peona! ever have I long'd to slake
> My thirst for the world's praises: nothing base,
> No merely slumberous phantasm, could unlace
> The stubborn canvas for my voyage prepar'd—
> Though now 'tis tatter'd; leaving my bark bar'd
> And sullenly drifting: yet my higher hope
> Is of too wide, too rainbow-large a scope,
> To fret at myriads of earthly wrecks.
> Wherein lies happiness? . . ." (I, 769–77)

Then follows the "pleasure thermometer" with which we are familiar.

In the lines just quoted, which serve as a kind of prologue, we can now discern the link between the love-dream and the "truth" about the gradations of happiness. The link can be paraphrased as follows: though other ardent creatures, desiring to believe in the veracity of their dreams, have suffered earthly wrecks of their heavenly hopes, he, Endymion, is convinced that his dream is veracious ("no merely slumberous phantasm"). To prove this, he will show how all happiness can be measured by its intensity, and that the happiness of love is far and away the chief felicity possible to man. So he goes on, many lines beyond the "pleasure thermometer," to exalt the happiness of love, even to declaring that

> this earthly love has power to make
> Men's being mortal, immortal . . . (I, 843–44)

that is, to make gods out of mortals. No, his dream cannot have deceived him, for he is convinced that it offers him

> A hope beyond the shadow of a dream, (I, 857)

while other signs witnessed in his waking hours make him

> scruple whether that same night
> Was pass'd in dreaming. (I, 860–61)

Endymion's dream thus gives every sign (to the dreamer at least) of being a veracious adumbration or prefiguration. Why, then, does it not come true immediately, as Adam's did? The simplest answer is that this would have spoiled the poem; Keats was saving the fulfillment of the dream for the climax of his book, and he had determined to write four thousand lines.[16] Between Adam's dream and Endymion's this is the only difference of much importance. The content of the two dreams (love) and their function (prefiguration) are the same. But most significant, so far as the problem of defining Keats's usage of "truth" is concerned, *Endymion* shows the same relationship between its hero's prefigurative dream and his value judgment as *Paradise Lost* shows between Adam's prefigurative dream and his value judgment. In a word, both judgments are ex post facto *defenses* of the prefigurative veracity of erotic dreams.

This is why, we may guess, Keats at one time cited "my first book" as an illustration of imaginative "truth" (Letter 31), and at another time called

---

16 "[*Endymion*] will be a test, a trial of my powers of imagination and chiefly of my invention which is a rare thing indeed—by which I must make 4000 lines of one bare circumstance and fill them with poetry . . . I may be asked—why endeavor after a long poem? To which I answer . . ." And he gives his answer: that a long poem is a pleasure to the reader, but more important: "a long poem is a test of invention which I take to be the polar star of poetry . . ." (Letter 25, pp. 52–53).

a single passage in this book *an* imaginative "truth" (Letter 42). Whether or not he realized that he was pointing to two quite different species of "truth," we can see that they were closely linked in his mind. Endymion could not afford to believe in his dream unless he could convince himself of its superlative value.

With this knowledge, it becomes feasible to resume the examination of Letter 31, the several illustrations of imaginative "truth" there given, and the general elaboration of the theory. Henceforth the defining process will be simplified by the discrimination of prefigurative *visions* from value *judgments*, or judgments of any kind for that matter. Usually, if not always, Keats furnishes a clue to this discrimination : "*a* truth" is a judgment, "truth" is a vision.

II. PREFIGURATIVE TRUTH

In the effort to discriminate one kind of imaginative "truth" from another in the last chapter, it was found necessary to give a brief description of the "truth" represented by prefigurative vision. That description can hardly be meaningful, however, and it will fail to convince rational minds unless Keats's prose explication is scrutinized more thoroughly, and unless the illustrations in *Paradise Lost* and *Endymion* are studied in more detail.

Since the prose explication (Letter 31) was only partially reproduced in the last chapter, it calls for full quotation at this point. The sentences are numbered to facilitate the explication which follows.

[1] O I wish I was as certain of the end of all your troubles as that of your momentary start about the authenticity of the imagination. [2] I am certain of nothing but of the holiness of the heart's affections and the truth of imagination—what the imagination seizes as beauty must be truth—whether it existed before or not—for I have the same idea of all our passions as of love they are all in their sublime, creative of essential beauty. [3] In a word, you may know my favorite speculation by my first book and the little song I sent in my last—which is a representation from the fancy of the probable mode of operating in these matters. [4] The imagination may be compared to Adam's dream—he awoke and found it truth. [5] I am the more zealous in this affair, since I have never yet been able to perceive how any thing can be known for truth by consecutive reasoning—and yet it must be. [6] Can it be that even the greatest philosopher ever arrived at his goal without putting aside numerous objections. [7] However it may be, O for a life of sensations rather than of thoughts! [8] It is 'a vision in the form of youth' a shadow of reality to come—and this consideration has further convinced me for it has come as auxiliary to another favorite speculation of mine, that we shall enjoy ourselves here after by having what we called happiness on earth repeated in a finer tone and so repeated. [9] And yet such a fate can only befall those who delight in sensation rather than hunger as you do after truth. [10] Adam's dream will do here and seems to be a conviction that imagination and its empyreal reflection is the same as human life and its spiritual repetition. [11] But as I was saying—the simple imaginative mind may have its rewards in the repetition of its own silent working coming continually on the spirit with a fine suddenness—to compare great things with small[1]—have you never by being surprised with an old melody—in a delicious place—by a delicious voice, felt over again your very speculations and surmises at the time it first operated on your soul—do you not remember forming to yourself the singer's face more beautiful than it was possible and yet with the elevation of the moment you did not think so—even then you were mounted on the wings of imagination so high—that the prototype must be here after—that delicious face you will see. [12] What a time! I am continually running away from the subject—sure this cannot be exactly the case with a complex

---

[1] This phrase, "to compare great things with small," though Keats did not enclose it in quotation marks, is a borrowing from Milton, where it occurs four times, sometimes with slightly altered wording. See *Paradise Lost*, II, 921–22; VI, 310–11; X, 306; *Paradise Regained*, IV, 563.

mind—one that is imaginative and at the same time careful of its fruits—who would exist partly on sensation partly on thought—to whom it is necessary that years should bring the philosophic mind—such an one I consider yours and therefore it is necessary to your eternal happiness that you not only drink this old wine of heaven, which I shall call the redigestion of our most ethereal musings on earth; but also increase in knowledge and know all things. [13] I am glad to hear you are in a fair way for Easter— you will soon get through your unpleasant reading and then!—but the world is full of troubles and I have not much reason to think myself pestered with many. . . . [14] You perhaps at one time thought there was such a thing as worldly happiness to be arrived at, at certain periods of time marked out—you have of necessity from your disposition been thus led away—I scarcely remember counting upon any happiness—I look not for it if it be not in the present hour—nothing startles me beyond the moment. [15] The setting sun will always set me to rights—or if a sparrow come before my window I take part in its existence and pick about the gravel. [16] The first thing that strikes me on hearing a misfortune having befallen another is this. [17] "Well it cannot be helped— he will have the pleasure of trying the resources of his spirit" . . .[2]

Perhaps the first thing to notice is that there are two Keatses in this letter—the one who fervently and hopefully proclaims his proposition founded on happiness (it might be called his faith), and the one who, particularly toward the close, soberly admits the inevitable unhappiness of human existence. It will presently be seen that these two Keatses are interdependent; the one psychologically grows out of the other. But for the time being we are mainly interested in the less sober, more excited and hopeful Keats. He it is who is responsible for the bold assertion that "what the imagination seizes as beauty must be truth," an assertion the elucidation of which comprises twelve of the seventeen sentences quoted.

Within these twelve sentences, however, "truth" is used in two senses— one of which is antithetical to the usage connecting the word with beauty. Midway in his exposition, Keats pauses to distinguish his beauty-truth, if we may so call it, from the "truth" of rational inquiry. Though he himself is unable to understand how rational inquiry ("consecutive reasoning"—Sentence 5) can establish truth, he is aware that common usage connects the word with such inquiry. He even goes so far as to admit the validity of rational "truth," and to contrast this truth (or "thoughts"—Sentence 7) with his own cherished "sensations" (Sentence 7). Thus he comes near to unsaying what he has just said so emphatically, namely, that "truth" is a product of the imaginative mind. Careful reading reveals, however, that the unsaying is more apparent than real, deriving partly, it may be supposed, from some uncertainty in his own mind, but mainly from deference to the rational outlook of Benjamin Bailey, student at Oxford and prospective theologian. The sentences that follow this expression of deference (9–11) are

---

[2] Letter 31, pp. 67–69.

sufficient proof that Keats's conviction is not wavering: "truth" may be the conventional name for the rational "thoughts" of Bailey and his kind, but "truth" and "authenticity" (in a sense not understood by Bailey) are infallible attributes of the imagination. So sure is he of this fact that he feels a duty to warn Bailey of the inadequacy of the latter's rational conception of truth.

Though rational minds may be inclined to come to the defense of Bailey here, such a defense would miss the point of Keats's argument. The "truth of imagination" is a species peculiar to the poet, and we must allow him to explain what he means, without intruding our conventional notions. He was having trouble enough in explaining his ideas to the logical-minded Bailey; we shall obscure his message if we quibble about the propriety of his usage.

After this prelude, we may proceed to examine Keats's meaning, sentence by sentence and phrase by phrase:

Sentence 1

Evidently the rational Bailey has expressed some doubt, in conversation or in a letter (not extant), about the "authenticity" (veracity) of the imagination.

Sentence 2

Keats may be uncertain about many matters, but he cherishes a strong conviction that the affections of the heart are "holy" and that imagination is "true." Plainly his faith posits a causal relationship between the affections and the imagination. Notice, however, the revelatory "*must be* truth"; Keats's faith seems to rest on an ardent *wish*. That he was to some degree conscious of the element of wishfulness in his thinking is clear in other sentences of the letter where he twice refers to his faith as "a *favorite* speculation." His criterion of "truth" is evidently what he *likes* to, and *needs* to, believe.

The beauty seized by the imagination is truth, he continues, "whether it existed before or not." A curious phrase, that; but later sentences will make it clear. When he tries to elaborate his idea, he falls back on the passions as material for imaginative contemplation. He mentions only love, however, suggesting that his main interest lies here, a fact which must be plain to all readers of *Endymion* (which he was writing at this time), especially when it is remembered that the "pleasure thermometer" (I, 777 ff.)[3] places love "at the tip-top" of all human pleasures.

---

[3] The "pleasure thermometer" passage was analyzed in chapter i.

Yet the final phrase of the sentence, "essential beauty," makes for perplexity. Is this a flying leap into the Platonic heaven, as commentators sometimes assume? Though the problem is too complex to discuss here,[4] it can safely be said that any notion of transcendental essence was probably far from Keats's mind. Later sentences of the letter will show that his thought adhered steadily to the sensuous, not the supersensuous, and to the particular, not the universal. In fact, "essential beauty" can be translated as the beauty of "essences," provided it is understood that "essences" in this usage is merely a loose synonym for "things of beauty" or "shapes of beauty"—mundane and concrete. On page 34 and the following pages this interpretation is amplified.

SENTENCE 3

"My favorite speculation" is the key phrase here. Keats's faith is a favorite, cherished belief, something he *wants* to believe in, rather than a categorical certainty. Evidently the "must be" of the original proposition was no accident. To argue that what must be, *is*, not only appears to be Keats's position here, but also was Endymion's position in the poem when he strove to convince Peona (and himself?) of the prefigurative veracity of his love-dreams. If wishes were truths, one is tempted to observe, all men would be seers.

What Keats means by "my first book" we have already learned: he refers to Endymion's prefigurative dream, and possibly also to the *defense* of his faith in the dream, namely, the "pleasure thermometer." As to "the little song" ("O Sorrow," *Endymion*, IV, 146 ff.), it is not easy to make clear, at this stage of the discussion at least, in what sense the Indian maid's lament

---

[4] Because it would involve, merely as the first of several ramifications, a thorough collation of all similar phrases in Keats's writings, such as "the principle of beauty" (Letter 60, p. 130), "the principle of beauty in all things" (Letter 186, p. 468), "love of beauty in the abstract" (Letter 90, p. 222), "the mighty abstract idea I have of beauty in all things," (Letter 94, p. 241), "the beautiful—the poetical in all things" (Letter 28, p. 60). Collation of these phrases would have to be followed by a careful study of some fifteen occurrences of the word "abstract" (with its derivatives), which Keats uses in a very special sense virtually equivalent to "imaginative" (an "abstraction" is *an image* for this poet!). As the inquiry is pursued further, the following conclusion more and more suggests itself: that Keats's ostensibly transcendental phrases were but loose labels for his *collective* notion of the manifold concrete beauties of the *finite* world—existing either as objects of perception or as images in the imagination. If the evidence for these statements is not offered here, it is because its bulkiness would deflect the course of the major inquiry, not because the collation and contextual study of terms has been neglected. See Appendix A for a full index to "abstract" and its derivatives.

represents "the truth of imagination." A first surmise might be that Keats intended to distinguish "fancy" from "imagination"; indeed the word "probable" suggests that he may not have been quite sure of the "truth" of the Indian maid's song and thus called it a product of "fancy" rather than of imagination. Such a surmise is without evidence to support it, however; for a collation of all occurrences of "imagination" and "fancy" in Keats's writings indicates that he apparently used the words interchangeably.[5] In view of these difficulties, it will be more profitable to study "O Sorrow" in its context in *Endymion* (see chapter iv, pp. 74 ff.).

SENTENCE 4

In the first chapter we dealt with this statement briefly, concluding that Adam's dream furnished the prototype both for Keats's "favorite speculation" and for the illustration of this in Endymion's prefigurative dream. Love, the love of man and woman, was the content of Adam's dream, as subsequently of Endymion's, and both Adam and Endymion constructed pleasure-ladders to prove that love was "the sum of earthly bliss." Two passages not previously quoted from *Paradise Lost* will show still further parallels between the faiths of Adam and Endymion. In answer to Adam's plea for "collateral love and dearest amity," God responds by promising that:

> What next I bring shall please thee, be assured,
> Thy likeness, thy fit help, thy other self,
> *Thy wish exactly to thy heart's desire.*
> (VIII, 449–51—italics mine)

The last verse gives the psychological equivalent of Keats's creed as expressed in Letter 31, though the writer of this letter, "all on fire" with his splendid idea, was probably less conscious of the wishfulness of his thinking than Milton was of Adam's. When Adam waked from his dream, he exclaimed:

> I wak'd
> To find her . . .
> When out of hope, *behold her, not far off,*
> *Such as I saw her in my dream,* adorned
> With what all Earth and Heaven could bestow
> To make her amiable. (VIII, 478–84—italics mine)

His heart's desire was now fact, not dream; "he awoke and found it truth," as Keats succinctly put it.

---

[5] See Appendix A for a concordance of "imagination" and "fancy" in Keats's prose.

SENTENCES 5 AND 6

Here is again revealed the psychological motive of Keats's creed. "I am the more zealous" in believing that imagination is true, he declares, because I am unable to comprehend rational inquiry. Rather a negative argument, this, though it is well known that Keats, like most poets, did his thinking intuitively and passionately rather than logically and sequentially. There is a "must be" here also, but it carries no force of conviction, being a kind of unwilling concession to alien, rational minds. Such minds, even the most philosophical, Keats feels, must have side-stepped "numerous objections." To his mind it seems that a straight line is the surest avenue to "truth"; one must not be thwarted by obstacles.

SENTENCE 7

"However it may be," let's not argue, Keats says in effect. I know what I want; I know what has value for me: it is the "life of sensations," not the life "of thoughts." This is the sentence that has won the poet many a puritanical frown and, quite as naturally, some ingenious defenders. By "sensations" he meant "intuitions," the latter say, evidently having in mind the "consecutive reasoning" of which Keats disapproves.[6] But there is no authority for this gloss, as a collation of all occurrences of "sensations" and its derivatives demonstrates. By "a life of sensations" Keats seems frankly to have meant a comparatively unreflective, predominantly sensuous and feelingful kind of aesthetic experience (our mind turns at once to such poems as *Endymion*, "Lamia," "The Eve of St. Agnes," and "I stood tip-toe . . . ," the last of which he called, revealingly enough, a "posey/Of luxuries"—ll. 27–28). In the words of the parable which he later invented, the "life of sensations" was "the infant or thoughtless chamber [of life], in which we remain as long as we do not think—We remain there a long while, and not-

---

[6] Cf. "intuitive perceptions of the higher nature" (Albert E. Hancock, *John Keats* [Boston and New York: Houghton Mifflin Company, 1908], p. 62), "intuitions of the mind and spirit" (Sidney Colvin, *John Keats, His Life and Poetry, His Friends, Critics, and After-Fame* [New York: Charles Scribner's Sons, 1917], p. 155), "intuition" (Ernest de Sélincourt, *The Poems of John Keats* [6th ed.; London: Methuen and Company, 1935], p. xxxviii), "intuitions of the mind" (Clarence D. Thorpe, *The Mind of John Keats* [New York: Oxford University Press, 1926], p. 12), "instinctive impulses" and "intuitions" (John Middleton Murry, *Keats and Shakespeare* [London: Oxford University Press, 1925], p. 29), "intuitions" as opposed to "concepts" (Lascelles Abercrombie, "The Second Version of *Hyperion*," *The John Keats Memorial Volume* [London: John Lane, The Bodley Head, 1921], p. 27), "individual, isolated intuitions" (Claude Lee Finney, *The Evolution of Keats's Poetry* [Cambridge: Harvard University Press, 1936], I, 243), "transcendental visions, or super-rational intuitions, of divine love, beauty, and truth" (Werner Beyer, *Keats and the Daemon King*, p. 125).

withstanding the doors of the second chamber ["the chamber of maiden-thought"] remain wide open, showing a bright appearance, we care not to hasten to it . . ."[7]

SENTENCE 8

Beginning with an "it" which presumably refers to the "life of sensations" in the preceding sentence, the first half of Sentence 8 concludes with the assertion that such a life is "a shadow of reality to come." That is, sensuous imaginative experience is a foreshadowing or prefiguration of subsequent, substantial reality. Adam's dream is still the prototype of Keats's thought. If we turn to *Paradise Lost*, we find that Keats's striking phrase, "a shadow of reality to come," is anticipated by Adam's description of an earlier prefigurative dream, a dream in which he beheld "the Garden of bliss" (VIII, 299 ff.) with all its luscious fruits, which aroused such appetite in the dreamer that he sought to pluck them:

> Whereat I *waked,* and found
> Before mine eyes *all real,* as the dream
> Had lively *shadowed.* (VIII, 309-11—italics added)

---

[7] Letter 64, p. 143. Keats's "life of sensations" shows a close resemblance to "the language of the sense" and the "sensations sweet" which Wordsworth valued so highly in "Tintern Abbey" (ll. 108, 27). And Keats's later description of this life as "the infant or thoughtless chamber" reminds one of the first (or perhaps the first two) of "the three ages of man" described in Wordsworth's poem. The two poets do not divide mental development into precisely the same stages, but they both envision a sensational stage as preceding a thoughtful stage. To what extent Keats may have been influenced by the "sensational" or "associationist" psychology of the day it is not easy to demonstrate (see J. R. Caldwell, *John Keats' Fancy* [Ithaca: Cornell University Press, 1945], esp. chap. ii, and Arthur Beatty, *William Wordsworth: His Doctrine and Art in Their Historical Relations* [2d ed.; Madison: University of Wisconsin Studies in English, 1927]). Keats's letters suggest that his general practice was to arrive at conclusions empirically rather than to accept anything at second hand.

The important fact to notice is that Keats had confessedly *not* reached the reflective stage when he wrote Letter 31, that he was still happy in more or less unmixed sensuous enjoyment, and that this sensuous enjoyment was largely comprised of such bodily feelings or emotions ("sensations") as "things of beauty" might evoke. The very context of "a life of sensations" would suggest as much, but the interpretation is corroborated by a collation of all occurrences of the word "sensations" in Keats's writings. With its derivatives, the word occurs thirty-one times in the prose and once in the poetry. Almost invariably it refers to a state of bodily feeling or emotion produced by direct sensory or by imaginative experience. Not once is there a suggestion of the meaning, "intuitions." Keats's pulses and nerves are implicit throughout. See the tabulation of the thirty-one occurrences of the word in the prose (Appendix A), and see the detailed consideration of the evidence in my article, "Keats's 'O for a life of sensations . . . !'" *MLN,* LXIV (April 1949), 239-44.

There can be little doubt that Keats is still thinking of the imagination and its accompanying "sensations" as prefigurative agents.

This is made still clearer in the portion of Sentence 8 which follows the em dash. Here Keats links up two "favorite speculations," revealing that his beauty-truth proposition is actually an auxiliary of another favorite belief, namely, that the "here after" (which can only be understood as postmortal existence) will be modeled on the best of earthly experience. Heaven will be better than earth in that it will have "a finer tone," but except for this refinement or intensification, and of course the endless prolongation, it will be an extension or "repetition" of earthly happiness. The notion is naïve, perhaps, but the history of the race furnishes many and enduring records of the same kind of thinking. Even the stern and intellectual Milton conceived Eden in this fashion. Keats's speculation, it is true, modifies the popular paradise in one respect: it is foreshown to the imagination (primarily to the imagination of poets, we may suppose), and is not drawn from direct, crude sense-experience. His heaven is thus an aesthetic realm—*imagination objectified*, as it were.

Now to return for a moment to a phrase near the beginning of Sentence 8, "a vision in the form of youth." The quotation marks are Keats's, but no editor has identified the quotation. Perhaps the words are an unconscious adaptation of a vaguely remembered quotation, but it is possible, too, that the source lay not in another mind so much as in the dark backward of Keats's own. Has not heaven always been conceived, more or less naïvely, as a region of eternal youth? Was not this the essential condition of the Olympian heaven, which was far more real and vivid to the poet than any Christian or ethical conception? Was not this the tragedy of Tithonus, who was granted immortality, youth denied? Then if Keats conceives of the felicitous moments of mortal imagination as a presage of their immortal repetition, and if Keats himself is a young man, an ardent one at that, and if he is at this very moment conducting a Latmian shepherd to such an everlasting consummation, is it not reasonably clear what he means by the vivid phrase, "a vision in the form of youth"? A *vision* which at the moment is accompanied with supreme happiness is also a *prevision*, a *prefiguration*, of an immortal, blissful, youthful hereafter.

As for the possible source, or at least a parallel, of the phrase, a bit of Keats's conversation on "the Greek spirit," as reported by his friend Joseph Severn, may furnish a clue:

Rome [Severn said], the real Rome would never have become a joy to me . . . had it not been for Keats's talks with me about the Greek spirit,—the Religion of the Beautiful, the *Religion of Joy*, as he used to call it . . . "I never cease to wonder at all that *incarnate Delight*," Keats remarked to me once . . . He made me in love with the real living spirit of the past. He was the first to point out to me how essentially modern that Spirit is: "It's *an immortal youth*," he would say, "just as there is no *Now* or *Then* for the Holy Ghost."[8]

If Keats spoke these ecstatic words while dying in Rome, we can hardly argue that they were the source of the phrase, "a vision in the form of youth," in Letter 31. Yet the idea may not first have come to the poet while he was in Rome. At least as early as March 1817, the Greek spirit as embodied in the Elgin marbles had moved him deeply, so deeply that his own mortal being seemed too narrow a room for adequate appreciation.[9]

Of course the words to Severn, coming from a dying man who had lost his faith in immortality, did not posit a hope of heaven. Until Tom Keats died (December 1, 1818), and probably for some time afterward, the poet had "scarce a doubt of immortality,"[10] but eighteen months later he wrote to the girl he loved: "I wish to believe in immortality."[11] His faith had weakened, and this is one reason, added to his general sobriety of outlook in 1819–20, that he did not tell Severn in Italy, while he lay there dying of consumption, that he would enjoy the Greek spirit again after death.

SENTENCE 9

Happiness in postmortal existence will be denied to those whose faith is placed in rational processes rather than in imagination and its prefigurative "life of sensations." It is not clear whether Keats means that *all kinds* of happiness will be denied to rational minds in the next life, or only that the repetition in a finer tone of earthly, aesthetic happiness will be so denied.

SENTENCE 10

Again Adam's dream is cited as the prototype of Keats's faith, but now he carries the explanation a step farther. Adam's dream "seems to be [to imply?] a conviction that imagination and its empyreal reflection is the same as human life and its spiritual repetition." Whose "conviction" is here referred to—Milton's, Adam's, or Keats's? The words suggest that Adam's dream is not merely an analogy but a *proof* of the prefigurative agency of imagination, and that he, Keats (and probably Milton also), accepts it as such.

---

[8] William Sharp, *Life and Letters of Joseph Severn* (London: Sampson Low, Marston and Company, 1892), p. 29. Except for *Now* and *Then*, the italics are mine.

[9] Cf. his sonnet "On Seeing the Elgin Marbles," printed March 9, 1817.

[10] Letter 98, p. 246.

[11] Letter 223, p. 500.

If this is so, how are we to interpret the perplexing phrase, "imagination and its empyreal reflection"? Does Keats mean that the mortal imagination is a mirror catching reflections, in favored moments, from the empyrean? Is his notion Platonic? On the contrary, a collation and contextual study of the several occurrences of "empyreal" (and "empyrean") will show that he has no thought of an illumination from a transcendental realm, but is simply looking forward to the enjoyment of postmortal existence. Of the four other occurrences of the word "empyreal" and "empyrean" in his writings, three refer unequivocally to the Greek heaven of Olympus. The other refers to imaginative meditation ("a tapestry *empyrean* full of symbols for his [the imaginative man's] spiritual eye"),[12] but hovers delicately and uncertainly between the literal and the figurative. The three uses of the word in reference to the Greek heaven, all of them in *Endymion*, are connected with Endymion's love-dreams and their prefigurative veracity. For example, while the hero dreams that he lies in erotic transport in the arms of his goddess-love, he hears her promise to him: "An immortality of passion's thine" (II, 808), and she vows to teach him "lispings *empyrean*," or "lispings immortal" (II, 819) as the original draft reads. Plainly, "empyrean" is a loose synonym for "immortal" or "heavenly." In much the same way, the god of Sleep dreams that "a young man [Endymion] . . . / Would at high Jove's *empyreal* footstool win / An immortality" (IV, 377–79). And later, after Endymion, carried to heaven while dreaming, wakes from a dream of Cynthia to behold her in the flesh, and yet is doomed for some mysterious reason to descend to earth again without her company—even then, sad as he is, he reaffirms the reality of the pleasures which the Olympian "empyrean" had given him, declares their superiority to "earthly" pleasures, and remains withal "more happy than betides mortality" (IV, 849–59).

To epitomize, "empyrean" in *Endymion* refers invariably to the joyous life of immortal beings. An approximate synonym would be "heavenly" or "immortal." The same synonyms will serve for another word in Sentence 10, viz., "spiritual." "Spiritual" appears seldom or never to denote the immaterial or supersensuous in Keats's usage. In contexts such as the present one, "spiritual" denotes the immortal, blissful sequel of earthly existence,[18]

---

[12] Letter 48, p. 103.

[18] See Appendix A for a concordance of "spiritual" in Keats's prose, and cf. especially the fruition of Endymion's long love-quest: he was "spiritualiz'd" (IV, 993), that is, immortalized or "deified," so that he could enjoy "an immortality of passion" (II, 808) with Cynthia. In general, Keats's usage of "spiritual" falls into such categories as: highly refined in thought or feeling, ethically excellent; pertaining to imagination; pertaining to immortality. Sometimes the last two meanings appear to be linked, as in Letter 31.

and at times Keats frankly equates the word with sensuous qualities.[14] He seems to see little difference between the "life of *sensations*" destined to be "repeated in a finer tone" (Sentences 7 and 8) and "human life and its *spiritual* repetition" (Sentence 10).[15]

Though this excursion to explain Keats's use of "empyreal" and "spiritual" may seem like a circuit round Robin Hood's barn, it is a necessary reminder that he frequently used words unconventionally. The rather special meaning of "spiritual" and "empyreal" confirms the interpretation of "imagination and its empyreal reflection" which might have been proposed (though perhaps not convincingly to Platonic minds) merely as a result of studying the context of the phrase. The context of the phrase amounts really to an equation, such an equation as Keats formulated in his original identification of "beauty" with "truth." That is, the "empyreal reflection" of the imagination *is* the "spiritual [i.e., immortal or postmortal] repetition" of human life. If it should be objected that Keats may really have intended an analogy when he wrote the equation, the meaning is still approximately the same: the "empyreal reflection" of the imagination is the postmortal or "spiritual" counterpart of the imagination, in the same way as "human life" (a larger category than imagination) enjoys its "spiritual repetition."

Though this may seem to exhaust Keats's meaning, there is one aspect of his theory, perhaps the most interesting, that has not been emphasized. It can be stated thus: not only is the "empyreal reflection" a counterpart of mortal imagination, but it is its logical product and consummation, incapable of coming into being without this mortal parent. In this sense mortal imagination becomes not merely prefigurative of, but *productive of*, immortal or empyreal reality. This is why—and the point is important—the product is called a "reflection" by Keats, and why I have chosen to call the parent imagination "prefigurative," though I might have added "parturient" and not have changed the meaning. The imagination does not *receive* "reflections" from the empyrean; the empyrean receives reflections from the imagination!

The expected idea would be that imagination opens itself to illuminations from a supersensuous realm, reflecting them like a mirror or recording them

---

[14] E.g., certain deities are said to reveal themselves to mortals, "every *sense* / Filling with *spiritual sweets* to plenitude (*Endymion*, III, 38–39). In the same way, "*immortal* bowers" are sometimes presented "to *mortal sense*" (*Endymion*, II, 438). In view of Keats's habitual usage of "spiritual," he could have written "spiritual bowers" without altering the meaning.

[15] It is of course true that the "spiritual repetition" of human life implied some sort of refinement of earthly pleasures, but whether Keats meant much more than intensification and enhancement of such pleasures by his phrase, "repeated in a finer tone," it would be difficult to demonstrate.

like a camera. Keats's idea is the very reverse: imagination is like a projector, throwing its sensuous, mortal images far out into the empyrean, projecting and extensionalizing them both in time and in space. At once some perplexing earlier words in the letter leap into clarity: "What the imagination seizes as beauty must be truth—*whether it existed before or not.*" That is to say, *the imagination creates not merely in a mental but also in an extensional, apocalyptic sense.* What it *envisions* will *be*, postmortally and eternally.[16]

SENTENCE 11

Though the initial adverbial clause has a questionable reference, the main function of the sentence is clear: Keats desires to give yet another illustration of his "favorite speculation," and to choose this illustration from a source outside poetry. Delaying for the moment the illustration, we turn to the question raised at the beginning of the sentence. There are two ideas in the sentence, one of them familiar and the other novel. What is puzzling is that the novel idea is introduced with the phrase "But as I was saying," as if Keats were now recapitulating a point previously made. Actually the point had not been made at all or even intimated, and the sudden importation of it here shows that the poet's mind was running faster than his pen.

Yet the connection of the novel idea with the one previously elaborated is not far to seek. In searching for another example than Adam's dream, one closer to the experience of ordinary beings, Keats hit upon the associative response to a familiar melody which the hearer would at some earlier time have heard as sung by a beautiful woman. When the melody is heard at a later time, the hearer recollects his first "speculations and surmises."[17] This is a normal associative process, made especially familiar in the retrospective poetry of Wordsworth and the associational psychology of the day. Had Keats's thought stopped with the recollected "speculations and surmises," or even with the refining process which made the singer's face "more beautiful than it was possible," there would be nothing original or surprising in his conception—except its total inconsistency with every other sentence in the

---

[16] The full meaning of the word "prefigurative" as I have applied it to Keats's beauty-truth identification should now be clear. The imagination, it would seem, does not merely foreshow to a poet the blissful sequel of mortal existence; it actually *creates* this sequel, or appears so to do.

[17] In an early poem Keats uses a similar illustration, but he does not carry it forward to the "prototype . . . here after" of Letter 31:

> . . . when I hear a lay
> That once I saw her hand awake,
> Her form seems floating palpable, and near . . .
> ("Ah! who can e'er forget . . . ," ll. 37–39)

letter! Unhappily, critics have sometimes seized upon this half-sentence as the clue to Keats's major theory. "It is all of it mere Wordsworthianism," says Garrod, epitomizing the entire letter, and citing Wordsworth's "emotion recollected in tranquility" as proof.[18] But actually no part of the letter except this half-sentence resembles Wordsworth's theory. For Wordsworth's theory is founded on *re*collection and *retro*spection, whereas Keats's theory is founded on *pro*spection and *pre*figuration, like Adam's and Endymion's dreams.

Readers who are not yet convinced should ponder carefully the latter half of Sentence 11. Here Keats's characteristic thought pushes through, and in a truly striking manner. There are not two ways to read his final triumphant words: "the prototype *must* be *here after*—that delicious face *you will* see." In heaven, the perfect realm, will exist the perfect face—not perfect in any abstract Platonic sense, not an Idea or Form, but simply a mortal, feminine countenance, concrete and sensuous, enhanced immeasurably in its mortal, earthly, corporeal beauty.

Thus the sentence does after all, if taken as a whole, recapitulate the theory with which the writer began. The phrase "But as I was saying" is justified by the second half of the sentence, if not (at first sight anyway) by the first half. It reaffirms, in a dramatic and bold image, the theory derived from Adam's veracious dream, that "What the imagination seizes as beauty *must* be [postmortal] truth—whether it existed before or not."

It is probably unnecessary to observe that excitement, hope, and wish combine in such pronouncements and are responsible for them. Even Keats was aware of this, or partially aware, for he incidentally confesses that his logic, if such it may be called, derives simply from impassioned feeling: the "elevation of the moment," the "being mounted on the wings of imagination so high" that disbelief is impossible. At such moments "the prototype *must be* here after," "beauty *must* be truth."

A conjecture may now be ventured as to how the novel idea of recollection crept into the first half of Sentence 11, the second half of which reaffirms the theory of prefiguration. Though in the hurry of writing Keats was seemingly unaware that the two halves of his sentence were not logically joined, it is reasonable to speculate that he saw in the process of recollective imagination (or even in imagination in general) a sign of a gradual and continuous refining of the original sense-experience. Each time this experience was imaginatively recollected, its beauty would be enhanced in the imagination. Each recollection would be a finer "repetition" of the original experience. And thus the individuals who cultivated imagination (the "life of sensations") on

---

[18] H. W. Garrod, *Keats* (Oxford: The Clarendon Press, 1926), p. 39.

earth would be prepared for the "happiness . . . repeated in a finer tone" in the next world. This last and culminating repetition would be existential, not mental—like the paradisal Eve and Cynthia who incarnated Adam's and Endymion's dreams.

Whether Keats's theory actually involved, or whether he had carefully thought out, such a continual refinement and upward gradation of imaginative pleasures, his words in Letter 31 and elsewhere do not make fully clear. Perhaps the hypothesis renders his thought more systematic and coherent than it really was. Nevertheless, similar ideas appear elsewhere in his writings, for example in the sketch of humanity's gradual refinement through imagination (Letter 48), and in the progressive aesthetic evolution of the natural and human world which forms the central theme of "Hyperion." To be sure, the tragic story of the Titans does not carry the evolution forward into heaven, but this may be the consequence of the fragmentary condition of the poem or, more plausibly, of the fact that a maturer, wiser poet felt it necessary to modify his "young minded" though still "favorite speculation."

Sentence 12

Keats here checks his yearning, hopeful imagination, and confesses that his sentiments have been the fruit of impassioned feeling, not of thought. As to the subject from which he says he is "continually running away," he cannot be referring to his "favorite speculation," which has really run away with him! Instead, he must have in mind the distinction, stated earlier in the letter, between the "consecutive" or rational mind, and his own imaginative, sensational mind. For it is to this distinction that he now returns, candidly admitting that the rational mind is more "careful of its fruits" than his own. Reason does not accept a conclusion dictated by feeling, though imagination is tempted to do so. The rational mind, when it allows some freedom to the imagination, is "a complex mind"; Keats's own unrational, "sensational" imagination is, by implication, a simple mind—at least in the present stage of its development.

There may be some deference in this confession, deference to the Wordsworthian, ecclesiastical Bailey; but there is sober wisdom also. When the "elevation of the moment" has passed, Keats's judgment becomes active and clear-sighted, and he disinterestedly analyzes the tendencies of his mind and temperament. That he did in fact look forward to the time when his own sensational mind would become the "philosophic mind," we know from his earlier definition of poetry in "Sleep and Poetry" (122 ff.), from his celebrated "simile of human life" in Letter 64,[19] and from his increasingly serious

---

[19] Pp. 143–45.

determination, throughout the ensuing year, 1818, to "get wisdom."[20] Nevertheless, for the present he is content with "half knowledge"[21] and the "life of sensations." Not only is he content, but he feels that Bailey must be warned of the insufficiency of his "complex mind." This insufficiency is a grave one, for "it is necessary to your *eternal happiness*" (italics mine), he warns Bailey, that you devote yourself at least partly to the sensational, imaginative life.[22]

What does Keats mean by Bailey's "eternal happiness"? The phrase can hardly refer to any kind of earthly, mortal happiness; Sentence 14 makes this certain, and of course the whole tenor of the letter has been determined by the prospect of "happiness repeated in a finer tone" in the next world. Therefore Bailey's "eternal happiness," if he is ever to enjoy it, can only be had in the "here after," like the "prototype" of the singer's beautiful face and the "empyreal reflections" of Adam's and Endymion's dreams.

We can profitably turn back at this point to a perplexing phrase in Sentence 2: "creative of essential beauty." This was earlier interpreted as creative of the beauty of "essences" ("things of beauty"), but at the time it was not indicated where these beautiful "essences" might be located. Since we now know that Keats's creed assumes an equation between mortal beauties as presented to the imagination and immortal beauties as extensionalized in an aesthetic elysium, the phrase "essential beauty" falls into its proper position as the second half of the equation. It refers to the postmortal counterparts of "essences" contemplated by the mortal imagination; for, as Keats specifically states, beauty becomes "truth" exactly because, and when, mortal imagination is "*creative of* essential beauty." As pointed out before, the beauty of "essences" in heaven seems not to be different in kind, but only in degree of pleasurableness and in eternality, from the beauty of mortal "essences." Keats's heaven is not a supersenuous but a superior sensuous realm; it is "happiness on earth repeated in a finer tone."

In this heaven he will see the "prototype" (the "essential beauty") of the singer's beautiful face which he imagined with such pleasure on earth. In heaven, lovers will be joined eternally and blissfully to their mates (as *Endymion* is largely devoted to proving), and the fondest love-dreams of Endymion and of all ardent lovers will be translated into everlasting reality. It is ever the poet's privilege, while yet stationed on earth and enjoying the life of imagination, to have glimpses of, and *ipso facto* to become "creative of," the postmortal beauties which he will henceforth enjoy everlastingly.

To return to Sentence 12, a word may be added about "this old wine of heaven," the figurative beverage indispensable to Bailey's happiness in the

---

[20] Letter 62, p. 134.
[21] Letter 32, p. 72.
[22] Sentences 8 and 9 contained a similar warning.

next world. The phrase appears to be a synonym for the pleasures of imagination and the "life of sensations" earlier described. Though Keats sometimes refers to poetry itself as a "wine,"[23] or to the "luxurious" parts of
Milton's verse as "cups of old wine,"[24] the "old wine of heaven" recommended
to Bailey appears to be the pleasurable "sensations" excited by such passages
of poetry, together with some consciousness of their heaven-presaging quality.
It is possible, of course, that Keats did not intend the "old wine of heaven"
to be synonymous with "redigestion" (= imagination and sensations?) but
with "ethereal musings," which is pretty surely a synonym for passages of
poetry, as numerous usages of "ethereal" with an unequivocal reference
testify.[25] The question of exact reference is not crucial, however; all we need
to know with certainty is that Keats was recommending the imaginative, sensational life to Bailey, that such a life would involve a devotion to poetry and
a redigestion of it or musing upon it, and that Bailey would be shut out of
heaven if he failed to live such a life.

Sentences 13–17

With Sentence 12, Keats appears to have completed the explanation of
his theory of imagination, and in Sentences 13–17 he turns to the subject of
unhappiness, which he regards as the necessary condition of mortality.[26]
There is some reason to believe, however, that what he says concerning unhappiness is rather closely related to his theory of imagination, which is of
happiness all compact. For if he starts with the premise that continuous
mortal happiness is impossible, and if at the same time he experiences
moments of exceeding joy, the apparent inconsistency can be resolved by
linking these moments with an assumed supramortal existence. Either they

---

[23] "Song" ("Hence Burgundy, Claret, and Port"), l. 6.

[24] Marginal note on Milton. See M. B. Forman (ed.), *The Poetical Works and
Other Writings of John Keats* (New York: Charles Scribner's Sons, 1938–39), V, 292.

[25] Passages of Shakespeare are called "ethereal" (Letter 53, p. 112); "the sun,
the moon, the stars, the earth and its contents" are described as "materials to form
greater things—that is to say *ethereal* things" [that is, poetry created by John Keats]
(Letter 15, p. 31; "mould ethereal" is a synonym for poetry (Letter 48, p. 103); from
scenery in Scotland, Keats will "learn poetry," transmuting such scenery "into *ethereal*
existence," that is, into poetry (Letter 71, p. 157); and "any one grand and spiritual
passage" in poetry . . . engenders ethereal finger-pointings . . . a tapestry empyrean
. . . ," etc. (Letter 48, p. 103). These "finger-pointings" are the fruit of such "redigestion" as Keats recommended to Bailey, for they occur only if a man "read a certain
page full of poesy or distilled prose, and let him wander with it, and *muse upon* it, and
reflect upon it . . ." (Letter 48—italics mine).

[26] The portion omitted in the quotation from Sentence 13 is an allusion to his
brother's illness and his own. It is not material to the discussion.

are emanations from a presently existing transcendental realm, or, as Keats preferred to believe, they are the creative germs of a felicitous hereafter. For the very reason that mortal minds, condemned by law to unhappiness, are permitted rare and superlative experiences, Keats argues that there *must* be a realm where such experiences will be continuous and eternal. Thus Sentences 13–17, though on first sight they seem to have little to do with the beauty-truth proposition, may in a sense be regarded as an indirect confirmation of it. At least they show why the poet clung so ardently to his "favorite speculation." It was, if we may so call it, a kind of "Christian" aesthetic, in which a man could *guarantee* his heaven by believing rightly and by living the appropriate kind of life on earth.

Did Keats always and uniformly adhere to such a faith? The records in his prose writings are few and scattered; his judgment was usually on hand to police his feeling. In his poetry he could allow himself more freedom, though as time passed and wisdom accumulated, the early optimism underwent a gradual modification and, finally, an almost total extinction. "Hyperion" marks a middle stage, "The Fall of Hyperion" the nadir of optimism. As late as December 1818, as we have seen, Keats had "scarce a doubt of immortality," but by 1820 (if not before), the shadow of death was upon him and his faith had weakened: "I wish to believe in immortality," he wrote to Fanny Brawne. Once a wish had been a criterion of truth; now it looked like a sign of illusion.

It will not be amiss, however, to give a few examples of Keats's prefigurative faith during its pristine phase of optimism. The extent to which this faith infuses *Endymion* will be shown in the next chapters, but it appears in other places as well, if somewhat sporadically. For instance, in "To My Brother George" Keats declares that glimpses of elysium are permitted to the rapt imagination of the poet. Though "no mortal [i.e., nonpoetic] eye can reach the flowers" of "that far seat of blisses,"

> The Poet's eye can reach those golden halls.[27]

Or as another poem expresses it, with clearer emphasis on the idea of prefiguration, the poet's spirit in fortunate moments

> with its *destined skies*
> Holds *premature* and mystic communings.[28]

The same faith appears to be implied in "Bards of Passion and of Mirth," a

---

[27] "To my Brother George," ll. 35, 44, 47.
[28] "The Poet," ll. 11–12. Italics mine.

generously concrete illustration of the poets' elysium as it is prefigured in the imagination of Keats. He envisions this elysium as a region

> Where the daisies are rose-scented,
> And the rose herself has got
> Perfume which on earth is not;
> Where the nightingale doth sing
> Not a senseless, tranced thing,
> But divine melodious truth . . .[29]

It might be argued that this elysium is a playful fiction rather than a veracious prefiguration, were it not that Keats introduces the poem with the prose explanation that "it is on the double immortality of poets."[30] By this he means that poets achieve immortality figuratively in their works (their "souls on earth"—ll. 2, 38) and actually in their postmortal existence (they have "souls in heaven too, / Double-lived in regions new"—ll. 3–4, 39–40). The same theme is developed in "Lines on the Mermaid Tavern," where the Elizabethan poets, now denizens of elysium, are represented as remembering fondly "mine host's Canary wine" and "dainty pies / Of venison" (ll. 6, 8), with the result that the Mermaid Tavern with all its earthly delights is transplanted to the zodiac, where the poets now sip "beverage divine" (l. 20). There is a gentle touch of humor in this zodiacal-elysian assembly, but the humor is hardly a sign of the author's disbelief.

No colorless, incorporeal, Platonic heaven beckons to the sensuous imagination of Keats, but an aesthetic elysium where "what we called happiness on earth [is] repeated in a finer tone," where daisies and roses and nightingales, and Canary wine and venison pies are supernal counterparts of their earthly species, where the beauty of (mortal) "essences" has become "essential beauty," transfigured and everlasting—all by virtue of the creativity of the mortal imagination![31]

Not often did Keats expose his ardent creed in the sober language of prose, where "consecutive" minds might pounce upon and censure his logic. To Bailey alone did he open his heart with any fullness. For this reason it is surprising to discover what amounts almost to a public confession (though not an elaboration) of the faith which he described to Bailey. In a newspaper

---

[29] "Bards of Passion and of Mirth," ll. 14–19.

[30] Letter 98, p. 265.

[31] In an article that explores Keats's ideas of elysium and their sources, G. Giovannini notices that Keats's elysium "conforms closely" to his " 'favorite speculation . . . that we shall enjoy ourselves here after by having what we called happiness on earth repeated in a finer tone . . .' " See "Keats' Elysium of Poets," *MLN,* LXIII (January 1948), 21–22.

essay, a piece of dramatic criticism, Keats was characterizing the verse of Shakespeare, and wrote:

A melodious passage in poetry is full of pleasures both sensual and spiritual. The spiritual is felt when the very letters and points of charactered language show like the hieroglyphics of beauty;—the mysterious signs of an immortal freemasonry! "A thing to dream of, not to tell!"[32]

The exclamation points are not accidental; they remind us of such an "elevation of the moment" as produced the "favorite speculation" of Letter 31. And, indeed, that favorite speculation seems to be repeated here in slightly different language; for "the mysterious signs of an immortal freemasonry" can only be construed as prefigurations (to the imagination) of fellowship in heaven. The meaning of the word "spiritual" is evidently the same as that in Letter 31, referring not to immateriality or ethical excellence, but simply to the *immortal* sequel of earthly existence. Once again the poet is resorting to his favorite logic: the intense sensational ("sensual") pleasures of imagination (and of its product, poetry) *ipso facto* prefigure a happy postmortal existence where these pleasures can be enjoyed without cessation and without satiety.

Did not Keats warn Bailey that, unless he devoted himself to poetry and the "life of sensations," he would cut himself off from "eternal happiness"? Not only Milton with his "conviction" concerning Adam's dream, but Shakespeare himself, or his splendid verse at least, seemed to the ardent and hopeful, as yet "young minded" Keats, the sign and promise of an elysian sequel to earthly existence.

Specious logic, rational minds will say. But perhaps the question has little to do with logic, which is no respecter of the feelings. If "beauty must be [or become] truth," the faith that decrees this miracle is not a product of the analytical reason, but of a fervent and rapt imagination, and of an unfaltering trust in "the holiness of the heart's affections."

---

[32] "On Edmund Kean as a Shakespearian Actor." See M. B. Forman, *The Poetical Works* . . . , V, 229. The quotation marks enclose a verse, not previously identified, that Keats either adapted or slightly misquoted from "Christabel": "A *sight* to dream of, not to tell!" (I, 253).

III. THE PREFIGURATIVE THEME IN *ENDYMION*
(BOOKS I-II)

"For the young there is nothing unattainable; a good thing desired with the whole force of a passionate will, and yet impossible, is to them not credible. Yet, by death, by illness, by poverty, or by the voice of duty, we must learn, each one of us, that the world was not made for us, and that, however beautiful may be the things we crave, Fate may nevertheless forbid them."[1] Written by a philosopher of the twentieth century, Bertrand Russell, these words describe youthful idealism in any age, and are particularly appropriate to the "young minded" author of *Endymion*. With remarkable swiftness this young-minded stage passed; mental maturity came to Keats almost in a matter of months. There are even signs in *Endymion*—one might almost call them frequent—of this sober wisdom which he was soon to attain. Yet in the main, *Endymion* is a fervent and sanguine testament of young love and its hopeful, prefigurative dreams.

In Letter 31, it will be recalled, Keats asserted that he had "the same idea of all our passions as of love they are all in their sublime creative of essential beauty." Of the non-amatory passions, however, he had nothing to say, and naturally enough, since he was at that very moment conducting a Latmian shepherd to the final and everlasting fulfillment of his "sublime" love-dreams. The principal theme of *Endymion* is the hero's quest of this everlasting fulfillment, a fulfillment which Cynthia summarily describes as "an immortality of passion" (II, 808). If to some readers the theme, thus stated, seems carnal and unidealistic, it must be recognized that Keats's frankness on this point is everywhere evident, that he was, of course, depicting love as he viewed it *through the imagination*, and that such love was "holy" to him. Hazlitt would have understood Keats's point of view, as can be seen in his defense of Juliet's "indelicate" sensuality in anticipating the pleasures of the marriage bed: "critics do not perceive that the feelings of the heart sanctify, without disguising, the impulses of nature."[2] And Poe carries the sanctification a step farther, implying (as Keats argued in Letter 31) that a youthful poet's dreams of love presage an answering experience in heaven: "The boyish poet-love is indisputably that one of the human sentiments which most nearly realizes our dreams of the chastened voluptuousness of heaven."[3]

---

[1] Bertrand Russell, *Mysticism and Logic* (New York: W. W. Norton and Company, 1929), p. 52.

[2] "Romeo and Juliet," *Characters of Shakespeare's Plays* (London: Oxford University Press, 1949), p. 118.

[3] Poe, "Lord Byron and Mary Chaworth," *The Poems of Edgar Allen Poe with a Selection of Essays* (Everyman ed.), p. 330.

Dreams of heaven. All men have such dreams, and poets are notably susceptible to them. In the person of Endymion, John Keats dreamed of, and finally attained, his own voluptuous heaven. But what is the precise relation of Endymion's dreams to the heaven he yearns for? G. Wilson Knight has some suggestive words on this point: "The complexities of the poem . . . concern the relation of waking life to a divine dream . . . Yet the dream turns out to be reality."[4] And again: "Shelley was a sleep-worshipper; Keats a positive fanatic."[5] True, if perhaps overstated; but Knight's words are passing intimations, not explanations.

Explanations become possible, however, if one correlates Letter 31 with *Endymion*. What the letter describes, the poem enacts. That is, the letter is a statement of Keats's prefigurative creed and the poem is an illustration. The illustration was probably not the consequence of deliberate planning, to be sure. For the poem appears to have been intended originally as an exercise in craftsmanship, "a test of invention which I take to be the polar star of poetry."[6] Keats was telling the simple truth when he confessed: "I must make 4000 lines [a number arbitrarily determined] of one bare circumstance and fill them with poetry."[7] It is not surprising therefore that the poem strikes many readers as a kind of "amiable confusion" (Saintsbury),[8] as "treasures poured forth with indistinct profusion" (Shelley),[9] or as "a thin and scanty tissue of . . . story . . . [wherein the poet's] imaginations go rambling and entangling themselves everywhere, like wild honeysuckles" (Jeffrey).[10] Saintsbury and Shelley and Jeffrey were right, in a sense; the poem is, particularly with respect to its imagery, its scenes, and its many digressions, a medley. In fact, Keats confessed to Shelley in 1820 that his "mind was like a pack of scattered cards" during the process of composition.[11]

He was not oblivious of his readers, however, for it was part of his intention to please them with little wildernesses of pleasant images, clusters of "things of beauty" (such as the marvelous underworld so elaborately described in Book II). As he says in the same letter that stresses the "4000 lines" and the "test of invention":

I may be asked—why endeavor after a long poem? To which I should answer—Do not the lovers of poetry like to have *a little region to wander in* where they may pick and choose, and in which *images are so numerous* that many are forgotten and found new in a second reading?[12]

---

[4] G. W. Knight, "The Priest-like Task: An Essay on Keats," *The Starlit Dome* (London: Oxford University Press, 1941), p. 263.

[5] *Ibid.*, p. 261.   [6] Letter 25, p. 53.   [7] *Ibid.*, p. 52.

[8] "A Reminiscence of Endymion," *The John Keats Memorial Volume*, p. 163.

[9] Shelley's letter to Keats, July 27, 1820.

[10] Review of *Endymion* in *The Edinburgh Review*, August 1820.

[11] Letter 227, p. 507.   [12] Letter 25, pp. 52–53. Italics added.

Thus *Endymion*, from one point of view, is a luxuriant exfoliation of images, a kind of mixed bouquet of "things of beauty," a "posey/Of luxuries,"[13] a paradise of dainty devices (sylvan, floral, nymphic, amorous, mythic, subterrestrial, submarine, lunar . . .). If this is one of Keats's purposes, and if he is also seeking to fill up four thousand lines, we can see why he had to keep Endymion on the move and to change the scene continually. Thus it is hardly necessary to look for allegorical meanings in Endymion's visit to the underworld (though here Keats may have taken a hint, more pictorial than allegorical, from the classic epic or the Cave of Mammon in *The Faerie Queene*), his undersea discoveries, and his magic ascent to Olympus and return to Mount Latmos. All the while the hero was seeing new sights and his poet was practicing his invention, while the reader, so Keats thought, would "have a little region to wander in."

There is, however, more in the poem than the fecund exfoliation of Keats's invention. First of all, there is the "bare circumstance," the Greek myth which is his primary subject. What he does with this myth, how he reshapes it to suit his faith in "the holiness of the heart's affections and the truth of imagination," forms a curious and revealing story. Did he set about this transmutation of the myth consciously? Probably not, though Letter 31 betrays a considerable awareness of what he was doing. In this letter Keats referred Bailey to two illustrations of his "favorite speculation" in *Endymion*. Probably he could have furnished further illustrations from the same poem if Bailey had requested them. These illustrations, not few in number, I propose to enumerate in the pages that follow. It will be necessary also to look unblenchingly at the love scenes which Keats regarded as "holy," for the nature of this love has generally been misconstrued, I believe, from 1880 to the present (the period of idealistic and neo-Platonic allegorizations).[14] Attention will also be called to the varying allegiance which Keats gives to his "favorite speculation": as the poem unfolds there is increasing evidence (not the least of which is the Cave of Quietude passage in Book IV and the

---

[13] Ll. 27–28, announcing the theme of "I stood tip-toe . . . ," Keats's first *Endymion*.

[14] This allegorization began with Mrs. Frances M. Owen and has been maintained, with varying shades of meaning, by Sidney Colvin, Ernest de Sélincourt, Robert Bridges, H. I'A. Fausset, J. M. Murry, Clarence D. Thorpe, A. W. Crawford, Claude Lee Finney, and Werner Beyer. Amy Lowell stands virtually alone in recognizing the frankly physical quality of the love which Keats describes, bravely calling the poem an "idealization of sexual love" (*John Keats* [Boston and New York: Houghton Mifflin and Co., 1925], I, 365). For a sampling of critical opinion from 1880 to 1947, see my articles: "The meaning of 'Fellowship with Essence' in *Endymion*," *PMLA*, LXII (December 1947), 1061, and "Endymion — A Neo-Platonic Allegory?" *ELH*, XIV (March 1947), 64.

resolution never again to "be by phantoms duped," IV, 619–55) that the poet is graduating from optimistic credence into sobriety and wisdom. Nevertheless the poem ends with the triumphant enaction of his "favorite speculation."

BOOK I

The most patent evidence of the prefigurative theme in Book I ("my first book") was glanced at in chapter i. But Endymion's prefigurative dream, there briefly epitomized, was not the first appearance of the theme. One item in the poet's list of exemplary "things of beauty" is worth noticing:

> The grandeur of the dooms
> We have imagined for the mighty dead. (I, 20–21)

Though this is not a positive assertion of belief, it is one of numerous indications in Keats's poetry, the best known of which is probably "Bards of Passion and of Mirth," that elysium was no mere fiction to him.

At I, 63, Keats turns to his story, describing the forest on Mount Latmos, destined to be the setting of the first and last episodes of the tale. Into this scene comes Endymion, soon to demand sympathy for his inward sorrow, but at first impressing many of the onlookers with his exceeding happiness:

> he seem'd
> To common lookers on, *like one who dream'd*
> *Of idleness in groves Elysian:*
> But there were some who feelingly could scan
> *A lurking trouble* in his nether lip. (I, 175–79)

(I have italicized the key words here. Italics in later passages are mine unless otherwise noted.) How any human being could wear this double and contrasting expression of countenance it is not easy to guess. But the poem soon makes it clear that in this initial appearance of Endymion, Keats has telescoped, with an obvious temporal inconsistency, two antithetical aspects of Endymion's recent experience: his incomparably felicitous love-dream of Cynthia (destined ultimately to be incarnated), and his grievous loss of that felicity when the dream faded. Thus the passage suggests the "favorite speculation" of Letter 31.

The shepherds now gather around a venerable priest, and a chorus chants an ode to Pan, whose festival the shepherds have come to celebrate. After the chorus completes its chant, the shepherds turn to the gaiety of dancing, seeming to the poet, who here conceives of them as living in a kind of Golden Age, to be "unconscious" gatherers of "time's sweet first-fruits" (I, 321). When the dancing leads at last to weariness, they seat themselves upon the turf and listen to stories. But some of the company are interested in more thoughtful matters, and they withdraw for contemplation:

> Who thus were ripe for high contemplating,
> Might turn their steps towards the sober ring
> Where sat Endymion and the aged priest
> 'Mong shepherds gone in eld, whose looks increas'd
> The silvery setting of their mortal star.
> There they discours'd upon *the fragile bar*
> *That keeps us from our homes ethereal;*
> And what our duties there: to nightly call
> Vesper, the beauty-crest of summer weather;
> To summon all the downiest clouds together
> For the sun's purple couch; to emulate
> In ministring the potent rule of fate
> With speed of fire-tailed exhalations;
> To tint her pallid cheek with bloom, who cons
> Sweet poesy by moonlight: besides these,
> A world of other unguess'd offices. (I, 355–70)

The "contemplative" elder shepherds here depicture their charmingly naïve conception of postmortal existence. "Our homes ethereal" are obviously not incorporeal or "spiritual," but a kind of enhanced play-world compounded of a rather childlike execution of the "rule of fate" and—here Keats's interest enters, rather anachronistically—tinting the cheeks of mortal maidens who read poetry by moonlight! The passage might be dismissed as an attempt to depict the childlike minds of a primitive people, were it not for the telltale "us" and "our" in I, 362–63. Like the interest in tinting the cheeks of feminine readers of poetry, these pronouns are not merely the result of a faulty historical sense; they are unconscious autobiographic confessions. Keats seems to share with his shepherds a hope of heaven. It is hardly accidental, furthermore, that between mortality and immortality, as Keats declares, there is only a "fragile bar." The implication seems to be that gifted spirits, perhaps even during mortality, can pass beyond the pale. "The poet's eye can reach those golden halls," as we were told in "To My Brother George"; to the poet, privileged by imagination, "that far seat of blisses" is ever and again visible.

The verses which follow those quoted above offer a close parallel to the "favorite speculation" of Letter 31:

> Anon they wander'd, by divine converse,
> *Into Elysium; vieing to rehearse*
> *Each one his own anticipated bliss.*
> One felt *heart-certain* that he could not miss
> His quick gone love . . .
> Another wish'd, mid that eternal spring,

> To meet his rosy child . . .
> Some were athirst in soul to see again
> Their fellow huntsmen . . .
> > Thus all *out-told*
> > *Their fond imaginations* . . . (I, 371–93)

Again it is easy to read these lines as Keats's attempt to depict the minds of a primitive pastoral people. But the question at once arises: if this was his only intention, if his own faith did not coincide with that of the shepherd folk, why did he write the ardent letter to Bailey? The parallels between the italicized passages in the verse and the "favorite speculation" so fervently elaborated in Letter 31 are too close to be the result of coincidence only. In the preceding verses, as we have seen, the telltale pronouns and the divine recreation of tinting the cheeks of maidens reading poetry betrayed Keats's strong interest in the elysian speculations of his "contemplative" shepherds. The significant expressions in the present passage—"heart-certain," "anticipated bliss," and "fond [i.e., loving][15] imaginations" are exactly echoed in Letter 31, where Keats argued that "the truth of imagination" is inseparable from "the holiness of the heart's affections," that imagination is "a shadow of reality to come," and that this reality to come (= elysium) is "happiness on earth repeated in a finer tone."

While the shepherds please themselves in "anticipated bliss" of heavenly reunion with those they loved on earth, Endymion is overborne by his secret grief, and "swoons off" (I, 398). This is a convenient anaesthesia, administered by the sympathetic Keats at almost every point in the poem where Endymion shows signs of acute suffering. A gentle and benignant companion soon appears: his sister Peona, who leads him away to a pleasant bower, where again he is "quieted to slumbrous rest" (I, 442). At once Keats apostrophizes sleep (I, 453–63), typically praising it less for the repose it brings (which presumably Endymion needed) than for the imaginary dramas which it unfolds. Dreamful, not dreamless, sleep appeals to the poet; for it is the "great key to golden palaces, . . . to all the mazy world / Of silvery enchantment." "Sleep and Poetry" was no accidental title of an earlier poem; according to Keats, dreamful sleep contains the very stuff of poetry and is, presumably, of happiness all compact. Until some time in 1818, there is scarcely a hint in his writings of the unpleasant aspect of dreams.

When Endymion awakes, Peona, like a faithful confidante, gently persuades him to tell the cause of his sorrow. It all began with a dream, he ex-

---

[15] Keats seems not to have meant "fond" in the sense of foolish or credulous, but of affectionate and loving: "fond imaginations" arise from the heart's fondnesses, its "holy" affections. This interpretation is supported by fourteen of the seventeen occurrences of "fond" and its derivatives in Keats's verse. See the Concordance.

plains, a vividly blissful dream in which his "dazzled soul" commingled with a "passionately bright" moon (I, 594) ; the moon then disappeared behind clouds, and suddenly a ravishing blonde female descended into his arms. "Such a paradise of lips and eyes" (I, 618) he had never seen and now can scarcely describe; her "passionate looks" (I, 657) raised him to unimaginable heights of ecstasy :

> madly did I kiss
> The wooing arms which held me. . . .
> I ev'n dar'd to press
> Her very cheek against my crowned lip . . . (I, 653–62)

Thus embracing, their bodies sank gently into a bed of flowers, and there in "our nest" (I, 670), says Endymion, they prolonged their ecstasy until "my sweet dream / Fell into nothing" (I, 677–78). To recover again this dream, and to convert it into everlasting reality ("an immortality of passion"—II, 808) is the cardinal motivation of Endymion throughout the remainder of the poem.

It may be remarked at this point that the emotional apogees in *Endymion,* from Keats's point of view at least, are invariably the physical embraces of the lovers. Bent as he is on celebrating the delights of physical love, Keats does not suffer his hero to be under any illusion as to the nature of his visitant. So far as Endymion is concerned, his dream-goddess is no allegorical creature; both he and she appear to be naïvely ignorant of Platonism or neo-Platonism or any kind of Idealism. Neither in the four thousand lines of the poem nor in any remarks to his friends did Keats leave a hint that he disagreed with Endymion's interpretation : poet and poet's hero were celebrating the joys of "boyish poet-love"; the mistress that their sleep bodied forth was a voluptuous woman bent on giving and receiving erotic pleasure.[16]

In the first draft of the poem, two verses (I, 646–47)—later emended— showed a striking parallel to the prefigurative truth of Letter 31 : Endymion's love-dream made him

> Sleepy with deep foretasting, that did bless
> My Soul from Madness, t'was such certainty.[17]

Even in the midst of his dream it appears that Endymion felt a sensation of sleepiness; evidently the extreme felicity of his experience suggested the familiar association with sleep or the trance-state. Still more important,

---

[16] For ample evidence of the erotic theme in *Endymion,* and for evidence against the familiar transcendental allegorizations, see Newell F. Ford, "Endymion—a Neo-Platonic Allegory?" *ELH,* XIV (March 1947), 64.

[17] See H. W. Garrod, ed., *Keats' Poetical Works* (Oxford: The Clarendon Press, 1939), p. 84. The spelling of "t'was" follows the manuscript.

however, is the "certainty" that this felicity is a prefiguration (a "foretasting"). Here is the familiar heart-logic seen in the letter to Bailey and in the "heart-certain," "anticipated bliss" of the contemplative shepherds.

When Endymion brings his dream-history to a close, he describes the melancholy loss of his dream, and then patiently listens to a homily from his sympathetic sister. Dreams are less than nothing, she propounds with Pertelotean skepticism, until she appears to have persuaded her brother of his illusions. "Shame and ruth" pass across his face, but only for a moment; color suddenly returns to his pallid cheek, and now it is Peona's turn to listen:

> "Peona! ever have I long'd to slake
> My thirst for the world's praises: nothing base,
> No merely slumberous phantasm, could unlace
> The stubborn canvas for my voyage prepar'd—
>   . . . my higher hope
> Is of too wide, too rainbow-large a scope,
> To fret at myriads of earthly wrecks.
> Wherein lies happiness? In that which becks
> Our ready minds to fellowship divine,
> A fellowship with essence . . ." (I, 769–79)

The first verses of this prologue to the passage on the gradations of happiness (I, 777 ff.—the value judgment examined in chapter i) are pregnant with unconscious confession: Endymion argues that his dream was "no merely slumberous phantasm" precisely because of its intense felicity, and because his hope is higher and stronger than that of other mortals. For the same reason he will discount the "myriads of earthly wrecks" suffered by others who were seduced by hope, because his own hope seems to exceed theirs! To consecutive minds this kind of "logic" might be called the hope-fallacy. Not so to minds whose convictions are rooted in the heart's affections.

After naming the four gradations of happiness and insisting that love, passionate love, is incomparably the highest felicity, Endymion rhapsodizes on this felicity through some fifty verses, coming finally to two assertions which suggest why he was so ardent a defender of the prefigurative veracity of his love-dream:

> I have ever thought that it [love] might bless
> The world with benefits unknowingly. (I, 826–27)

The benefit to the lovers themselves, Endymion boldly adds, is that love actually triumphs over death, not figuratively but literally:

> 'Now if *this earthly love has power to make*
> *Men's being mortal, immortal*; to shake
> Ambition from their memories, and brim
> Their measure of content; what merest whim,

> Seems all this poor endeavour after fame,
> To one, who keeps within his stedfast aim
> *A love immortal, an immortal too.*   (I, 843–49)

The last verse would be clearer if Keats had written:

> A love everlasting, the love of *an* immortal,

that is, of his dream-goddess. Cautious minds may object that the poet here allows his hero inconsistently to anticipate his ultimate apotheosis; but though this knowledge may partially underlie the assertion, Endymion's language has a universal application. He is stating a principle, a law of love, and Keats seems to be concurring with him—just as Endymion's words describing the gradations of happiness were claimed by Keats as a general "truth" (Letter 42).

It is a daring statement, surely, that the love of mortals guarantees the immortality of lovers, but Keats's theme is exactly this, as the Glaucus-Scylla episode in Book III, with its multitudinous resurrection of dead lovers, and Endymion's own apotheosis in Book IV, make progressively clear.[18] And we can be sure that this faith is shared by both poet and hero, because the first *Endymion* ("I stood tip-toe . . .") proclaims it in Keats's own, not his characters', words,[19] and because Letter 31 was written by Keats, not by Endymion.

Like "consecutive" men, Peona is troubled at such high claims. She has had no love-dreams to make her "heart-certain" of immortalization, and needs to be reassured by her brother. He thus corrects her skepticism:

> Look not so wilder'd; for *these things are true,*
> And never can be born of atomies
> That buzz about our slumbers, like brain-flies,
> Leaving us fancy-sick. No, no, I'm sure,

---

[18] To intrepret the immortality of lovers (referred to in I, 843–49) as the figurative immortality of posthumous fame would be erroneous for another reason: the passage deliberately contrasts the immortality mentioned with the immortality of fame.

[19] In "I stood tip-toe . . ." Keats declares that his purpose is to "tell but one wonder of thy [Cynthia's] bridal night" (l. 210), and then describes this wonder as the miraculous gift of health and joy to ill and melancholy mortal lovers (ll. 221–35), followed by a guaranty of their continuous and eternal happiness:

> Therefore no lover did of anguish die:
> But the soft numbers, in that moment spoken,
> Made silken ties, that never may be broken.   (ll. 236–38)

This is not so dramatic as the multitudinous resurrection of lovers' corpses in Book III of *Endymion*, but it is clear that the wondrous potency of love accomplished both miracles.

> My restless spirit never could endure
> To brood so long upon one luxury,
> Unless it did, though fearfully, espy
> *A hope beyond the shadow of a dream.*
> My sayings will the less obscured seem,
> When I have told thee how my waking sight
> Has made me scruple whether that same night
> Was pass'd in dreaming. (I, 850–60).

"A hope beyond the shadow of a dream"—what is this but the verse equivalent of the phrase in the letter to Bailey: "a shadow of reality to come"? The "reasoning" is also the same as that in the letter, and reiterates the heart-logic of the gathered shepherds earlier in the poem. Of hope and wish, nurtured in the heart, "truth" is born; such is the creed of poet and poet's hero.

Patient, unpoetic Peona listens quietly while her brother describes three visions of his dream-lady subsequent to the dream. A triple confirmation of a pleasurable dream scarcely justifies skepticism, and this is why Book I can end with a recapitulation of Endymion's faith in the veracity of dreams:

> There is a paly flame of hope that plays
> Where'er I look, (I, 984–85)

even though for Peona's sake he will "bid it die."

But Endymion's creator was of another mind, meaning to keep that flame alive until "the shadow of reality to come" should be succeeded by the substance of reality arrived.

Book II

Keats begins his second book with a repetition of the eulogy of love which Endymion spun forth from the value judgment concerning happiness. There is little difference between the two passages in what they say about love; what is significant is that the induction to Book II is in Keats's own words, proving again that he and his hero share a single faith. The entire history of great deeds, he asserts, is as nothing when compared with the poets' stories of love. It can even be said with confidence that all aspects of history save the amorous are guilefully overvalued:

> Hence, pageant history! hence, gilded cheat!
> Swart planet in the universe of deeds! (II, 14–15)

Thus the entire Trojan War is an idle tale not worth the attention, except for the love story of Troilus and Cressida.

> Yet, in our very souls, we feel amain
> The close of Troilus and Cressid sweet. (II, 12–13)

Not the sad ending of that story interests Keats, but "the close" (i.e., the embrace)[20] of lovers. And so his task in *Endymion,* as he conceives it, is to tread "the path of [passionate] love and poesy"; soldierlike, he is "striving to uprear Love's standard on the battlements of song" (II, 38–41).

This is typical of the young Keats's conception of love. Despite the traditional allegorical interpretations, there is scarcely a suggestion of Heavenly Love in the whole of *Endymion,* except in the sense—a very important one, though Keats does not make it explicit—that physical passion as contemplated by the imagination is more ideal than physical passion directly experienced. Indeed, this may be what he meant by the words in Letter 31, that "I have the same idea of all our passions as of love they are all *in their sublime* creative of essential beauty." *Endymion* is the story of love in its sublime, of love exalted and worshiped by the *imagination* of hero and poet. Such love is holy because its seat is in the heart and because the heart's affections are the source of the supremest happiness of earth and the guaranty of a superior felicity in heaven.[21]

Nevertheless, the mode in which Keats's imagination envisions the sublime love of Endymion and Cynthia is not sublime or ideal in the sense of spiritual or nonphysical. This is a crucial point, obvious enough to the reader who is willing to take Keats at his word, but frequently obscured to those who read *Endymion,* as it has so long been read, *sub specie allegoriae.* If the allegorical premises are surrendered, an invariable rule can be discerned throughout the poem: in Keats's judgment the sublimest moments are those in which Endymion and Cynthia lie in erotic embrace. These passages often contain the weakest poetry, to be sure, but Keats supposed them to be the high points of his poem, higher than his poetic capacity could adequately describe. We have witnessed as much already in Book I, where Endymion enjoyed his pristine love-dream; but the subsequent embraces are even more telltale, especially the one in II, 707 ff. where, confessing that he is incapable of matching the amorous ecstasy with words, Keats desperately beseeches "Old Homer's Helicon" to come to his aid!

After the induction to Book II, the poet conducts Endymion on mazy journeys, ever searching for the substance of his dream. Pursuing a butter-

---

[20] The word is so defined by Woodhouse and corroborated by Ernest de Sélincourt, *The Poems of John Keats,* 6th ed., p. 430.

[21] Cf. what Keats said about the heart on another occasion: "I wish, at one view, you would see my heart toward you [i.e., Charles Brown]. 'Tis only *from a high tone of feeling* that I can put that word on paper—*out of poetry.*" (Letter 155, p. 397—italics mine).

fly, which is metamorphosed into a naiad who kisses her hand to him, the shepherd receives from her a message of hope:

> thou must wander far
> In other regions, past the scanty bar
> To mortal steps, before thou cans't be ta'en
> From every wasting sigh, from every pain,
> Into the gentle bosom of thy love (II, 123–26)

Endymion's goal, evidently, is escape from mortality; the "scanty bar" that separates him from endless bliss with his beloved is the same as the "fragile bar / That keeps us from our homes ethereal" (I, 360–61).

While these words might have restored him to confidence and unwavering hope, it is not thus that Endymion reacts. Instead he is puzzled, and sits down to meditate upon the "fancied city of delight" which leads many a hopeful man to failure and disillusionment. Words like these are prophetic of the soberer poet of later years; momentarily divorced from his naïve and wishful creed, Keats allows Endymion to speak words of mature wisdom:

> But this is human life: the war, the deeds,
> The disappointment, the anxiety,
> Imagination's struggles, far and nigh,
> All human; bearing in themselves this good,
> That they are still the air, the subtle food,
> To make us feel existence, and to show
> How quiet death is. (II, 153–59)

If age is mental rather than chronological, Keats was scarcely younger when he wrote these sober words than when he sketched his philosophy in the "Vale of Soul-Making" in 1819.[22] One of the minor themes of Endymion is this sober wisdom which mistrusts fervent hopes and prefigurative dreams. Keats's mental age advanced rapidly during the months given to the poem, but his new wisdom was vacillatory, permitting such emphatic contradictions as the rapt letter to Bailey. Moments could undo, or seem to undo, the experience of months. Such was the poet's fate even in the years that followed, though the self-deceptions occurred less frequently in proportion as he came to perceive, and to resign himself to, the limitations of mortality.

Despite his moment of resignation, however, Endymion is unwilling to surrender his dream, for

> I can see
> Naught earthly worth my compassing. (II, 161–2)

Only his "thrice-seen love" (II, 168) is worthy of service, he avers, and he prays to Cynthia for help (not knowing, of course, the identity of his dream-

---

22 Letter 123, pp. 334 ff.

love). Almost at once his spirit is elevated in ecstasy and escapes the "fragile bar":

> by all the stars
> That tend thy bidding, I do think the bars
> That kept my spirit in are burst—that I
> Am sailing with thee through the dizzy sky!
> How beautiful thou art! (II, 184–88)

As the trance dissolves, Endymion stands tremblingly on earth, and hears a voice from a deep cavern:

> now, as deep profound
> As those are high, descend! He ne'er is crown'd
> With immortality, who fears to follow
> Where airy voices lead: so through the hollow,
> The silent mysteries of earth, descend! (II, 210–14)

Without the courage that banishes skepticism, the voice declares (and without trust in dreams and imagination, it is implied), Endymion cannot attain immortality and its lasting happiness. Had not Keats's message to Bailey been the same—that heaven awaits those alone who trust the imagination? "Consecutive" men do not go to heaven because they do not trust "airy voices."

Still quaking from his aerial ecstasy, and more alarmed than calmed by the voice from the cavern, Endymion heeds the imperious words, and flees beneath the earth. Through spacious, fantastically wrought underground passages he proceeds, lighted by innumerable gems. So far as the story is concerned, there seem to be but two reasons for conducting Endymion thither: to prove his fidelity in love despite delays and frustrations, and to give the poet a chance to fill in his predetermined four thousand lines. Many similar divagations scattered through the four books can as plausibly be explained by these two motivations.

Absorbed in contemplation of the beauties of the underground passages, Endymion fails to see other beauties which stir his poet:

> He saw not fiercer wonders—past the wit
> Of any spirit to tell, but one of those
> Who, when this planet's sphering time doth close,
> Will be its high remembrancers: who they?
> The mighty ones who have made eternal day
> For Greece and England. (II, 249–54)

The attitude here expressed is the familiar one—no mere fiction to Keats— that poets live in elysium after death. He envisions the great poets of Greece and England as not merely idle in their postmortal existence; along with other employments, theirs will be the privilege, since no others will be capable, of transmuting the wonders of this perishable underworld to imperishable poetry!

While Endymion is exploring these labyrinthine halls beneath the earth, he discovers a statute of Diana in a temple, does brief obeisance to her, and wanders onward. Up to this time the beauties of the place have diverted him from thought of his sorrow. But he grows weary of this lone enjoyment of beauty, weary even of its abundance, and at last sits down before a wild, tenebrous cavern:

> There, when new wonders ceas'd to float before,
> And thoughts of self came on, how crude and sore
> The journey homeward to habitual self!
> A mad-pursuing of the fog-born elf,
> Whose flitting lantern, through rude nettle-briar,
> Cheats us into a swamp, into a fire,
> Into the bosom of a hated thing. (II, 274–80)

In Keats's first draft the motivations are clearer still; for there the fog-born elf

> Cheats us into a swamp, cuttings and shreds
> Of old vexations plaited to a rope
> Wherewith to drag us *from the sight of hope,*
> *And fix us to our earthly baiting-ring.* (II, 279–80 ff.)[23]

Thus when Endymion's hope (and Keats's, also?) dies or is frustrated, he falls into periods of melancholy and distrusts the visions whose prefigurative veracity he had defended to the skeptical Peona. But it can hardly be Endymion alone that the passage refers to. From the point of view of the creative poet, when "the elevation of the moment" passes and rapture cools, the attention is recalled from the blissful concentration on the aesthetic object, and "thoughts of self," of *"habitual* self," and of the everyday, unimaginative world of fact, repossess the mind. The record of this oscillation, often painful and disturbing, between the ecstatic absorption in an aesthetic object and the unecstatic aftermath, runs throughout Keats's writings. It may be attributed to an extraordinary capacity for perfervid imaginative experience, to the natural and proportionately strong desire to prolong such felicitous moments, and to the incapacity, so long as one is mortal, to be successful in this.

Endymion's disillusioned confession constitutes the very obverse of the staunch faith in the letter to Bailey and in the first book of *Endymion.* Yet the distrust of optimism grows in importance as the poem develops, even though destined to be contravened by the resurrection of lovers in Book III

---

[23] See Garrod, *Keats' Poetical Works,* p. 104.

and by Endymion's deification in Book IV. Considered as data for the mental biography of Keats, however, every doubt of the "authenticity" of the imagination is prophetic of the maturer poet who in 1819 turned, at times almost violently, against "the dreamer tribe" and its wish-made world. "La Belle Dame" (if it is in any sense autobiographical), "Lamia," and "The Fall of Hyperion" confirm this tendency which in 1817 finds occasional and tentative utterance. And the "Ode to a Nightingale" returns, though less bitterly, to the thought and very wording of Endymion's disillusioned soliloquy.[24]

As the poem continues, the hero bewails his solitude, regarding himself as "an exiled mortal" (II, 316). Longing for a return to his familiar earthly haunts, and praying to Diana, he is miraculously rewarded with a metamorphosis of his marble surroundings into green foliage and flowers. At once hope is reborn and he continues his journey, soon to be rewarded with a still more miraculous adventure. In a sumptuous bower he discovers a sleeping youth of rare and voluptuous beauty. While Endymion gazes wonderingly upon Adonis' luxuriously sensuous bower, his poet enumerates its things of beauty, from lilies and lavish vines to minstrel Cupids. One of the latter has a message for the visitor:

> be of happy cheer!
> For 'tis the nicest touch of human honour,
> When some ethereal and high-favouring donor
> *Presents immortal bowers to mortal sense;*
> As now 'tis done to thee, Endymion. (II, 435–39)

The "ethereal" donor is an immortal (Cynthia or Venus?), and has signalized the human shepherd's fidelity in love by permitting him a glimpse of heaven. Manifestly this honor is not an end in itself: it promises ultimate happiness to the wanderer and is thus a kind of equivalent in direct experience of a prefigurative vision. It serves the same function, on a smaller scale, as the Glaucus-Scylla episode in Book III, where the legions of dead lovers are resurrected.

Endymion is instructed to recline upon the flowers and taste of a variety of luxurious fruits, while the minstrel Cupid narrates Adonis' history,

> telling how the sea-born goddess pin'd
> For a mortal youth. (II, 458–59)

---

[24] Cf. the closing stanza of the "Ode to a Nightingale" (even the rhymes and the figure of speech are the same):

> Forlorn! the very word is like a bell
> To *toll me back from thee to my sole self!*
> Adieu! the *fancy cannot cheat so well*
> As she is fam'd to do, *deceiving elf!*

Adonis was unresponsive,

> content to see
> An unseiz'd heaven dying at his feet. (II, 463–64)

At this the sympathetic Endymion, pricked on by his poet, is about to "call /
Curses upon his [Adonis'] head" (II, 471–72), but is inhibited by the Cupid
who continues his story. After the boar slew the insouciant Adonis, Venus
distractedly implored the help of Jupiter, who wept like Pluto when Orpheus
pled for his Eurydice, and straightway

> decreed he [Adonis] should be rear'd
> Each summer time to life. Lo! this is he,
> That same Adonis, safe in the privacy
> Of this still region all his winter-sleep.
> *Aye, sleep*; for when our love-sick queen did weep
> Over his waned corse, the tremulous shower
> Heal'd up the wound, and, with a balmy power,
> *Medicined death to a lengthened drowsiness:*
> *The which she fills with visions*, and doth dress
> In all this quiet luxury. (II, 447–86)

In deference to the omnipotence of love, Adonis' death was thus commuted
to a sleep, the sleep itself being filled with prefigurative visions of amorous
bliss! Keats is not interested in the naturalistic symbolism of the myth or
in Spenser's metaphysical Garden of Adonis; he treats it as a simple history
of true love, and purposely locates it here in his second book to renew Endymion's faith in the veracity of his dream.

Thus a portion of heaven—an erotic heaven—has been revealed to Endymion. Through half of each supernal year Adonis sweetly dreams of "the
first long kiss" (II, 491) and "embracements warm" (II, 533); the other
half *enacts* what he dreamed. The Adonis episode is, in short, a kind of parallel of Adam's dream, and another seeming proof of "the truth of imagination." Adonis' sleep prefigures heaven, and his waking *is* heaven. Likewise
Endymion, in being permitted to visit this "immortal bower" with his "mortal
sense," enjoys a double apocalypse: the vicarious one of Adonis, and the
personal one of his own promised felicity.

But on vision alone Endymion is not required to depend; for presently
Venus herself approaches, Adonis awakes, and the lovers are rapturously
joined. Pitying Endymion's loneliness, she reassures him:

> Endymion! one day thou wilt be blest;
> So still obey the guiding hand that fends
> Thee safely through these wonders for sweet ends. (II, 573–75)

While Venus and Adonis float away into the air, the questing shepherd sets
forward again, suffused with hope. Coming to the end of his path, he prays

to Jupiter, who sends a large eagle which, reversing Chaucer's journey, carries Endymion downward through a mighty chasm to "a jasmine bower, all bestrown / With golden moss" (II, 668–71):

> His every sense had grown
> Ethereal for pleasure; 'bove his head
> Flew a delight half-graspable; his tread
> Was Hesperean; to his capable ears
> Silence was music from the holy spheres. (II, 671–75)

One would guess that he must be in such an "immortal bower" as "ethereal donors" sometimes reveal to "mortal sense." If his senses are "ethereal for pleasure" and his tread "Hesperean," he must be capable of godlike pleasures. He says as much a few lines later: "I feel immortal" (though he is perplexed that immortality and the embrace of his beloved are not synonymous).

In a moment this perplexity is obliterated by an erotic embrace. Feeling "endued / With power to dream deliciously" (II, 707–8), Endymion throws himself onto a mossy bed. But before sleep arrives, his long-cherished love-dream comes true for his *waking* consciousness:

> Stretching his indolent arms, he took, O bliss!
> A naked waist: "Fair Cupid, whence is this?"
> A well-known voice sigh'd, "Sweetest, here am I!"
> At which soft ravishment, with doting cry
> They trembled to each other.—Helicon!
> O fountain'd hill! Old Homer's Helicon!
> That thou wouldst spout a little streamlet o'er
> These sorry pages; then the verse would soar
> And sing above this gentle pair . . . (II, 712–20)

That either Homer or Helicon responded to Keats's desperate plea will seem doubtful to some readers, for Endymion's passion mounts quite un-Homerically as the lovers lie delightedly "fondling and kissing" (II, 735). As if to make the theme of his poem emphatically clear, as if indeed he foresaw the neo-Platonic interpreters of a later day, Keats causes Endymion to particularize the physical attractions of Cynthia. Beginning with her face, he singles out "those lips, O slippery blisses," backtracks to her "twinkling eyes," then rises, or struggles to rise, to the *summum bonum*, the "tenderest, milky sovereignties" of her breasts (II, 758–59). At this point, the sovereign moment of his ecstasy, he swoons, signifying that with the contemplation of Cynthia's breasts he has reached—and passed—the highest point of human bliss. His senses are saturated and perforce must rest.

Except for the desirability of veiling what a young poet has rather ineptly if feelingfully described, there can be no reason for importing a neo-Platonic allegory into such a passage, any more than Plato can enlighten us on Keats's ecstatic eulogy of a beautiful woman whom he had seen at Vauxhall:

> In vain! away I cannot chace
> The melting softness of that face,
> The beaminess of those bright eyes,
> *That breast—earth's only Paradise.*
> ("Fill for me a brimming bowl," ll. 13–16)

We need to remember, of course, that Keats was young and relatively inexperienced both as poet and lover, and also that he was describing love as his imagination idealized it. Such love was sacred to him, however weak or Leigh Huntian his verses might appear. Porphyro and Madeline, Lycius and Lamia, Keats and Fanny Brawne (in the "Bright star" sonnet, for instance) enjoy the same experiences as Endymion and Cynthia, but these cause no distress for the sensitive reader. Why? Not because Keats was more spiritual in his later poems, but because he had learned good taste and had gained control of his language. In short, he was no longer an apprentice poet.

Prior to Endymion's swooning, there was a moment in which he expressed his supreme desire in words that revealingly tie together two diverse eras of Keats's life. Addressing his unknown beloved, Endymion exclaims:

> O known Unknown! from whom my being sips
> Such darling essence, wherefore may I not
> Be ever in these arms? in this sweet spot
> Pillow my chin for ever? ever press
> These toying hands and kiss their smooth excess?
> Why not for ever and for ever feel
> That breath about my eyes? (II, 739–45)

No one who has read the "Bright star" sonnet can fail to see its prototype in these lines, where both the words and the ideas are almost exactly parallel. The breast of the loved one, whether Cynthia or Fanny, is regarded by the lover, whether Endymion or Keats, as a luxurious pillow for the male head, and as the source of breathing which communicates pleasing sensations. But the cardinal idea in the minds of both lovers is their ardent yearning to prolong the ecstasy of physical love through all eternity. This desire to prolong supreme moments of earthly happiness forever, finds frequent expression in Keats's writings, and is obviously related to the "favorite speculation" of Letter 31, where prolongation is admitted to be impossible, but postmortal "repetition" is fervently upheld.

When we return to the text we find Endymion listening to the longest speech that Cynthia at any time utters (II, 761–824). Her endeavor is to persuade him, whom she has revived from his swoon with kisses, that she is passionately and enduringly in love with him, but that certain conditions in heaven make it as yet impossible for her to reveal her identity or to snatch him immediately into heaven. She confesses being "ashamed" (II, 787) of what the other gods will think, especially Jove and Minerva, if she, famous for her chastity, should be found a victim of passionate love.[25] Furthermore, she fears she may forfeit her "crystalline dominion" and the worship that she has long enjoyed. "But what is this to love?" she then defiantly exclaims (II, 795), longing to have Endymion "press [her] sweetly" forever (II, 798). Her cult and worship, even her reputation on Olympus, are as nothing to the ecstasies of love. Who is Minerva after all, and how happy is she in her chaste wisdom? "Now I swear at once / That I am wise [to be in love], that Pallas is a dunce" [to be "wise" but loveless] (II, 799). Yet who knows, in fact, whether Pallas herself may have a secret lover: "Perhaps her love like mine is but unknown" (800). If so, not Pallas but Cynthia is the dunce: "O I do think that I have been alone / In chastity" (801–2).

No Galahad is Keats's Cynthia. Her confessed enlightenment might well be regarded as a sufficient assurance to the anguished shepherd, lying in her arms all this while, of their eventual union and eternal felicity. But even a lover's words ought to be sealed by some sacred ritual to be wholly believed in. Since Endymion is not a Christian, the Bible is out of the question; very properly, therefore, Cynthia seals her vow with a soft kiss:

> Sweet love,
> I was as vague as solitary dove,
> Nor knew that nests were built. Now a soft kiss—
> Aye, by that kiss, I vow an endless bliss,
> *An immortality of passion's thine.* (II, 804–8)

Like Juliet, as Keats thought of her story at the beginning of this book ("weaning / Tenderly her fancy from its maiden snow"—II, 28–29), Cynthia confesses that the supreme experience of a woman, in heaven as on earth, is her transition from the state of maidenhood to that of passionate love. Still more important, the fate which she promises to Endymion is a verification of his dream, and in its wording might fittingly stand as the major theme of *Endymion*. No quest of ideal, Platonic beauty is this "immortality of *passion*" which, through the four books of the poem, the hero strenuously seeks and ultimately wins.

---

[25] More ethically minded than either Cynthia or Keats, Matthew Arnold was impressed with Cynthia's defection from chastity:

> the conscious thrill of *shame*
> Which Luna felt . . .
> When she forsook the starry height
> To hang over Endymion's sleep. . . .
> ("Isolation. To Marguerite," ll. 19–24)

When Cynthia leaves him, Endymion subsides into an anesthetic swoon, but later awakes to melancholy thoughts of remembered happiness and present solitude. After a time he is startled by the sudden irruption of two rushing streams, the one madly pursuing the other. Then a voice impassionedly calls upon Arethusa, yearning to encircle "her waist," to steal "in between her luscious lips" and "kissing breasts" (II, 940, 942, 947). The voice is that of Alpheus the pursuing river, and to his entreaties the fleeing Arethusa answers that Diana's edict is the cause of their love's frustration. Then the streams sink into a chasm, and Endymion prays to his own beloved, who is, of course, though unknown to him, the same Diana or Cynthia:

> he wept, and said: "I urge
> Thee, gentle Goddess of my pilgrimage,
> *By our eternal hopes,* to soothe, to assuage,
> If thou art powerful, these lovers' pains;
> And make them happy in some happy plains."   (II, 1013–17)

May Alpheus and Arethusa be rewarded with everlasting love in elysium—this is his prayer. Such a boon he might properly have requested for himself, and doubtless this is the reason that he speaks of *"our* eternal hopes." For hope not only "springs eternal in the human breast," but by its very existence seems to promise *eternity* to *all* imaginative minds. This is the heart-logic—or hope-logic—that motivated the letter to Bailey and the major theme of *Endymion.*

Once again sleep comes to the shepherd-prince, this time for a different purpose: Keats magically shifts the scene, and when the curtain of sleep is lifted, Endymion beholds "the giant sea above his head" (II, 1023). Book II is at an end.

A backward glance over the book reveals at once its structure and purpose. Disregarding the decorative effect ("the little region to wander in") of the lavish description of the underworld, the major *foci* of the book, so far as the plot and the prefigurative theme are concerned, are the Adonis episode and the embrace of Endymion and Cynthia. Endymion's visit to the bower of Adonis serves him as the equivalent of a prefigurative dream. Cynthia's visit to Endymion, not in dream but in actuality, promises him "an immortality of passion." Thus the two episodes have a single aim, the chief difference being that Endymion is first a spectator, then an actor.

In Book I he told Peona that he had been visited during his dreams. Now he can say that he has actually, consciously entered into heaven, if only for a brief time. To a degree, then, his dreams have already come true. The Alpheus-Arethusa episode is a weak epilogue intended to round out the one thousand lines of the book, showing once again that passionate love is the crown and sum of things.

Keats probably intended, and then forgot, to unite Alpheus and Arethusa at a later point in the poem. This would be a logical consequence of Cynthia's renunciation of chastity and of her approaching union with Endymion; it would also be a verification of the theme that love "bless[es] / The world with benefits unknowingly." In Book III the poet dramatically illustrates this principle by making Endymion's love the agent of a multitudinous resurrection of dead and faithful lovers, but the less miraculous union of Alpheus and Arethusa fails to take place. They do not reappear in the poem.

IV. THE PREFIGURATIVE THEME IN *ENDYMION* (BOOKS III-IV)

The induction to Book III consists of an oddly irrelevant diatribe against the tyrannic governors of Keats's own day, which leads the poet to contrast these earthly rulers with the deities who dwell beyond earth's confines. Though

> few of these far majesties, ah, few!
> Have bared their operations to this globe—(III, 34–35)

to the poet-mind, it seems, they sometimes reveal themselves,

> every *sense*
> Filling with *spiritual* sweets to plenitude. (III, 38–39)

It was thus that Adonis' "immortal bowers" were disclosed to Endymion's "mortal sense," though now Keats speaks in his own person, not one of his character's. And he proceeds to an encomium of Cynthia as the most attractive of all the deities who have poured their "spiritual [= immortal] sweets" into "mortal sense." In her lunar embodiment Cynthia touches all earthly things with her beauty, so that, for example,

> The sleeping kine,
> Couch'd in thy [her] brightness, *dream of fields divine.* (III, 57–58)

This curious prescience of elysium on the part of cattle is not merely an expression of the pathetic fallacy; it is an extension of Keats's "favorite speculation" from the dreams and imagination of mankind to the dreams of animal kind.

After one hundred lines of induction, devoted largely to the adoration of Cynthia in lunar embodiment, Keats resumes his story. Cynthia's beams pierce the depths of ocean and guide Endymion on his way. He has not proceeded far, however, before he pauses to apostrophize the moon in a well-known passage (III, 142 ff.). Partly appropriate to the pastoral life of the shepherd-prince, and partly derived from Keats's own interest in the moon and all things beautiful, partly, too, influenced by the famous mystic passage in "Tintern Abbey," these lines appear to identify "all my ardours" with Endymion's principal ardor for the moon itself. There is no hint of the Wordsworthian idea of immanence, however; Keats may have enjoyed "elevated thoughts," but these seem not to have derived from any sense of a divine "presence" diffused pantheistically through the material world. With the influence of "Tintern Abbey" subtracted (it is largely a matter of diction and form of statement), Keats appears to be writing a kind of equivalent of the "pleasure thermometer" in Book I. All beautiful things are *associated with* the beauty of the moon, we might say in paraphrase, because they have all afforded pleasure to the poet, and because the moon has afforded the supreme pleasure. Inseparable from the lunar pleasure, of course, is Endymion's erotic dream-goddess, causing him to climax his enumeration of "ardours" with "the charm of lovely women" (III, 169). As he confesses in the following verses, his "strange love" (III, 176) ever emerges from his image of the moon; and she brings "a nearer bliss" (III, 175), making his interest in the moon (as separate from her) "an *under*-passion" (III, 179). The love of male for female is thus the *summum bonum,* Endymion and Keats seem joined in believing.

Almost at the very moment when he is exalting his beloved, Endymion discovers that he is not alone upon the floor of the sea. It is not Cynthia who relieves his solitude, but an aged, melancholy man sitting "upon a weeded rock" (III, 193). When he sees Endymion he rises excitedly, and "in a voice of solemn joy" exclaims:

> Thou art the man! . . .
> O Jove! I shall be young again, be young .˙. .
> With new-born life! . . .
> O, I am full of gladness! (III, 233–52)

Unacquainted with the old man's history or the purport of his words, Endymion starts back in dismay and fear but soon yields to pity. The tears come and he kneels before the aged Glaucus.

Although the long episode which follows (III, 187–1032) is of signal importance in understanding the theme of Keats's poem, it has often perplexed critics, as Sidney Colvin freely admits. The standard interpretations, however, usually overcome this perplexity by reading a "moral" of sympathy, unselfishness, and the like into Endymion's experience with Glaucus:

The whole long Glaucus and Scylla episode filling the third book [Colvin writes], . . . has to many lovers and students of Keats proved a riddle hard of solution . . . But bearing in mind what we have recognized as the general scope and symbolic meaning of the poem, does not the main purport of the Glaucus book, on closer study, emerge clearly as something like this? The spirit touched with the divine beam of Cynthia—that is aspiring to and chosen for communion with essential Beauty—in other words the spirit of the Poet—must prepare itself for its high calling, first by purging away the selfishness of its private passion in sympathy with human loves and sorrows, and next by acquiring a full store alike of human experience and of philosophic thought and wisdom.[1]

---

[1] Sidney Colvin, *John Keats* . . . (New York: Charles Scribner's Sons, 1917), p. 194.

Without pressing the transcendental nature of Endymion's quest, de Sélin-court agrees with Colvin as to the "moral" of the Glaucus episode:

. . . the episodes of Arethusa and of Glaucus could have no possible justification in the scheme of the poem had they not been introduced to emphasize the conception, already presented in *Sleep and Poetry*, that only by human sympathy can the poet reach the summit of his power.[2]

The words of Thorpe are similar; he regards Endymion's collaboration with Glaucus as

an act of human love and sympathy that prepares the poet's spirit for the next higher experience, a complete union of the soul with the heart of humanity, . . . the last step to the altar of high poetic insight . . .[3]

Plausible as these allegorizations are, they all pass over one cardinal fact: that if Keats intended the episode to be such a symbolic homily to his hero, he neglected to leave any hint to this effect.

The problem of his meaning can be much simplified if one does not begin with the premise, long orthodox in criticism, that the poem is an allegory, idealistic or specifically neo-Platonic, of the poet-soul in quest of transcendental Beauty. Allegorization becomes unnecessary when the episode is read without such a premise, yet bearing in mind "an immortality of passion" as the hero's cardinal objective, the prefigurative function of the Adonis episode in Book II, and the parallel to the poem's prefigurative theme in Letter 31.

Since the Glaucus episode occupies ll. 187–1032 of Book III, it can be assumed that Keats did not intend it as a digression and that he meant it to illustrate his primary theme. From the outset it is clear that he intended to instruct both his hero and his readers, for this reason causing Glaucus to explain why he and Endymion were destined to meet. Glaucus' first words are joyous because he foresees a metamorphosis of his age and sorrow to youth and happiness. His next words tell Endymion that the cause and warrant of this transfiguration are love:

> Though thou know'st it not,
> Thou art commission'd to this fated spot
> For great enfranchisement. O weep no more;
> I am a friend to love, to loves of yore:
> Aye, hadst thou never lov'd an unknown power,
> I had been grieving at this joyous hour. (III, 297–302)

The "loves of yore" to which he refers are the dead lovers to whom his sor-

---

[2] De Sélincourt, *The Poems of John Keats* (6th ed.; London: Methuen and Company, 1935), p. xli. The interpretation is repeated on p. 438.

[3] Clarence D. Thorpe, *The Mind of John Keats* (New York: Oxford University Press, 1926), p. 60.

rowful years have been devoted and whom we shall soon meet in the flesh. What Endymion is first of all to understand, however, is that his own fidelity in love to his unknown Cynthia has brought good to other beings. Glaucus' life is rendered happier, and soon hundreds of other lives will enjoy new happiness, all because Endymion was faithful in love. This idea has appeared earlier in the poem and will appear again; it consists in the conviction that love "bless[es] / The world with benefits unknowingly."

But it is necessary to know Glaucus' autobiography to understand the causes of both his past suffering and his destined happiness. He begins thus:

> My soul stands
> Now past the midway from mortality. (III, 314–15)

Already Glaucus is regaining youth and taking on immortality at the same time. Soon it will be seen that the cause of this double transformation is love.

One thousand years ago, Glaucus tells Endymion, he was a youthful fisherman, enjoying a simple Arcadian existence. Gradually his contentment gave way to longings which he endeavored to satisfy by plunging beneath the sea and exploring "the ceaseless wonders of this ocean bed" (III, 392). Then he met Scylla, whom he loved "to the very white of truth" (IV, 402). But Scylla fled her lover even as Arethusa fled Alpheus, and Glaucus sought aid of Circe.

Instead of acquiring Circe's help in his pursuit of Scylla, however, he succumbed to the irresistible loveliness of an unknown woman (actually Circe), who brought him "more bliss than all / The range of flower'd Elysium" (III, 427–28). Scylla was forgotten in this "long love dream" (III, 440). Yet his new beloved was not exemplary for constancy and one day deserted him. Rushing out to find her, he came upon a horrid scene amid the forest, where uncouth animal shapes did strange obeisance to his beloved. Glaucus was fascinated and horrified. While he watched, a sighing elephant advanced, beseeching the lady's mercy in human voice:

> I sue not for my lone, my widow'd wife;
> I sue not for my ruddy drops of life,
> My children fair, my lovely girls and boys!
> I will forget them; I will pass these joys;
> Ask nought so heavenward, so too—too high:
> Only I pray, as fairest boon, to die. (III, 545–50)

Plainly, this elephant-man was once a human father and husband, monogamous and faithful. His present fate is evidently the result of his having paid court to Circe while he was wedded to another. Is not this Keats's way of saying that the man has committed love's cardinal sin, infidelity, and that what he now suffers is the consequence of this sin? And may we not assume as much for the other animals (formerly men) who grovel in the power of this magician (actually Circe, as Glaucus learns in a moment)? An expert narrator would have pointed up the theme of infidelity, but we know that Keats disliked "obtrusiveness" in poetry, and that in the craft of narration he was still an apprentice.

When Glaucus realized that he was in the power of Circe, "that curst magician" (III, 555), he sought vainly for three days to escape. But notice here that Keats does not dwell on the sensuality of Circe or those who serve her, as one might expect; in his conception she is a cruel, capricious, and jealous witch, seducing honorable young men and breaking up happy couples! Everywhere she pursued Glaucus, taunting him with his desire to return to a "breast more lily-feminine," that is, Scylla's (III, 577). Filled with jealousy and calling him a "sea-flirt" (III, 581), she cursed him with one thousand years of sorrowing, solitary old age, after which time he must die:

> Thou hast thews
> Immortal, for thou art of heavenly race:
> But such love is mine, that here I chase
> Eternally away from thee all bloom
> Of youth, and destine thee towards a tomb. (III, 588–92)

This is an unexpected, but wholly consistent, inversion of Keats's favorite theme: unfaithful love can ungod a god even as faithful love can deify a mortal.

Before crippled age destroyed his youthful vigor, Glaucus swam furiously through the sea, only to discover the floating dead body of Scylla, victim of Circe's wrath. Lovingly he carried her to a crystalline cavern—where Endymion will shortly go, says Glaucus—and left her in a niche. Almost at the same moment youth fled his bones and decrepit age possessed him.

Passing over the desolate years of his punishment, Glaucus tells Endymion

> How a restoring chance came down to quell
> One half of the witch in me. (III, 644–45)

It happened this way: one day he beheld a ship upon the horizon; then a storm arose and the ship went down with all its "poor struggling souls" (III, 659). As will appear presently, the passengers on this ship symbolized all earthly lovers whom death had cheated of happiness. Glaucus longed to rescue them, but his old age (the penalty for his infidelity) prevented:

> O they had all been sav'd but crazed eld
> Annull'd my vigorous cravings; and thus quell'd
> And curb'd, think on't, O Latmian! did I sit
> Writhing with pity, and a cursing fit
> Against that hell-born Circe. (III, 661–65)

The implication is that had he remained faithful in love he could have rescued the shipwrecked lovers from death, for then he would have retained his youth and strength. Or in terms of a leitmotiv in the poem, true love does good to the rest of the world.

While Glaucus bewailed his inability to save the lovers from death, an old man's hand emerged from the sea, holding forth a scroll and a wand. The hand withdrew, but Glaucus retained—and still preserves, he says—the scroll and the wand. Eagerly he read the scroll and soon found hope for release from Circe's curse:

> a shine of hope
> Came gold around me, cheering me to cope
> Strenuous with hellish tyranny. Attend!
> For thou hast brought their promise to an end. (III, 685–88)

Endymion is requested to listen to the happy promise contained in the scroll, for here lies the secret of the gladness that Endymion himself has brought to Glaucus:

> In wide sea there lives a forlorn wretch,
> Doom'd with enfeebled carcase to outstretch
> His loath'd existence through ten centuries,
> And then to die alone. Who can devise
> A total opposition? No one. So
> One million times ocean must ebb and flow,
> And he oppressed. Yet he shall not die,
> These things accomplish'd: —If he utterly
> Scans all the depths of magic, and expounds
> The meanings of all motions, shapes and sounds;
> If he explores all forms and substances
> Straight homeward to their symbol-essences;
> *He shall not die.* Moreover, and *in chief,*
> He must pursue this task of joy and grief
> Most piously; —*all lovers tempest-tost,*
> *And in the savage overwhelming lost,*
> He shall deposit side by side, until
> Time's creeping shall the dreary space fulfill:
> Which done, and all these labours ripened,
> *A youth, by heavenly power lov'd and led,*
> *Shall stand before him*; whom he shall direct
> How to consummate all. The youth elect
> Must do the thing, or both will be destroy'd. (III, 689–711)

If Glaucus is to escape death (and Endymion also, it seems!), he must perform several tasks, but his poet immediately forgets all the others in the "chief" one: the service to "all lovers tempest-tost." This last phrase, together with a variation of it in III, 722 (quoted below) and Glaucus' obedient collecting of the dead bodies, confirms the symbolism previously suggested for the shipwrecked creatures. They are lovers cheated of happiness by death.

After Glaucus has read the hopeful message on the scroll, Endymion enthusiastically exclaims, "We are twin brothers in this destiny!" (III, 713), and is answered by a confident Glaucus:

> "Look!" the sage replied,
> "Dost thou not mark a gleaming through the tide,
> Of diverse brilliances? 'tis the edifice
> I told thee of, where lovely Scylla lies;
> And where I have enshrined piously
> *All lovers, whom fell storms have doom'd to die*
> Throughout my bondage." (III, 717-23)

Led by the elder man, Endymion enters the jeweled cavern and beholds to his astonishment thousands of lovers lying "in silent rows" (III, 735). Still more remarkable is their appearance in death, with

> patient lips
> All ruddy, —for here death no blossom nips. (III, 739-40)

Like Juliet in the tomb they seem to sleep in beauty. Though the men do not know it yet, exactly this is the condition of the "dead" lovers.

Excitedly the old and young man perform the complex ceremony which the scroll prescribes, Endymion doing his part with unexpected ease which moves Glaucus to cry:

> What, is it done so clean?
> A power overshadows thee! O, brave!
> *The spite of hell is tumbling to its grave.* (III, 758-60)

Quickly the old man directs Endymion to strew certain leaves on his, Glaucus', face, and afterward on the recumbent lovers. In a twinkling Glaucus becomes a smiling youth, and steps to a "beauteous corse" (Scylla), pressing its cold hand. Scylla sighs, Endymion applies the magic leaves, the nymph arises, and Endymion leaves the restored lovers "to their joy." He moves onward between the rows of the dead, scattering his leaves:

> And, as he pass'd, each lifted up his head,
> As doth a flower at Apollo's touch.
> *Death felt it to his inwards*: 'twas too much:
> Death fell a weeping in his charnel-house.
> The Latmian persever'd along, and thus
> *All were re-animated.* There arose
> A noise of harmony, pulses and throes
> Of gladness in the air—while many, who
> *Had died in mutual arms devout and true,*

Sprang to each other madly; and the rest
Felt a high certainty of being blest.
They gaz'd upon Endymion. Enchantment
Grew drunken, and would have its head and bent. . . .
The two deliverers tasted a pure wine
Of happiness, from fairy-press ooz'd out.
Speechless they eyed each other, and about
The fair assembly wander'd to and fro,
Distracted with *the richest overflow*
Of joy that ever pour'd from heaven. (III, 785–806)

Those who "died in mutual arms devout and true" are immediately resurrected to everlasting bliss, while those who were unfavored with so romantic a death but have been no less faithful, have to wait only a few moments until their mates are rounded up (until "each their old love found"—III, 824). No faithless lovers are among this multitude, none save Glaucus, whose long penance is now paid. He is a "new born god" (III, 807), and Scylla's death has been only a "dream" (III, 809). Death, man's eternal enemy, direst foe of lovers' happiness, has now been overcome, and hell's tyranny is abolished. And how was this miracle wrought? By the steadfast devotion of a shepherd-prince to his beloved. In other words, fidelity in love can conquer not only the power of a witch who justly if cruelly punishes infidelity in love, but it can bless all the world, at least all the loving world, with benefits unknowingly. As Christ brought salvation to men by atoning for their sins, so the faithful Endymion brings salvation to lovers by atoning for Glaucus' sin. True, he is not, like Christ, conscious of his mission, but his unwavering devotion to Cynthia works the same miracle as Christ's unswerving devotion to God.

Yet the dead lovers were not precisely dead, Keats intimates, describing them as "ripe from hue-golden swoons" (III, 861). Evidently death was, in virtue of their amorous fidelity, converted into a kind of swoon or sleep full of pleasant (and prefigurative?) visions. Such had been Adonis' reward, his death being "medicined . . . to a lengthened drowsiness" filled with prefigurative love-dreams. The implication is that death, like dreamful sleep, thus becomes for faithful lovers a prefiguration of eternal felicity.[4]

The host of revived lovers now offers thanks to Neptune and, more enthusiastically, to Cupid and Venus, the latter of whom pities and blesses Endymion when she learns that he alone is "not yet / Escap'd from dull mortality's harsh net" (III, 906–7). The rejoicing lovers then hail Cupid

---

[4] Cf. Shelley, whose Witch of Atlas
> Could medicine the sick soul to happy sleep,
> And change eternal death into a night
> Of glorious dreams. (ll. 178–80)

as the power that has "fann'd away" "all death-shadows" (III, 981–82) and as the "God of *warm pulses*, and dishevell'd hair, / And *panting bosoms bare!*" (III, 984–85). These words are rather difficult to construe transcendentally.

Meanwhile, the irony of Endymion's situation begins to tell. Among the legions of joyous couples he alone is without his mate. He is "there far strayed from mortality" (III, 1007), painfully conscious that immortality without love is worse than death. But from his distress he is released by a convenient swoon, during which Cynthia's voice promises him that his present fate is only temporary:

> Immortal bliss for me too hast thou won.
> Arise then! for the hen-dove shall not hatch
> Her ready eggs, before I'll kissing snatch
> Thee into endless heaven. Awake! Awake! (III, 1024–27)

Thus another prefigurative dream—the most assuring yet vouchsafed— promises heaven to the faithful lover. When he awakes, the scene shifters have been at work again, and he is surrounded by a pleasant forest with a placid lake before him. Gone is the sea, and he stands upon the earth.

So ends the third book, leaving but one or two observations to be made. Keats deliberately altered the old Glaucus-Scylla myth in two ways: (1) Glaucus' punishment at the hands of Circe is the consequence not of his sensuality but of his inconstancy. That the same is true of the other men who fell into the witch's power, that they had deserted wives and lovers— according to Keats the cardinal sin in love's religion—is a plausible inference. If Keats has perhaps not made sufficiently lucid his reinterpretation of the myth, one needs to remember that the love which he contrasts with Circe's is not less physical; it is *constant* love, and therein lies its incomparable superiority. (2) Keats declined to allow Scylla to die as a result of Circe's curse. This was her fate, along with a hideous transformation, according to the mythical story, but Keats was determined to open the doors of heaven to faithful lovers. Consequently Scylla's death was, like Adonis', a pleasurable swoon, one long prefiguration of "an immortality of passion."

Glaucus alone of all the resurrected lovers was punished. Glaucus alone was disloyal, losing his immortality thereby. But after long penance the sentence was revoked by the steadfast devotion of young Endymion, restoring godhead to Glaucus and granting everlasting bliss to all faithful lovers, proving unanswerably that love "bless[es] / The world with benefits unknowingly," and can, though earthly itself, win immortality for its loyal devotees.

In view of this simple and obvious interpretation of the Glaucus episode, so consistent with all other parts of the poem and with its oft reiterated theme, not to speak of the "favorite speculation" of Letter 31, it will hardly seem necessary to convert Keats's ingenuous love story into a mystical allegory, or to find a moral of sympathy and self-sacrifice in the hero's collaboration with Glaucus.

Book IV

After the grand climax of Book III—the reunion of all lovers who had died during ten hundred years, the Bacchanalian rejoicing, and the choric hymn from thousands of couples praising the "sovereign power of love"— it is difficult to imagine how even the most skillful poet could keep his hero and heroine much longer disjoined and yet hold the attention of the reader. But Keats, long before he reached this point, even before he began his poem, had determined to "make 4000 lines of one bare circumstance and fill them with poetry." "A long poem is a test of invention which I take to be the polar star of poetry," he had added in self-justification.

Having invented his personal version of the Glaucus story, and reached a climax beyond what he had perhaps foreseen, he was still committed, according to his plan, to the "invention" of another one thousand lines. His primary problem, of course, was how to prolong Endymion's celibacy and yet not alienate the reader. The solution that he found is not always lucid and not always consistent, but in brief it may be said to depend on two motifs: Cynthia's need for concealing her identity, and her desire to test Endymion's fidelity. Perhaps it occurred to the poet that Endymion had not yet been tempted; was his amatory fidelity really as unshakable as it seemed? Glaucus, for example, had been subjected to the wiles of Circe; why should not Endymion be tempted by the voluptuous Indian maid, just to prove that he was strong enough to withstand her attractions, and so to be worthy of Cynthia's everlasting affection?

If it could be demonstrated that Keats was familiar with Drayton's *Endimion and Phoebe*, as Amy Lowell and C. L. Finney believe that he was,[5] it could be argued that Keats got his idea for the Indian maid from the Phoebe incognita of the elder poet. For in Drayton's poem Phoebe (Cynthia) adopts the disguise of a nymph in order to avoid frightening mortals (Endimion especially) with her effulgence and in order to carry on her wooing of Endim-

---

[5] Finney, *The Evolution of Keats's Poetry*, I, 252 ff., and Amy Lowell, *John Keats* (Boston and New York: Houghton Mifflin Company, 1925), I, 330 ff.

ion more adroitly.[6] Endimion is at first unyielding, protesting his fidelity to Phoebe, but soon he falls under the nymph's spell and swears eternal constancy to her. At once she reveals her true identity and they are joined in everlasting love.

We should remember, too, that Keats's Cynthia has a further reason for concealing her identity. In her most extended and passionate speech (II, 761–824), she informed Endymion that she dared not reveal to the gods her love for him. Beset by shame and fear, she hesitated to lose her reputation for chastity and her cult of worship by falling victim to passionate love. Then, convincing herself that lying in Endymion's arms was superior to the lonely virtue of chastity, she vowed "an immortality of passion" to her shepherd-lover and sealed it with a kiss. It would be strange if she should break that vow now; yet in the meantime she must bring herself to break a vow in heaven: her dedication to virginity. " 'Tis but to atone / For endless pleasure, by some coward blushes" (II, 787–88), she assures herself—but this will take time and courage. She is still a modest maiden (until recently ignorant "that nests were built"—II, 806), and she must be strong enough to brave the frowns or smiles of the gods when her defection becomes known.

In Book IV Keats reminds us of Cynthia's internal struggle, though he does it somewhat left-handedly, and in the person of the Indian maid, so that readers have not generally seen a connection between the Indian's words and those of Cynthia in Book II. When Endymion is on the point of joining himself to the Indian girl for life, she mysteriously withdraws, even though she has just finished a hyperbolic eulogy of passionate love!

> I may not be thy love: I am forbidden—
> Indeed I am thwarted, affrighted, chidden,
> By things I trembled at, and gorgon wrath.
> Twice hast thou asked whither I went; henceforth
> Ask no more! I may not utter it . . . (IV, 752–57)

Whither, indeed, has she gone on these occasions but back to Olympus? Her words are an almost certain confession (to the reader if not to Endymion) of her true identity. The Indian maid is evidently the disguise that Cynthia has adopted for the purpose of visiting her earthly lover; she is using a standard ruse in such matters, often resorted to by Jupiter in his amours, and only less frequently by the other Olympians. Cupid in his visits to Psyche and Lohengrin in his visits to Elsa also had to conceal their identity. In "Lamia" Keats takes for granted the necessity of an immortal's playing

---

[6] See "Endimion and Phoebe," ll. 103 ff., 181 ff., 225 ff., 229 ff., 303 ff., 555 ff., 611 ff., 663 ff., 975–92, in *The Works of Michael Drayton*, ed. J. W. Hebel (Oxford: B. Blackwell, 1931–41), Vol. I.

incognita when she loves a mortal; Lycius confesses that he has not even ventured to ask the name of his goddess-love (Lamia) :

> Sure some sweet name thou hast; though by my truth
> I had not ask'd it, ever thinking thee
> Not mortal but of heavenly progeny . . .[7]

As for the Indian maid's mysterious interdict on love, it apparently derives from the same internal struggle as Cynthia described in Book II : she has not yet found a way to renounce her long established and public dedication to celibacy and chastity.

This view of Cynthia and the Indian maid, whose roles have been so perplexing to commentators, should go far to simplify the interpretation of Book IV. Whether Cynthia desired to test her lover's fidelity or to visit him incognita, or whether her motives were mixed, or whether Keats was striving valiantly to spin out another thousand lines before bringing his lovers to their everlasting embrace, or whether, as more probable, all these things were combined, not always pellucidly, in the "young minded" composition of a first long poem, need not be decided with finality. But something like this seems to have been the germ of the "invention" which stretched the story to a round four thousand lines, though it must be admitted that the poet was at times rather careless of the dramatic relations of his characters, trusting to thaumaturgy to get him out of any difficulty.

Without denying the difficulties confronting them, critics have tended to regard the Indian maid as a type of sensuous beauty, designedly contrasted with, and ultimately fused with, Cynthia the type of transcendental Beauty. Or proceeding from the moral of "sympathy" and "sacrifice" that they attach to the Glaucus episode, they reason that Endymion's love for the Indian girl constitutes an enlargement of his humanitarian sympathy (since she sings a song of sorrow and he is moved to compassion), which finally renders him worthy of mystic wedding with the Ideal Beauty.

Endymion's relations with the Indian Lady in Book IV [writes Thorpe] are not merely representative of the sensual love of man for woman . . . the union with the Indian Maiden is the marriage of the soul of a poet with the spirit of sorrow and suffering in the world . . . Keats believed that the poet must find in the tragedy of the world his poetic salvation . . .[8]

Likewise, Colvin associates Endymion's "earthly passion" for the Indian maid with "human pity and desire," and concludes that this passion "was one all the while, had he but known it, with his heavenly passion born of

---

[7] II, 81 ff. (draft). Cf. Garrod's edition.

[8] Clarence D. Thorpe, *The Mind of John Keats*, pp. 60–61.

poetic aspiration and the soul's thirst for [transcendental] Beauty."[9] De Sélincourt follows much the same line, though without insisting on the transcendental elements, and carries the hero's "awakened human sympathy" beyond his "self-absorbed" love for both Cynthia and the Indian lady, to a courageous "renunciation" and "purification," until finally he is "spiritualized" and "at peace."[10] Plausible as these interpretations might be in a poem like Shelley's "Alastor," it is not easy to forget Endymion and Cynthia's clearly stated objective: "an immortality of *passion*." Nor does Endymion's association with the Indian maid, who celebrates the revelry of Bacchus' crew and utters hyperbolic eulogies of physical love,[11] appear to be an object lesson in human sympathy.

If we regard her instead—and Keats gradually lets us in on the secret— as a disguised embodiment of Cynthia, a form assumed by the latter for the purpose of secretly visiting her lover and testing his fidelity, there will be little need to invent a "spiritual" allegory. In fact, the fervent adulations of physical love spoken by the Indian maid will then be understood by the reader as a re-expression of the central theme of the poem, coming actually from the disguised Cynthia. Certain problems of dramatic motive and consistency will arise from time to time, but these may be ascribed in the main to Keats's inexperience, even his inattention, to such matters, and to his easy trust in the old "machinery" of mythological poetry, in which metamorphoses of characters, sudden aerial journeys, unexplained changes of scene, and general thaumaturgy were accepted conventions.

Let us now turn to the story. As Endymion chances upon the lamenting Indian girl, he hears her implorations for the toying hands and sweet lips of a lover (IV, 47 ff.), and then is addressed by his poet in strange fashion, who simultaneously warns him of Cynthia's jealousy and urges him to enjoy the "panting" beauty and "warm delight" of the Indian girl! (56 ff.) She continues her plaint, and for a moment imagines, as she notices a hyacinth growing beside her, a blissful wedding with the resurrected Hyacinthus:

> [Oh] that woodland Hyacinthus could escape
> From his green prison, and here kneeling down
> Call me his queen, *his second life's fair crown!*
> Ah me, how I could love! (IV, 68–71)

Without troubling to ascribe this wish to flirtatiousness, real or affected (on

---

[9] Colvin, *John Keats*, pp. 203–4. Whenever Colvin uses the word "Beauty" with a capital "B" and in such a context, he means "transcendental" or "immortal" or "essential" Beauty, as he elsewhere variantly calls it. See pp. 172, 180, 182, and *passim*.

[10] De Sélincourt, *The Poems of John Keats*, pp. 443, 445.

[11] As in IV, 71–85, 738–47, for example.

the part of the disguised Cynthia), or to the poet's own carelessness in treating the dramatic relations of his characters, we can see here another sign of the prefigurative theme of the poem. Had the girl's wish come true, not only would Hyacinthus have enjoyed a postmortal, erotic existence, but he and his beloved would have been re-enacting the happy fate of Venus and Adonis —a fate which Keats and Endymion regard as the *summun bonum*.

Some readers will want to know why the Indian girl is lamenting if she is really Cynthia, why she presently sings the song "O Sorrow," and why she tells Endymion that she has followed Bacchus' crew all the way from the banks of the Ganges. I am afraid no very satisfactory answer is at hand. Of course the maid explains that she took up with Bacchus to gain surcease from love-sorrow, adding that she had been "cheated by shadowy wooer from the clouds" (IV, 190). Whether this is a womanly fiction invented to win over the wondering shepherd it would be perilous to say, but women have been known to employ such ruses. Did not the Wyf of Bathe win Jankyn, her fifth husband, by a fictional appeal to his pity?

> I seyde I mette of hym al nyght,
> He wolde han slayn me as I lay upright, . . .
> But yet I hope that he may do me good . . .
> And al was fals; I dremed of it right naught.

Chaucer was, of course, obliging enough to let the reader in on the trick, whereas Keats, like a true romantic (or an inept narrator), preferred an air of mystery. The Wyf may be an inappropriate analogue, however; someone is sure to remind us that she lacks high romantic seriousness!

Other reasons might be offered for the Indian girl's far home and her lyric lamentation. If Cynthia has adopted the disguise of an Indian, she obviously needs to explain her presence in Greece to the Latmian shepherd; Keats conveniently provides for her "past" by joining her to Bacchus' company on the god's return from his renowned conquest of the East. For a goddess, we must remember, all things are possible—fictional as well as real journeys whenever the spirit bids. Why, however, does she choose to play the part of a sorrowing lover when she comes upon the scene? Well, she has reason enough if she *is* Cynthia, in that she is still cut off from wedded union with her shepherd beloved. Also it may suit her pleasure to draw out and explore the shepherd's capacity for tenderness and amorous compassion. Is there a bit of Rosalind in her?

After wishing that she might be the postmortal bride of Hyacinthus, the Indian girl dilates on the wonders of love in words that remind us of the earlier rhapsodies of Endymion and Keats:

> Ye deaf and senseless minutes of the day,
> And thou, old forest, hold ye this for true,

> There is no lightning, no authentic dew
> But in the eye of love: there's not a sound,
> Melodious howsoever, *can confound*
> *The heavens and earth in one to such a death*
> *As doth the voice of love*: there's not a breath
> Will mingle kindly with the meadow air,
> Till it has panted round, and stolen a share
> Of passion from the heart! (IV, 76–85)

Love is the highest value, the supreme happiness, we have been told before; love makes mortals immortal. The message is the same when it comes from the lips of this maid, for she, too, declares that love links earth and heaven.

As Endymion listens he melts with love and, ignorant as he is, protests that he is not being unfaithful to Cynthia:

> *Goddess! I love thee not the less*: from thee
> By Juno's smile I turn not—no, no, no—
> While the great waters are at ebb and flow,—
> I have a triple soul! O fond pretence—
> For both, for both my love is so immense,
> I feel my heart is cut for them in twain. (IV, 92–97)

Yet his ignorance, from which Keats will not allow him to be released till the end of the poem, gives the appearance of infidelity, and he is full of grief,

> Grief born of thee, young angel [the Indian girl]! fairest thief!
> Who stolen hast away the wings wherewith
> I was to top the heavens.   (IV, 108–10)

There is no doubt in his mind that infidelity to his first love will doom him to mortal, earthly existence, just as it doomed the god Glaucus to "crazed eld." Yet as for real infidelity, Keats has guarded against that in two ways: (1) Endymion's affection for the Indian maid is actually an affection for the disguised Cynthia, though, of course, he is kept in the dark as to this disguisement (it is hard to find any other reason for Keats's compelling the perplexed hero several times to declare his essential innocence); (2) Endymion never embraces the Indian maid, as he did Cynthia—in fact, he scarcely touches her. For this forbearance we may suppose Cynthia to be properly grateful.[12]

At this point in the poem the problem of Endymion's essential innocence is diverted for a time while the Indian maid sings her lament, "O Sorrow."

---

12 That Keats does not make the fact of disguisement sufficiently clear to the reader, and that on at least one occasion he treats the women as if they were two separate beings (IV, 430–61) must be counted a serious fault. But evidently he valued surprise higher than lucidity and consistency.

It will be remembered that this song was cited by Keats in Letter 31 as one of two examples from his own poetry of the beauty that is "truth." When glossing the letter we omitted consideration of this song because of certain difficulties in explaining it at that point, but now we can attempt an explanation. The song reads thus:

> O Sorrow,
> Why dost borrow
> The natural hue of health, from vermeil lips?—
> To give maiden blushes
> To the white rose bushes?
> Or is't thy dewy hand the daisy tips?
>
> O Sorrow,
> Why dost borrow
> The lustrous passion from a falcon-eye?—
> To give the glow-worm light?
> Or, on a moonless night,
> To tinge, on syren shores, the salt sea-spry?
>
> O Sorrow,
> Why dost borrow
> The mellow ditties from a mourning tongue?—
> To give at evening pale
> Unto the nightingale,
> That thou mayst listen the cold dews among? (IV, 147–63)

The remaining two stanzas carry the same thought farther with more illustrations. It can hardly be said that the thought is esoteric, though to call it "truth" may startle orthodox minds. Paraphrased, the thought seems to be as follows: there is, or may be, a kind of law of aesthetic compensation in the universe, specifically: the natural world becomes more beautiful as a consequence of the sorrow of lovers. Now aside from the consolation that this may bring to generous-minded lovers, it is another way of stating one of Keats's favorite themes: that "love bless[es] / The world with benefits unknowingly."

It might be argued that Keats intended this "truth" as only a pretty fiction. That is what it looks like to a casual reader, and another poet, or Keats at a later period, might have frankly called it such. Nevertheless in the letter to Bailey he called it "truth," "truth" seized through beauty. The interrogative form of the song would seem, then, to be more a device of expression than a confession of uncertainty.

We must now ask ourselves whether this "truth" is a value judgment or a prefigurative vision of existence. Manifestly it is not a value judgment, but a truth about existence, a "law" of the operation of the universe. Such a law the poet has visualized in his imagination, for he has "seized" it in the guise of images, images of those parts of the natural world whose beauty derives from or is enhanced by the sorrowing of lovers. In a sense, then, the truth might be called a *vision*, even though the visionary *process* is not superficially evident to the reader. But is this vision a prevision, a prefiguration such as we have been taught to expect? Can we say that its "prototype must be here after"? The wording of the song suggests a present, not a future, reference.

Perhaps a prefigurative poet calls for foresighted readers. Was not "Hyperion" coming to birth in Keats's mind even before he completed *Endymion*? Later in Book IV he promises:

> Thy lute-voiced brother will I sing ere long. (IV, 774)

He was thinking of Apollo, the hero of his later poem. How far he had gone in evolving the theme of the later poem cannot be known, but as all readers know, that poem takes sorrow, not felicity, for its subject. Out of such sorrow, much more severe than what the Indian girl suffered, is generated eternally a new and increasing beauty in the physical world. None of the Titans except Oceanus can foresee this "law" of aesthetic compensation. But to Oceanus' (imaginative?) mind it comes as a vision of "eternal truth" (II, 187); throughout the universe it operates as an "eternal law" (II, 228). This eternal law is clearly analogous to the law that the Indian girl describes, though her utterance of it is more tentative. In the familiar prefigurative way, then, the imagination of Oceanus, like that of the Indian maid, has seized a vision of beauty which is "truth."

The Indian maid's song does not make clear whether the law of aesthetic compensation is flashed upon the imagination as "a shadow of reality *to come*," or as a vision of presently operative reality. Whether the "truth" of her song has a present or future reference, however, is less important than that it represents the poetic imagination in its familiar role of *extensionalizing* its happy visions, thus converting beauty into "truth."

When the Indian girl finishes her song, she relates her experiences with Bacchus' lusty crew, in a passage famous for its exuberant realism. The vinolent company failed to heal her love-sorrow, she sighs piteously. At this, what can poor Endymion do but melt in sympathy? Yet his sympathy is divided against itself, for any tenderness to the Indian girl smacks of disloyalty to Cynthia. "I must not think—by Phoebe, no!" he exclaims (IV, 303), meaning that he must obliterate Cynthia (Phoebe) from his mind if he is to love the earthly maiden without remorse of conscience. But to forget Cynthia is not possible, he knows; and as if giving voice to his fears, a warning of "Woe to that Endymion!" (IV, 321) sounds ominously from the forest. The god Mercury alights suddenly on the earth and strikes it with his wand; two winged steeds arise magically, and Endymion, without a word of query or a moment's hesitation, mounts one steed and places his companion on the other. High into the air sail the steeds, but presently they fall into slumber, as do also their passengers.

Keats explains that the slumber was caused by their entering the magnetic field of Somnus, who "for the first time" (IV, 371) since his birth had come out of his forlorn cave—all because he had a prefigurative dream!

> into his depth Cimmerian
> There came *a dream*, showing how a young man,
> Ere a lean bat could plump its wintery skin,
> Would at high Jove's empyreal footstool *win*
> *An immortality*, and how espouse
> Jove's daughter . . .   (IV, 375–80)

Somnus is journeying to heaven "to hear the marriage melodies," scheduled "one hour" hence (IV, 382–83). How is this optimistic prescience to be reconciled with the ominous warning of "Woe to that Endymion!" less than fifty lines back? It is to be feared that no reconciliation is possible; Keats evidently didn't trouble himself about such inconsistencies. Nor did he trouble to fulfill Somnus' dream with promised immediacy; Endymion forthwith enters heaven and beholds Cynthia face to face, but Keats, instead of winding up his poem with a grand flourish, perversely drives a wedge between the lovers. If he ended his poem here he would have only 3,500 lines, whereas he had long since resolved to "make 4000 lines of one bare circumstance"!

As the still sleeping Endymion and the Indian maid enter heaven on their winged steeds, Endymion dreams of being in heaven and conversing with the gods and then, climactically, of springing into Dian's (Cynthia's) arms. Now at last he is acquainted with her true identity, and as he seeks to embrace her he wakes from his sleep, and to his glad astonishment

> *Beheld awake his very dream*: the gods
> Stood smiling . . .   (IV, 436–37)

Adam's delicious fate was now his own: his happy love-dreams had proved their prefigurative veracity.

By all rights the poem should have ended at this point with a simple account of the transformation of the Indian girl to her original self, Cynthia. But Keats was bent on writing another five hundred lines, and therefore resorted to a magician's trick. When Endymion beholds both Cynthia and the Indian girl (as if they could be separately and corporeally visible at the same time!), Keats compels him to kiss the Indian girl in order to rouse

Cynthia's jealousy and stave off their final union! "He could not help but kiss her" (IV, 449), declares Keats, though two seconds before

> His heart leapt up as to its rightful throne,
> To that fair shadow'd passion [Cynthia] . . .
> (IV, 445–46)

Obviously Endymion is a helpless puppet and Keats is capriciously pulling the strings.

Meanwhile, the reader must not suppose that the hero has really sinned; to make sure of this, Keats causes him to protest his innocence:

> Bright goddess, stay!
> Search my most hidden breast! By truth's own tongue,
> *I have no daedale heart*: why is it wrung
> To desperation? (IV, 457–60)

Cynthia is not appeased, however; she weeps and melts away. But presumably the reader is expected to stick by the hero and to ignore the illogicality of the situation, for this is the third strenuous reminder from Endymion that he is not guilty of genuine infidelity and that he is under the sway of mysteriously resistless powers. "I feel as true as innocence," he adds a few lines later (IV, 474); why he should be tortured in this way he cannot understand.

The winged horses now carry him earthward, with the discreetly mute Indian girl at his side. But as the moon rises, it (Cynthia, that is) works a spell on his companion, and now it is the Indian girl's turn to melt into thin air. Deserted by both his women (or by one in her Indian embodiment), Endymion surrenders all hope of happiness and enters the mental "Cave of Quietude," delineated by Keats in one of the sanest and soberest passages of the poem. The following verses are typical:

> . . . few have ever felt how calm and well
> Sleep may be had in that deep den . . .
> Dark Paradise! . . . *where hopes infest*;
> Where those eyes are the brightest far that keep
> Their lids shut longest *in a dreamless sleep.*
> (IV, 524–42)

The Cave of Quietude lies beyond the realm of grief and pain, entered not by those who strive but by those who have given over striving. No longer do they trust in the veracity of hope or of dreams; in this dark paradise hope would "infest," and sleep can be enjoyed only if "dreamless." Not a "young minded" but a mature-minded poet was vouchsafed this insight, which indirectly controverts the leading theme of the poem.

Yet Endymion cannot now be denied the bliss which his dreams have so often promised him; both the myth which the poet is following and the leading theme of the poem, so often proclaimed, require a happy consummation. Accordingly Keats does his best to persuade the reader that Endymion's dreams were veracious after all. For example, while Endymion sleeps in the Cave of Quietude, supposedly reconciled to the deceptiveness of dreams and hopes, the reader is allowed to see a floating host of the gods (not visible to Endymion) who sing a kind of prothalamion to Cynthia's coming wedding, summoning all of the deities of heaven to the ceremony. Keats represents Endymion as asleep when the singing occurs, but after giving the words of their song, adds: "More Endymion heard not" (IV, 611–12), as if he had magically heard the reassuring words in his sleep! Evidently Keats regarded the incident as an auditory equivalent of a prefigurative vision.

Down to earth the winged horse carries Endymion, forsaken by both his women. Formerly it had been his aim to live "beyond earth's boundary, . . . [where] / Sorrow is but a shadow" (IV, 620–21), but now it seems that he has lost heaven irrecoverably as a punishment for his "daedale heart." Then suddenly he is aware, as he steps on earth, of the Indian girl who had dissolved away in mid-air. Unable to renounce his affection for her, yet still feeling no guilt of infidelity (even though he believes that Cynthia has discarded him for the appearance of such guilt!), he decides that he and the Indian girl can perhaps work out their happiness together. At least she is no intangible dream, such as Cynthia now appears in retrospect:

> Let us aye love each other; let us fare
> On forest fruits, and never, never go
> Among the abodes of mortals here below,
> Or be by *phantoms* duped. . . .
>   . . . I have clung
> To nothing, lov'd a nothing, nothing seen
> Or felt but a great dream! . . .
>   *Against his proper glory*
> *Has my own soul conspired*: so my story
> Will I to children utter, and repent.
> *There never liv'd a mortal man, who bent*
> *His appetite beyond his natural sphere,*
> *But starv'd and died.* My sweetest Indian, here,
> Here will I kneel, for thou redeemed hast
> My life from too thin breathing: gone and past
> Are cloudy phantasms.   (IV, 626–51)

If Keats were careful of the dramatic relationships of his characters, he could not allow Cynthia to remain impassive while Endymion calls her a "phantom," "a nothing," a "cloudy phantasm" that has "duped" and "cheated" him. With this accusation the hero moves perilously close to love's cardinal sin, infidelity. Yet it is clear that the poet did not see any sin in his hero's words, and this may be explained by the fact that they are only partially motivated by the hero's situation. Intrinsically they are the poet's protest, milder presages of which have been scattered through the poem, against the fallaciousness of dreams. One's mind is carried forward to the more outspoken distrust of dreams in later years, especially in "Lamia" and "The Fall of Hyperion."

It is death, not fuller life, Keats now sees, that lies beyond the "fragile bar" of mortality, and perhaps the bar is not fragile after all. "Against his proper glory has my own soul conspired": the limitations of mortality are not dissolvable merely because hope and wish delude the yearning heart. Truth is not dream, and wisdom lies in a sober resignation to the unecstatic conditions of mortality. Here alone, if happiness is for man, let him look for it. This is the lesson which finally has been learned, and it is the poet rather than his hero who has learned it. For the hero will cross the bar in the end and become immortal, giving a final proof by miracle that dreams prefigure heaven.

In lines that follow the passage quoted, Endymion shows that he is not fully persuaded of his poet's wisdom, and indeed the poet himself seems reluctant to accept it. After denouncing dreams, Endymion confesses that he still cherishes his dream of Cynthia and will not relinquish its memory. If he cannot immediately enter into heaven, if mortality forbids this, there is still some reason to hope for a deferred recompense:

> The hour may come
> When we will meet in pure elysium. (IV, 657–58)

If this happens he can say, of course, that his dreams will have come true after all.

Obviously Keats needs to prepare his hero for his approaching deification and cannot allow him to remain an intransigent skeptic. Had not Endymion resurrected the thousands of lovers and saved a god from decrepitude precisely because of his steadfast faith? Surely he cannot be joined to his own celestial beloved if his faith vanishes.

The hapless Endymion does not, however, share his poet's knowledge of the identity of his two loves, and therefore tries to persuade himself that mortal felicity is possible with his Indian companion. In this self-persuasion he is not very successful, and his hopes are extinguished when the girl announces mysteriously that she cannot be his mate. Just before she speaks these fatal words, however, she rather inconsistently bursts forth in a fervent eulogy of passionate love ("how far above . . . / All earthly pleasure, all imagin'd good, / Was the warm tremble of a devout kiss"—IV, 741–44). From childhood till now this has been her faith, she declares, and such ecstasy does the thought of the warm kiss bring that at times she falls into seventy-two-hour swoons! (IV, 738–47). The seeming inconsistency of this passage in its context is probably due to Keats's decision to bring the main theme of the poem, the "sovereign power of love," again into prominence.

The poet appears to be at cross-purposes with himself, however, when the Indian girl passes abruptly from her osculatory fervor to the declaration: "I may not be thy love; I am forbidden—" (IV, 752). Why she is forbidden she does not explain, except to say that she is "thwarted, affrighted, chidden" (IV, 753). There is some mystery in her goings and comings, and Endymion must not inquire into it:

> Twice hast thou ask'd whither I went: henceforth
> Ask no more! I may not utter it . . . (IV, 755–56)

As we saw earlier, this taboo is apparently Keats's way of telling the reader that the Indian girl is really Cynthia incognita, not yet released from her cult of chastity, and that whenever she disappears she returns to her native haunts on Olympus. As for the taboo imposed upon a mortal when he is having an affair with an immortal, this motif is familiar enough in myth, as Orpheus or Psyche or Elsa (in *Lohengrin*) may remind us.

One who is reading the poem for a second time may surmise that Keats has brought his lovers to such a state of intimacy that they must shortly leap either into marriage or some new frustration. Since there are still two hundred fifty verses to write if the goal of four thousand is to be reached, a wedding is out of the question, hence the Indian girl's mysterious retreat. Clearly the story must be read without insistence on logical or consistent motive in this masquerading girl, licensing the poet to dispose by magic of any impediments he may run into.

As Endymion subsides into a despairing silence, his author steps forth to apologize to the reader for the delays in "enskying" the hero, and then adds that his sympathy with the lovelorn Endymion has often been so close that he has mourned with him:

> Yes, moonlight Emperor! *felicity*
> *Has been thy meed for many thousand years;*
> Yet often have I, on the brink of tears,
> Mourn'd as if yet thou wert a forester;—
> Forgetting the old tale. (IV, 776–80)

For thousands of years Endymion has lived in heaven, Keats here reminds himself; his days of love-sorrow are long since over. It is possible that the words are figurative, but the prefigurative theme of the poem and of Letter 31 encourage a fairly literal interpretation. If Keats could enter heaven at this moment, he would find Endymion and Cynthia in each other's arms!

As the story is resumed, Endymion is pictured sitting in motionless dejection, staring at heaps of dead leaves. The irony of this dejection is pointed up by the poet, who reminds us that the oblivious shepherd sits in the very place where "he took his first soft poppy dream" (IV, 786). Scarcely accidental, this reminder is intended as a good omen. Meanwhile, the Indian girl, so in the dumps a moment before, smiles, "pleasing her eye with all his sorrowing" (IV, 798–99). What can this mean but that she, like the poet, optimistically sees the end of the poem approaching, and, being Cynthia in disguise, looks forward to a climactic changing of her "costume"?

Appropriately at this point the sister of Endymion reappears and seeks to dissuade him from his grieving. She possesses some knowledge of a mysterious happiness destined for the Latmian people:

> Why shouldst thou pine
> When all great Latmos so exalt will be?
> .   .   .   .
> O Hermes! on this very night will be
> A hymning up to Cynthia, queen of light;
> For the soothsayers old saw yesternight
> *Good visions in the air,*—whence will befal,
> As say these sages, *health perpetual*
> *To shepherds and their flocks;* and furthermore
> *In Dian's* face they read the gentle lore:
>   (IV, 805–33)

Though Endymion remains ironically unconscious of the significance of Peona's words, they can mean only one thing to readers who have seen this theme before. It is the principle of the first book applied in a new form, having first been proved in the resurrective miracle of Book III and then in the aesthetic law of compensation of "O Sorrow." In the words of its first enunciation, love "bless[es] / The world with benefits unknowingly." The Latmian people will henceforth enjoy perpetual health as a consequence of Endymion's faithful love. And the augury of this Golden Age is a prefigurative vision granted to the soothsayers by Cynthia herself. Was it not the "contemplative" shepherds at the Pan festival in Book I who speculated on their "own anticipated bliss" and "the fragile bar / That keeps us from our homes ethereal"? That bar may not yet be passed by the Latmians as a whole, but their life henceforth will be nearer to the life of heaven. And all this because of the love between Endymion and Cynthia!

Though the reader becomes increasingly optimistic along with the cheerful Peona and the smiling Indian girl, Endymion lugubriously announces that he will retire to a hermit's cave. His Indian companion is advised to live with Peona, who alone will have permission to visit him. Love between mortals is pleasurable, he admits, but for himself there is only one love that will satisfy his desire. Frustrated in his passion for Cynthia, he will surrender to no lesser being and will dedicate to her his life of solitude and chastity:

> Let it content thee, Sister, seeing me
> More happy than betides mortality.
> A hermit young, I'll live in mossy cave,
> Where thou [Peona] alone shalt come to me.
>   (IV, 858–61)

The Indian maid agrees to match him in celibacy and "white Chastity" (IV, 883), appropriately consecrating her life to Diana (Cynthia). One might wonder if Keats is linking up his lovers' mutual surrender of desire with the ethical lesson of the Cave of Quietude, meaning to reward them only after they have proved themselves worthy by casting out desire. Not a line or a word suggests that this is his intention or that he at all remembers the solemn lesson of that passage. Instead his purpose seems to be merely to keep his hero in suspense, to spin out a round four thousand lines, and—of key importance—to prove once again that Endymion is guiltless of infidelity. For his firm resolution to live like a hermit in devotion to his empyreal mistress has proved beyond doubt that his heart is inherently monogamous.

Directing Peona and the Indian maid to leave him, he promises to meet the pair for a final farewell in the evening "behind great Dian's temple" (IV, 914). Then he practices the hermit for several hours, though Keats benignantly allows him to recline upon the grass, where he remains in a kind of waking swoon "all the long day" (IV, 920). In the evening he rises and walks toward Diana's (Cynthia's) temple, chides himself briefly for having believed that he could cross "the fragile bar" into eternity (IV, 937–44), and then, with a sudden accession of his old hope-logic, swears by several gods successively that

> I did wed
> Myself to things of light from infancy;
> And thus to be cast out, thus lorn to die,
> Is sure enough to make a mortal man
> Grow impious.   (IV, 957–61)

Without a moment's interval, as if in response to this agonized protest of the hermit, Cynthia's choir is heard near by (IV, 964–68). This serves as another prefigurative assurance to the reader, though not to Endymion, who is listening to his own thoughts.

In this abstraction he is discovered by the amiable Peona and her Indian companion, both of whom are smiling (probably in the fashion of bride and bridesmaids!). In playful irony Peona then asks Endymion what wish he would like to have fulfilled "ere we all are laid on bier" (IV, 973). He replies:

> Sister, I would have command
> If it were heaven's will, on our sad fate. (IV, 975–76)

Evidently it is heaven's (or Keats's) will, for the wish instantly becomes reality. The Indian maid is transfigured before Endymion's eyes, magically metamorphosed into Phoebe (Cynthia). And a second metamorphosis—apotheosis, in fact—joins Endymion with the undying gods. The long delay, says Cynthia, resulted severally from her own "foolish fear," from "decrees of fate," and from the necessity of conferring immortality on her mortal lover (IV, 989–93).[18] Now that all is well, she tells Peona that the lovers will "range these forests" (IV, 993), which henceforth will be "safe . . . As was thy cradle" (IV, 999). The lovers exchange three kisses and vanish. At IV, 1003, with almost mathematical accuracy, the poem has come to its sudden, if long deferred and repeatedly prefigured, consummation.

   Now to sum up. The substance of *Endymion* is love, "holy" but passionate, and given such "young minded" Keatsian turns as these: (1) The happiness from love excels all other types of happiness (the "pleasure thermometer" is but one of several proofs). (2) Love "bless[es] / The world with benefits unknowingly." (3) Devoted, ardent, faithful lovers can earn "an immortality of passion" for themselves, either by being apotheosized (like Endymion) or by being resurrected to eternal bliss (like the legions of dead lovers). (4) The happy dreams of lovers, like the cherished imaginings of poets, are prefiguratively veracious: their "beauty must be truth" (though occasional moments of skepticism invert this faith).

   These conclusions are in harmony with Keats's first trial of the Endymion story, "I stood tip-toe." The windup of that poem describes a miracle almost as wonderful as those in the longer poem:

> Cynthia! I cannot tell the greater blisses,
> That follow'd thine, and thy dear shepherd's kisses. (ll. 239–40)

Almost speechless at the thought of such amorous rapture, Keats could only report that "no lover did of anguish die," that sorrowing lovers were suddenly healed and rushed immediately, "nigh foolish with delight," into each

---

18 Keats's word for this apotheosis is "spiritualiz'd," by which he means "immortalized." Cf. the context, and previous definitions of "spiritual" in the Keatsian sense (chap. ii). "Spiritualiz'd" has been mystically construed by some allegorizers; see for example de Sélincourt, *The Poems of John Keats*, p. 445; H. I'A. Fausset, *Keats: A Study in Development* (London: Martin Secker, 1922), p. 61; Beyer, *Keats and the Daemon King*, pp. 139–40; and others.

other's arms, and that lovers' vows "made silken ties, that never may be broken" (ll. 236, 228, 238). And why did this miracle happen? Simply because "a Poet, sure a lover too," "wept that such beauty [Cynthia's] should be desolate [celibate]" and "in fine wrath" chose to memorialize poetically her "bridal night" (ll. 193, 202, 203, 210).

Keats was a better poet, in selected passages at least, when he composed his second *Endymion*. But traces of "mawkishness," "great inexperience," and "immaturity" were to be found there, as he candidly confessed in his Preface. For the poem was the product of "a space of life between" boyhood and manhood—adolescence, in short—in which "the soul is in a ferment" (Preface). This ferment was largely responsible for his frequent lapses of taste, and it was inseparable from his adulation of passionate love and the spell that this cast upon him. Cynthia's farewell to chastity, coupled with the immortalization of her earthly lover, seemed to him the *summum bonum* and filled him with ineffable enthusiasm.

Thus his poem, though part of its drama occurs in heaven, can hardly be called an allegory of Heavenly Love, any more than the "Song of Songs" or "Venus and Adonis" or "The Eve of St. Agnes" is such an allegory. Keats's shepherd-lover is not, like the Poet in Shelley's "Alastor," in search of the Absolute, nor does he seek a mystic salvation in a quest of the infinite, like Novalis and the Germans in their emblem of the Blue Flower.[14] As to the allegories which have been proposed for the poem since 1880, their gratuitousness may be a corollary of the fact that they did not originate until more than half a century after the poet's death, and that neither Keats nor any of his friends or contemporaries left the slightest hint of an allegorical purpose.

Let us freely admit that *Endymion* is, or contains, many elements which a description of its theme and plot leaves out of account. As many readers have felt, the poem is a kind of amiable miscellany, a paradise of dainty devices mingling myth and nature and passion, a garden of rambling honeysuckles and mazy journeys, a storied framework for clustered "things of beauty," earthly, subterranean, submarine, aerial—"a little region to wander in," as Keats himself described it. For these qualities it will continue to be read as a generous and zestful illustration of its celebrated opening line, and as a fervent and fruitful outpouring of a youthful imagination kindled by the manifold beauties of the world.

Granted all this—and we readily grant it and rejoice in it—we can hardly deny that in so far as the poem has a primary theme and a plot, this theme and plot are indissociable from the ardors and pleasures of youthful love and

---

[14] See Robert M. Wernaer, *Romanticism and the Romantic School in Germany* (New York and London: D. Appleton and Company, 1910), chap. xiv.

from the "favorite speculation" of Letter 31. Why should it be needful to "spiritualize" Keats's interest in the most stirring of human emotions? No one is embarrassed by, or seeks to allegorize, "The Eve of St. Agnes." May it not be that the "perfection of loveliness" in the language of the later poem— not to speak of its more skillful narrative, its pictorial richness, and the compressed, tense, suspensive drama of it—allow us to accept it without a thought of veiling the passion and the passion's consummation? Will not Hazlitt's defense of Juliet express Keats's state of mind in both *Endymion* and "St. Agnes," the almost religious fervor of his love, in such a way as to make all allegories and "spiritualizations" needless: "the feelings of the heart sanctify, without disguising, the impulses of nature."

"The holiness of the heart's affections" was the very cornerstone of Keats's aesthetic. Out of this holiness grew his faith in "the truth of imagination," and thus he turned to other poets for confirmation of his "favorite speculation" (Adam's dream in *Paradise Lost* and the "immortal freemasonry" of Shakespeare's verse), while he evolved his own argument and illustration in Letter 31 and in *Endymion*. What is more normal and natural than that his youthful imagination should fall rapturously in love with feminine beauty, and that like the youthful Shakespeare and Milton he should sing his hymn to love?

> And when Love speaks, the voice of all the gods
> Makes Heaven drowsy with the harmony.
> Never durst poet touch a pen to write
> Until his ink were tempered with Love's sighs.
>> (*Love's Labour's Lost*, IV, iii, 344–47)

V. THE PREFIGURATIVE THEME: PARALLELS AND INFLUENCES

By this time it must be clear that the concept of prefigurative truth, which we have studied in Keats's prose explication (Letter 31) and poetic representation (*Endymion*), was not an idiosyncrasy of a single mind or temperament. Though Keats gave it personal and vivid expression, and being a poet insisted on the pre-eminent value of imagination and the "life of sensations," he was repeating the optimistic creativity of the human race in its immemorial yearning for paradise. Of this he seems to have been more or less conscious, as the declared interdependence of his two "favorite speculations" in Letter 31 makes clear, and as the induction to his last great poem, written at a time when his youthful optimism had virtually disappeared, also suggests:

> Fanatics have their dreams, wherewith they weave
> *A paradise for a sect*; the savage too
> From forth the loftiest fashion of his sleep
> *Guesses at Heaven*: pity these have not
> Trac'd upon vellum or wild indian leaf
> The shadows of melodious utterance.
> But bare of laurel they live, dream and die;
> For Poesy alone can tell her dreams,
> With the fine spell of words alone can save
> Imagination from the sable charm
> And dumb enchantment.
> ("The Fall of Hyperion," I, 1–11)

Poetry and religion and primitive imagination are equally concerned with paradise, that is to say, but the latter two are comparatively inarticulate, at least with respect to "melodious utterance."[1] He had written in a similar vein more than a year previously, without being so explicit as to articulateness:

Many a man can travel to the very bourne of heaven, and yet want confidence to put down his half-seeing. Sancho will invent a journey heavenward as well as any body.[2]

Sancho is the practical man par excellence, but he shares with all men the hope of immortality, and he is, by virtue of his imagination, an embryonic poet. More cautious perhaps than when he wrote Letter 31, Keats called

---

[1] It is a little surprising to find Keats alluding to his prefigurative faith at the commencement of the poem which contains his almost violent condemnation of "the dreamer tribe." But perhaps the violence was conditioned by the very preciousness of the faith which had long nourished him, and which he was now reluctantly renouncing.

[2] Letter 44, p. 96.

Sancho's heavenward journey a "half-seeing" rather than (prefigurative) truth, even though this half-seeing reached to "the very bourne of heaven."

If in searching for the sources of Keats's prefigurative faith we were to cull from the books that he read all expressions of belief in a paradisal immortality, we should never make an end. Nor would such quotations always illustrate the psychology which is our principal concern. In this psychology two facts stand out: (1) The poet's credence springs from "the elevation of the moment" (and the remembered elevation of past moments, probably), from a perfervid state of aesthetic ecstasy. (2) The poet's elysium is modeled on his most treasured aesthetic experiences on earth, and consists of these "repeated in a finer tone."

It is this feelingful faith in the prefigurative veracity of blissful imaginings —aesthetic rather than religious or philosophical—that characterizes the citations to follow. It might be said at the outset that such a faith, particularly where some difficulty in credence wars with the poet's will to believe, could well be taken as one criterion of the Romantic point of view. One could cite such a definition of Romanticism as that by Hoxie N. Fairchild: "the endeavor, in the face of growing factual obstacles, to achieve, to retain, or to justify . . . [the] illusioned view of the universe and of human life."[3]

In idealistic and philosophical minds this endeavor often results in the view that the sensible appearances of art are signs of a true and transcendent, but nonsensuous, reality. Hegel and Schelling are typical. In poets with an inclination to mysticism and didacticism the validity of transcendental illumination may be upheld and poetry will then lean toward the ethical and "spiritual." In their different ways Wordsworth, Coleridge, and Shelley keep company here. It is not, however, with the transcendental view of art that we shall be concerned in this chapter. For the highest reality to Keats, at least to the "young minded" Keats, was a rich and intense sensuousness, and the postmortal elysium which he envisioned was an unmystic, unphilosophical extensionalization and refinement of the "life of sensations" on earth.[4]

Now it appears almost certain that Keats's faith in his aesthetic elysium

---

[3] Hoxie N. Fairchild, *The Romantic Quest* (New York: Columbia University Press, 1931), p. 251.

[4] In one way or another, every critic of Keats has testified to the conspicuous sensuousness of his poetry, though many of them have preferred to allegorize or mysticize this sensuousness into something "spiritual." To the latter tendency the words of Hoxie N. Fairchild should be opposed: ". . . if spirituality implies a rising above the senses, Keats was not a spiritual man . . . Keats seldom if ever worshipped spiritual beauty in the accepted meaning of that term, but he worshipped sensuous beauty so intensely that it acquired quasi-spiritual values in his mind."—Fairchild, *The Romantic Quest*, p. 406.

was encouraged, if not in fact suggested, by Leigh Hunt's similar faith. Thomas Campbell and even Samuel Rogers also offer interesting parallels. Before citing the evidence from these writers, however, it may be well to give some specimens of the same tendency of mind in writers not known to Keats, simply to show that the pattern appears with some frequency, particularly among writers affected by the Romantic point of view. At times they tend to "take a dream for a truth," or to yearn for "the instant made eternity," to borrow Browning's pertinent phrases.[5]

Three passages, from De Sénancour, Tennyson, and Poe, are representative. On a somber day in March, the hero of De Sénancour's *Obermann* happens upon a jonquil in bloom, and at once his dejection evaporates in a glad vision of heaven:

It was the strongest expression of desire: it was the first perfume of the year. I felt all the happiness destined for man. That inexpressible harmony of souls, the phantom of the ideal world, arose in me complete. Never did I experience anything so great and so instantaneous . . .[6]

Later he confesses that the ideal realm here envisioned probably has no counterpart in reality, but he insists that the vividness of the experience and his ardent desire to believe in its prefigurative veracity have never faded.

The passage from Tennyson is from his earliest volume, *Poems by Two Brothers* (1827). The poet is addressing an imagined, idealized friend:

> But where art thou, thou comet of an age,
> Thou phoenix of a century? Perchance
> Thou art but of those fables which engage
> And hold the minds of men in giddy trance?
> Yet, be it so, and be it all romance,
> The thought of thine existence is so bright
> With beautiful imaginings and the glance
> Upon thy fancied being such delight,
> That I will deem thee *Truth*, so lovely is thy might![7]

Though no assumption about postmortal existence accompanies this equation of imagined beauty with Truth, the parallel with Keats's "favorite speculation" is in other respects close. Tennyson is more self-conscious, perhaps, more aware of the possible illusoriness of imagination, but this imagination brings him "such delight" that he cannot refrain from calling it "Truth."

---

[5] "The Statue and the Bust," 1. 155, and "The Last Ride Together," 1. 108.

[6] De Sénancour, *Obermann*, Letter XXX (my translation from the Édition Critique by G. Michaut [Paris, E. Cornély et cie., 1912–13], pp. 102–3). William James cites the passage in *The Varieties of Religious Experience*.

[7] Quoted by Harold Nicholson in *Tennyson, Aspects of His Life, Character, and Poetry* (London: Constable and Company, 1923), p. 58. The passage does not appear in the usual editions of the poems and is not tabulated in the Concordance.

Poe goes even further than Tennyson, untroubled by rational caution. He speaks as emphatically as Keats in Letter 31, confidently linking the mortal imagination with postmortal existence:

> An immortal instinct, deep within the spirit of man, is . . . a sense of the Beautiful . . . Man is naturally possessed with a thirst unquenchable . . . This thirst belongs to [derives from] the immortality of Man. It is at once a consequence and an indication of his perennial existence. . . . Inspired by an ecstatic prescience of the glories beyond the grave, we struggle . . . to attain a portion of that Loveliness whose very elements, perhaps, appertain to eternity alone. . . . we weep . . . at our inability to grasp *now*, wholly, here on earth, at once and for ever, those divine and rapturous joys, of which *through* the poem, or *through* the music, we attain to but brief and indeterminate glimpses.[8]

Both Poe and Keats base their credence on rapture, not on logic.

In the search for parallels to and possible influences upon Keats's prefigurative faith, as found in the books that he is known to have read (or probably read), it seems logical to look first among his contemporaries or recent predecessors. Yet he may have caught some hints from such earlier writers as Spenser, Drayton, and Milton, as well as from Wordsworth, Coleridge, and Shelley, in whom the correspondences are sometimes close enough to have reinforced the faith which, as was said earlier, bears closest relationship to that of Leigh Hunt. But whether or not the exact derivation of his faith can be demonstrated, it should be instructive to observe the more or less close correspondences to it that a rapid chronological survey, not intended to be exhaustive, can furnish. The chronology will be slightly disrupted for the sake of bringing Rogers, Campbell, and Hunt together at the end of the chapter.

How enrapturing was Spenser's poetic otherworld to the young Keats has often been told. It must at times have seemed to him as if Spenser had envisioned such a sensuous heaven as he would like to inherit. In any event, Spenser had given a prefigurative love-dream to Arthur, a dream which sent Arthur on just such an unremitting quest as Keats later assigned to Endymion:

> For-wearied with my sports, I did alight
> From loftie steed, and downe to sleep me layd . . .
> Me seemed, by my side a royall Mayd
> Her daintie limbes full softly down did lay:
> So faire a creature yet saw never sunny day.
>
> .   .   .   .
> From that day forth I cast in carefull mind,

---

[8] Essay on "The Poetic Principle," *The Poems of Edgar Allen Poe with a Selection of Essays* (Everyman ed.), pp. 97–98.

> To seeke her out with labour, and long tyne,
> And never vow to rest, till her I find . . .
> (Faerie Queene, I, ix, 13–15)

Around this dream, and Arthur's ceaseless quest to prove its veracity and so fulfill his fondest desires, Spenser intended to construct his entire poem. Though the poem was never finished and the reader tends to forget this early statement of purpose, Spenser planned ultimately to verify the dream, joining in lasting love Arthur and the Queene of Faery.[9]

Of course Arthur's dream may be only an artistic device and does not indicate that Spenser regarded dreams or imagination as veracious, but it may have helped to confirm Keats in his faith, just as he accepted Adam's dream in *Paradise Lost* as "a conviction" that happy dreams come true in heaven. One may surmise, too, that Spenser's opulently sensuous imagination, like Keats's, must unconsciously have pictured heaven after its own likeness, however strong his insistence on ethical perfection.

When we come to one of the post-Spenserians, Michael Drayton, we find a detailed description of the poets' heaven. "The Muses Elizium," uncomplicated with moral allegory, is a frank and sumptuous picture of the delights which await poets on the other side of death. The following stanzas give a generalized summary of the sensuous particulars:

> A paradice on earth is found,
>   Though farre from vulgar sight,
> Which with those pleasures doth abound
>   That it Elizium hight.
>
> Where in delights that never fade
>   The Muses lullèd be . . .
>
> Decay nor Age there nothing knowes,
>   There is continuall Youth,
> As Time on plant or creatures growes,
>   So still their strength renewth.
>
> The Poets' Paradice this is,
>   To which but few can come;
> The Muses' onely bower of blisse
>   Their Deare Elizium.
> (ll. 1–6, 97–104)

Without essaying to judge where, along the sliding scale of emotion and credence, Drayton's attitude lay, we can see at once that his portrayal of

---

[9] Claude Lee Finney mentions Arthur's dream in connection with Endymion's dreams, but regards the dreams of both heroes as neo-Platonic symbols. See Finney, *The Evolution of Keats's Poetry*, I, 304–5.

elysium is strikingly like Keats's in "Bards of Passion and of Mirth" and (we shall come to this later) the "Ode on a Grecian Urn." It is significant, too, that Leigh Hunt follows Drayton rather closely in his depiction of the poets' heaven, and makes it clear that he regards such a heaven as no mere fiction.[10]

In some respects the young Milton was like the young Keats, save that the Puritanical impulse in him was strong. Teeming with energy and sanguinely persuaded of the excellence of his calling, he cast off restraint in some of his Latin poems, proudly proclaiming the glory and divinity of poetry and the heavenly meed of poets. An exuberant passage from "Ad Patrem" is typical (given here in prose translation):

> You should not despise the poet's task, divine song, which preserves some spark of Promethean fire and is the unrivalled glory of the heaven-born human mind . . . when we return to our native Olympus and the everlasting ages of immutable eternity are established, we shall walk, crowned with gold, through the temples of the skies and with the harp's soft accompaniment we shall sing sweet songs to which the stars shall echo and the vault of heaven from pole to pole.[11]

As here envisioned, heaven will be an aesthetic realm where poets will ever-lastingly sing their songs.[12]

The loving treatment of Adam and Eve in their sensuous, indolent, hedonistic paradise is another indication, though more or less unconscious, that the imagination of a poet, especially of a sensuous poet, is irresistibly attracted by the idea of paradise. Though Paul Elmer More ignores other aspects of *Paradise Lost*, there is much truth in his assertion that "the true theme is Paradise itself: not Paradise lost, but . . . that ancient ineradicable longing of the human heart for a garden of innocence, a paradise of idyllic delights."[13] Then More goes on to show that Tennyson preferred Milton's

---

[10] The classic source of this tradition of the poets' elysium is in the *Aeneid* (VI, 637 ff.), where heroes and poets relive "the joy they felt alive." Virgil's Fourth Eclogue, if Keats read it, would have encouraged him in his prefigurative faith, particularly in the cosmic evolution sketched in "Hyperion." It is significant that Virgil is the only classic writer who dared to place the Golden Age in the future. See H. A. Burd, "The Golden Age Idea in Eighteenth Century Poetry," *Sewanee Review*, XXIII (1915), 172–85.

[11] Translated by Merritt Hughes. See *Paradise Regained, the Minor Poems, and Samson Agonistes* (New York: Doubleday, Doran and Company, 1937), pp. 275–77.

[12] For similar descriptions of the destiny of poets and poetry, and for descriptions of poetic ecstasy, see "Elegy V" and "Mansus." One of Milton's aims, as he declared in "Il Penseroso," was to "attain / To something like Prophetic strain" (ll. 173–74)—an aim which Keats also strove for, as shown in his "Lines on Seeing a Lock of Milton's Hair."

[13] "The Theme of 'Paradise Lost,'" *Shelburne Essays*, Fourth Series (New York: G. P. Putnam's Sons, 1907), pp. 243–44.

Eden to his empyrean, and he might have cited Keats's preference for
Milton's "exquisite passion for . . . poetical luxury, . . . the Elysian fields
of [his] verse."[14]

"Comus" is a poem ostensibly devoted to the recommendation of chastity,
but it is likely to impress the aesthetic reader rather as a series of lyric flights
and scenes of sensuous opulence. Except for a few final verses recommending the love of virtue, the poem closes with a rapt flight into a sensuous
heaven:

> *The dances ended, the Spirit Epiloguizes.*
>
> *Spirit.* To the Ocean now I fly,
> And those happy climes that lie
> Where day never shuts his eye
> Up in the broad fields of the sky:
> There I suck the liquid air
> All amidst the Gardens Fair
> Of Hesperus, and his daughters three
> That sing about the golden tree:
> . . . there eternal Summer dwells . . .
> And drenches with Elysian dew
> (List mortals, if your ears be true)
> Beds of Hyacinth and Roses
> Where young Adonis oft reposes,
> Waxing well of his deep wound
> In slumber soft . . .
> But far above in spangled sheen
> Celestial Cupid . . .
> Holds his dear Psyche sweet intranc't
> After her wand'ring labours long,
> Till free consent the gods among
> Make her his eternal Bride,
> And from her fair unspotted side
> Two blissful twins are to be born,
> Youth and Joy: so Jove hath sworn.
>
> (ll. 976–1011)

The spirit of scholarship and of allegory can of course demonstrate that
Milton's purpose in these splendid lines was to celebrate idealized love and
its sanction in heaven. Probably true, the imaginative reader concedes, but
adds: the sensuous poet overwhelmed the moralist in this passage. Surely
Keats savored the "poetical luxury" of these verses, reading them with decided relish, pictorial, sensuous, and "elysian." To him the Attendant Spirit
must have seemed no mere guardian of a girl's chastity, but the very spirit of
poetry, capable of scaling heaven and dwelling with the gods. Elysium, he

---

[14] See M. B. Forman, *The Poetical Works* . . . , V, 292.

would have inferred from the resplendent words, flashes into poetic minds during moments of aesthetic transport. Such moments must be a sign, then, a "conviction," that the real elysium, sustainedly, perennially possessible, lies beyond the mortal sphere, ever beckoning to poets of ardent faith.

During the eighteenth century there are many examples, especially among the so-called precursors of Romanticism, of attitudes similar to Keats's "favorite speculation." These attitudes are often mingled with the Christian anticipation of the future life, or with the Shaftesburyan scheme of a universe of perfect harmony and beauty, or with some other doctrine of the time.

Akenside will serve as an example. It is not known whether Keats read *The Pleasures of the Imagination*, but if he did, he must have found that Akenside was enough of a poet, and sufficiently enjoyed his imaginative flights, to forget about his didactic purpose in considerable sections of his poem. In the following passage he lets himself soar:

> Fancy dreams,
> Rapt into high discourse with prophets old,
> And wandering through Elysium, Fancy dreams
> Of sacred fountains, or o'ershadowing groves,
> Whose walks with godlike harmony resound:
> Fountains, which Homer visits; happy groves,
> Where Milton dwells: the intellectual power,
> On the mind's throne, suspends his graver cares,
> And smiles: the passions, to divine repose,
> Persuaded yield: and love and joy alone
> Are waking: love and joy, such as await
> An angel's meditation.   (I, 162–72, enlarged ed.)

What would have appealed to Keats is the vision of elysium captured by the imagination, the godlike love and joy and music in a bucolic setting, where the great poets dwell throughout eternity. And he would not have been troubled by Akenside's cautionary "Fancy *dreams*" while "the *intellectual* power . . . *suspends* his graver cares." For the "sensations" of Keats's dreaming imagination (in 1817, at least) were more precious to him than "thoughts," and a truer avenue to a poet's eventual elysium.

As the eighteenth century drew to a close, Cowper and Crabbe gave signs of the shift in poetic outlook. While Crabbe contemptuously dismissed the "sleepy bards" who sought to perpetuate "the flattering dream" of the Golden Age,[15] Cowper sighed over the loss:

> Would I had fall'n upon those happier days
> That poets celebrate; those golden times
> And those Arcadian scenes . . .
> (*The Task*, IV, 513–15)

---

15 *The Village*, I, 17.

Reason and good sense compelled him, however, to admit that wish and truth were not identical, and therefore poets who believed in the Golden Age were judged to have "impos'd a gay delirium for a truth."[16]

But the roots of the illusion were stronger than Cowper's or Crabbe's critical axes. The heart watered them and they flourished, while the dry blade of reason reluctantly withdrew. As the century neared its close, a young man, William Blake, saw seraphic visions amid the smoke and grime of London itself, and did not cease to see the visions when youth left him. To some he may seem to have been the victim of hallucinations, but his axioms, proclaimed *ex cathedra coeleste*, as it were, merely expressed in extreme form the tenets of the new era. Nature is as nothing when measured against imagination, he declares: "Imagination is Eternity."[17] Doubt is anathema: "Everything possible to be believ'd is an image of truth."[18] "O that men would seek immortal moments!"[19] And so on. Of course the realm which Blake's imagination revealed to him was a spiritual realm, not the sensuous elysium which Keats envisioned, but both realms revealed themselves in corporeal images and through the channels of feeling and hope, not of reason.

Though the admixture of transcendental concepts is strong in Coleridge and Wordsworth, the strength of their credence in a future state may owe more to intense aesthetic delight than is always realized. Both poets find "religious meanings in the forms of Nature,"[20] but the religion may at times be little more than the sense of joy which leaps to an assumption of heaven. The song of a lark and the comfortable rays of the sun, simple sensations as these are, lift Coleridge to visions of the afterlife. The lark and the sun soothe his nerves until he falls into a half-somnolent state:

> And so, his senses gradually wrapt
> In a half sleep, he dreams of better worlds . . .
> ("Fears in Solitude," ll. 25–26)

Later in the same poem (ll. 176–91) Coleridge gives thanks for the beauties of the English countryside, which he regards as the source of

> Whatever makes this mortal spirit feel
> The joy and greatness of its future being.
> (ll. 190–91)

---

[16] *The Task*, IV, 528.

[17] "The Ghost of Abel," Introduction.

[18] "Proverbs of Hell," in *The Marriage of Heaven and Hell*.

[19] Quoted by Logan Pearsall Smith, *A Treasury of English Aphorisms* (London: Constable and Company, 1947), p. 61.

[20] "Fears in Solitude," l. 24.

As might be expected from the man who defined the origin of poetry as "emotion *recollected* in tranquillity," and who made the retrospective imagination prominent in so many of his poems, Wordsworth did not often cast his eye into the future. Nor was he stirred by any hope of a social revolution (after the subsidence of his youthful political ardor) which would revive the Golden Age on earth. Yet in the verses from *The Recluse* which he included in the Preface to *The Excursion* in 1814, he regards "Paradise, and groves / Elysian, Fortunate Fields" not as "a history only of departed things," but as "a simple produce of the common day" provided one is "wedded to this goodly universe / In love and holy passion."[21] One basis of this creed may be transcendental, but the transcendental is itself largely dependent on the simple, feelingful pleasure of aesthetic experience.[22]

There are many instances in *The Excursion*, which Keats judged one of the "three things to rejoice at in this age,"[23] of this mixture of aesthetic delight with "religious meanings." For example, the splendor of a sunset over a majestic panorama of lakes and mountains stirs one of the characters to thank God for "this local transitory type / Of thy eternal splendours" (IX, 619–20), and to confirm his faith in immortality. The passage has a theological cast, but if one reads the rapturous description preceding the words of thanksgiving, he will better understand how Keats probably read this poem, as he read Spenser and Milton, not for sermon but for delight. The thanksgiving would then seem to him a natural response to an incomparable aesthetic experience and a recognition that heaven would be designed after such earthly models.

Throughout Shelley's poetry the dream of the Golden Age (with its moral and social connotations) and, less often, of an elysium for himself and his beloved, is prominent. Hence the themes of his major poems, together with the devices for revealing the future to the characters of the poems, illustrate the faith that his imagination holds in vaticination. *Queen Mab, The Revolt of Islam,* "The Witch of Atlas" (less seriously), *Prometheus Unbound,* and *Hellas* all announce and to some extent delineate the Golden Age that is to be, and "Epipsychidion" fancifully discovers an arcadian isle where the spirit of the ancient Golden Age is preserved, and where the poet and Emilia Viviani will spend an amorously elysian existence.[24]

---

[21] Ll. 47-55. See *The Poetical Works of Woodsworth*, rev. ed. (London: Oxford University Press, 1950), p. 590.

[22] One may of course prefer a more technical interpretation, viewing Wordsworth's aesthetic experiences as more or less deliberate *exempla* of his version of eighteenth-century doctrines such as Shaftesburyanism or associationism.

[23] Letter 36, p. 79.

[24] The nature of the love which Shelley dreams of sharing with Emilia in this isle is of course debatable. By "amorously elysian" I do not mean to emphasize sex.

One might trace with some profit the correspondences between Shelley's and Keats's attitudes to sleep, dreams, and imagination. G. Wilson Knight has sought to do this so far as the imagery is concerned,[25] but the tendency of both poets to assume a kind of equation between blissful dreams and imagination, on the one hand, and an everlasting realm of felicity, on the other, has not been fully explored. For example, when Shelley views the awful majesty of Mont Blanc, ecstasy lifts him to "a trance sublime" (l. 35), and almost automatically this ecstatic trance evokes impressions of another realm into which he and his ecstasy have been absorbed, the mysterious realm of sleep itself:

> Some say that gleams of a remoter world
> Visit the soul in sleep,—that death is slumber,
> And that its shapes the busy thoughts outnumber
> Of those who wake and live.—I look on high;
> Has some unknown Omnipotence unfurled
> The veil of life and death? or do I lie
> In dream, and does the mightier world of sleep
> Spread far around and inaccessible
> Its circles?   (ll. 49-57)

"Do I wake or sleep?" Keats had wondered when the voice of the nightingale faded upon his imaginative ear. With both Keats and Shelley the intense rapture of imaginative experience tends to detach them from the feeling that the objective world is real, and to persuade them that superlative imaginative moments may be portions of some superior realm, near allied to sleep and death. In fact, the Platonic Shelley goes beyond Keats in speculating on the likeness of sleep's realm to death's kingdom, death's dream-kingdom.

Keats seems to have written without benefit of Plato, and he was not a social reformer, but he would have recognized the resemblances to his own faith in such passages of Shelley's *Defence of Poetry* as the following, had he lived to read them: "Poetry is the record of the best and happiest moments of the happiest and best minds," and "Poets are . . . the mirrors of the gigantic shadows which futurity casts upon the present . . ."[26]

In Byron the prefigurative imagination seldom speaks with credent voice. The cry of mockery is often cynically ready to break in. Yet the Romantic mood occasionally carries him near to credence, as when he writes that dreams "look like heralds of eternity,"[27] or when, seeking to describe the incom-

---

[25] G. W. Knight, *The Starlit Dome.* See the essays on Shelley and Keats.

[26] *Shelley's Defence of Poetry*, edited by L. Winstanley (Boston: D. C. Heath and Company, 1911), pp. 50-51, 58.

[27] "The Dream," l. 11.

parable beauty of Zuleika, he can find no analogy so apt as love's dream of heaven:

> Dazzling as that, oh! too transcendent vision
> To Sorrow's phantom-peopled slumber given,
> When heart meets heart again in dreams Elysian,
> And paints the lost on earth revived in Heaven.
>
> (*The Bride of Abydos*, I, 162–65)

A little more ardor, and Byron's credence might have rivaled Keats's. Sorrow's slumber may be "phantom-peopled," but the phantoms compose a "too transcendent vision" to encourage disbelief.

When Byron describes the Apollo Belvedere, one is reminded of Keats's ecstasy in envisioning the Grecian Urn, as well as of Endymion's quest of an immortal erotism:

> . . . in his delicate form—a dream of Love,
> Shaped by some solitary nymph, whose breast
> Long'd for *a deathless lover* from above
> And madden'd in that vision—are expresst
> All that ideal beauty ever bless'd
> The mind with in its *most unearthly mood*,
> When each conception was *a heavenly guest*—
> *A ray of immortality*—and stood,
> Starlike, around, until they gather'd to a god!
>
> (*Childe Harold*, IV, clxii)

The italics are not in the original, but they emphasize the deificatory quality which Byron sees in the statue and which he attributes to the ardent love-dream of a girl. In the following stanza he even declares that the statue, though "made by human hands, *is not of human thought.*" The Venus de' Medici inspires him in much the same way: "dazzled and drunk with beauty," he feels that "the veil of heaven is half undrawn."[28] He may be speaking figuratively or hyperbolically, of course, but he seems to say, at least with reference to the Apollo Belvedere, that a maiden's hopeful dream of love is bodied forth in a sculptured shape which answers to an actual heavenly personage. As Keats would say, "the prototype must be here after."

The mature Byron, to be sure, is best known for his mockery and anti-Romanticism. The Saturnian Age of Gold is irreverently dismissed in "Beppo":

> Oh, for old Saturn's reign of sugar-candy!—
> Meantime I drink to your return in brandy.
>
> (lxxx, 7–9)

And in "The Blues" (a satire of bluestockings and literary personages), a

---

[28] *Childe Harold*, IV, xlix–l.

trenchant dialogue strips bare the cardinal Romantic illusion. Lady Blue-
bottle exclaims:

> Oh! my dear Mr. Botherby! sympathize!—I
> Now feel such a rapture, I'm ready to fly,
> I feel so elastic—"*so buoyant—so buoyant*!"

and two of the men reply:

> For God's sage, my Lady Bluebottle, check not
> This gentle emotion, so seldom our lot
> Upon earth. Give it way: 'tis an impulse which lifts
> Our spirits from earth; the sublimest of gifts . . .
> 'Tis the Vision of Heaven upon Earth: 'tis the gas
> Of the soul; 'tis the seizing of shades as they pass,
> And making them substance; 'tis something divine . . .
> (ll. 129-41)

Another passage, though it was aimed primarily at Wordsworth and
Coleridge, throws a realistic light on *Endymion* and its author. When Don
Juan had been experiencing ecstasies from the contemplation of nature and
the stars, Byron ascribed these ecstasies not to any transcendental element in
the soul, but to glands and hormones (as we would say today):

> 'Twas strange that one so young should thus concern
> His brain about the action of the sky:
> If *you* think 'twas philosophy that this did,
> I can't help thinking puberty assisted.
> (Canto I, xciii)

Keats himself confessed in his preface that adolescence ("a space of life between") was partly responsible for *Endymion*.

Byronic scoffing was not, of course, characteristic of the age. Even in
minds like those of Samuel Rogers and of Thomas Campbell, where eighteenth-century moderation had not fully capitulated to the tides of Romantic
feeling, striking evidence can be found of the prefigurative attitude.

Rogers' *The Pleasures of Memory* might be expected to follow a consistently retrospective theme. In the analyses preceding each book the expectation is borne out; but in the poem itself, as frequently happens when
poets are rapt with their imaginative visions, there are some instances of the
now familiar pattern: that an experience of bliss on earth is accepted as an
argument *per se* for a future existence fashioned after the earthly model.

Similar to the Romantics' wonted attitude to dreams is Rogers' conception of memory as almost exclusively blissful (a "blooming Eden").[29]

---

[29] See *Poetical Works*, with a memoir by E. Bell (London: George Bell & Sons,
1892), p. 20. Subsequent references are to the same edition.

Even the scourged Congo slave can remember happy scenes, and in doing so he connects them with heaven:

> Memory bursts the twilight of the mind,
> Her dear delusions soothe his sinking soul,
> When the rude scourge assumes its base control;
> *And O'er Futurity's blank page diffuse*
> *The full reflection of her vivid hues,*
> 'Tis but to die, and then, to weep no more,
> Then will he wake on Congo's distant shore;
> Beneath his plantain's ancient shade *renew*
> *The simple transports that with freedom flew.*
>
> (II, p. 18)

The slave's happy memories are projected into an empty future, filling it with substance—a future that is but the "reflection" of memory's and fancy's hopeful visions. To be sure, Rogers calls these memories "dear delusions," but one wonders whether he really believed they were delusions, for elsewhere in the poem he confidently assumes the soul's immortality. Furthermore, it is not only the slave that builds a heaven from memory's Eden, but during dreams "Fancy's bright Elysium flows," and Memory, "the immortal friend," is beheld hovering "o'er sleeping Innocence,"

> Whispering seraphic visions of her heaven. (III, p. 19)

This heaven is later depicted with more detail:

> But is Her [Memory's] magic only felt below?
> Say, thro' what brighter realms she bids it flow;
> To what pure beings, in a nobler sphere,
> She yields *delight but faintly imaged here;*
> All that till now their rapt researches knew,
> Not called in slow succession to review;
> But as landscape meets the eye of day,
> At once presented to their glad survey!
> *Each scene of bliss revealed, since chaos fled,*
> And dawning light its dazzling glories spread;
> Each chain of wonders that sublimely glowed,
> Since first Creation's choral anthem flowed . . .
>
> (III, p. 27)

In another world, then, Memory is not Memory but Presence. Her operation on earth is "faintly imaged" from her immortal, rapturous Being there. Yet her heaven is not a creation antedating the earth's existence; it is fashioned from "each scene of bliss" upon the lowly earth. From the mortal point of view, then, heaven is but a projection and extensionalization of the best of earth: as Keats wrote in Letter 31, "happiness on earth repeated in a finer tone," "imagination and its empyreal reflection."

Like Rogers, Thomas Campbell was one of the leading poets of the day, enjoying the approval of the critics and a wide reading audience. That Keats had read the very popular *The Pleasures of Hope* cannot be proved, though the probabilities are on this side.[30] He had evidently read *Gertrude of Wyoming*,[31] and there is so close a correspondence between one verse of "Sleep and Poetry," where he is defining the essence of poetry:

'Tis might half slumb'ring on its own right arm (1. 237)

and a verse in *The Pleasures of Hope*, where Campbell is defining the source of political freedom:

The might that slumbers in a peasant's arm (I, 460)[32]

that Keats's verse is more likely a reminiscence than a mere coincidence.

In *The Pleasures of Hope* there is a poignant wavering between an ardent wish and a not quite eradicable doubt, reminding one of the similar vacillation in *Endymion*. In Campbell's poem this fluctuation produces two antithetic usages of "truth," very much as we found in Keats's Letter 31. There Keats argued that truth was the product of imagination, but he also allowed the word, though reluctantly, to the product of "consecutive reasoning." In the same way Campbell equates "Truth" with Hope, yet several times uses it in an opposite sense. Two other words share this fluctuation: "Wisdom" and "Science" (also "Reason" in one instance):

	Total Number of Occurrences[33]	Usages Connoting Hope	Usages Opposed to Hope
Truth	12	8	4
Wisdom	6	1	5
Science	3	1 (or 2?)	1 (or 2?)
Reason	1	0	1

It can be seen at a glance that Truth is on the side of Hope, whereas Wisdom appears to be their foe, though in one instance Wisdom has changed her allegiance. The tabulation corroborates the impression of the reader, who feels that Campbell is striving to face the facts and yet to uphold his favorite view of things. He would like to allow Hope and Wisdom and Science to share Truth among them, but he sees that Wisdom and Science too often

---

[30] C. L. Finney asserts, without offering evidence, that Keats's early poems were influenced by *The Pleasures of Hope*.—Finney, *The Evolution of Keats's Poetry*, I, 59–61.   [31] Letter 172, p. 452.

[32] References are to the edition of the poems by J. L. Robertson (London: Oxford University Press, 1907).

[33] The passages from which this tabulation is constructed may be found in Part I, 22, 286, 340, 349–50, 415, 421, 428, 439; and Part II, 77–78, 169, 317–18, 347, as well as in I, 17, 273, and II, 9, 213–14, 319–20, 325–26, 353, 394.

dwell in darkness and doubt, which are fatal to Hope. Therefore Truth *must* be on the side of Hope!

A few illustrative passages may help to make clear the antithetical usages in *The Pleasures of Hope*, and to reveal the main theme and direction of the poem. Part I delineates many of the consolations of hope for the ordinary man, and especially the alliance of hope with Genius (to which several sections are devoted) ;[34] but perhaps more space is given to a sanguine, earthly future for humanity, a future wherein freedom will have forever exiled tyranny, bringing in a new Golden Age. Part II dwells affectionately on the pleasures of love, and strenuously argues that hope, joined with imagination, promises to human beings a blissful immortality.

A few lines after the opening of Part I, Campbell suggests that a utopian future awaits humanity. This future is promised by Hope though denied by Wisdom: Wisdom may be "true," but she is "too severely true"!

> . . . if she [Wisdom] hold an image to the view,
> 'Tis Nature pictured too severely true.
> With thee, sweet Hope! resides the heavenly light
> That pours remotest rapture on the sight.
> (I, 15–24)

Science, Wisdom, and Reason misconceive Nature, Campbell contends, because their approach is cold and feelingless ; they have "the lukewarm passions of a lowly mind" (II, 298).

Hope, on the other hand, is "the pledge of Joy's anticipated hour" (I, 18), the "angel of life" (I, 53), "bright Improvement" (I, 321), a "creative spirit" (II, 55), "heart-warm wishes, true to happiness" (II, 60), a *"talisman . . . to snatch from Heaven anticipated joy"* (II, 69–71), "Daughter of Faith" (II, 261), and so on. In fine:

> Souls of impassioned mould, she speaks to you! (II, 204)

Part II opens with an apostrophe to the power of Love such as Keats would have read with high approval.

> Till Hymen brought his love-delighted hour,
> There dwelt no joy in Eden's rosy bower!
> (II, 25–26)

There are, of course, some "barren hearts" that have never yielded to the enchantment of love ; theirs is a "loveless wisdom" linked to "self-adoring pride," declares the poet, and he adds almost vengefully: "Fire, Nature,

---

[34] Again the parallel with Keats's Letter 31 is close, for the prelude to the famous statement of the "holiness of the heart's affections and the truth of imagination" consists of some observations on "genius and the heart."

Genius, never dwelt with you !" (II, 12). The young Keats who made poetry
the offspring of love would have been pleased by this.

Sensing the strength of the opposition, Campbell pleads first with the
loveless, then with the hopeless and pessimistic, then—more vehemently—
with the agnostic and the scientific. He cannot ignore the unhopeful aspect
of "Truth's historic page" (II, 169), but the future will be, he insists, the
product of "Hope's creative spirit" (II, 55). Regardless of the remote, mundane utopia, which can give little satisfaction to those who must die before
it has arrived, Hope and Imagination together project—and promise—a blissful postmortal existence for every imaginative and hopeful individual:

> Above, below, in Ocean, Earth, and Sky,
> Thy fairy worlds, Imagination, lie,
> And Hope attends, companion of the way,
> Thy dream by night, thy visions of the day !
> In yonder pensile orb, and every sphere
> That gems the starry girdle of the year;
> In those unmeasured worlds, she bids thee tell,
> Pure from their God, created millions dwell,
> Whose names and natures, unrevealed below,
> We yet shall learn, and wonder as we know . . .
>   (II, 189–205)

The heaven that Campbell envisions is less sensuous than Keats's aesthetic
elysium, but it is foreshown to him in the same mirrors: Imagination and
Hope. These two are "inseparable agents," as he declares in his prose analysis preceding the poem.

If Hope and Imagination are inseparable agents, and if Hope is a "creative spirit," it follows that heaven is not merely foreshown to, but may in
some measure be created by, the Imagination. Had not Keats insisted that
the imagination "is creative of essential beauty"? Like Keats, Campbell links
his argument to the heart's affections; our memories and dreams of loved
ones convince us, he feels, "of rapture yet to be" (II, 457), for:

> If fate unite the faithful but to part,
> Why is their memory sacred to the heart?
> Why does the brother of my childhood seem
> Restored awhile in every pleasing dream? (II, 463–66)

"The holiness of the heart's affections," Keats had likewise reasoned, is its
own sign and proof of the life hereafter. The heart, the imagination, and
dreams are the poet's trinity. If truth is not in these, where is it to be found?

In his formative years, no literary personage was closer to Keats than
Leigh Hunt. The younger poet read *The Examiner* regularly, he read Hunt's
poetry, and his debut in print was owing to the interest of Hunt. The two

met frequently, either at Hunt's house or at literary gatherings where Hunt was present. Two of Hunt's books were found in Keats's library as it was inventoried by Woodhouse after the poet's death: *Juvenilia* and *The Descent of Liberty*. It has long been recognized that Hunt was Keats's first literary guide after Cowden Clarke. The influence that Hunt exerted on the younger poet's verse-form and diction has always been acknowledged, and critics frequently remind us that Keats's early conception of poetry was largely molded by Hunt's disapproval of the morbid and his cultivation of the cheerful, and by his notion that poetry is a kind of bower of sensuous "luxuries." Although it is true that Hunt's sentimentality and mannerisms sometimes vexed Keats after he had known him longer, their friendship did not cease, and there is no reason to suppose that the impressionable younger poet automatically threw off all vestiges of the Huntian influence as soon as admiration was modified with vexation.

All this does not have to be argued; it is repeated here as a prelude to the consideration of Hunt's influence on Keats's "favorite speculation." This is an aspect of the relation between the two poets that has not engaged the attention of critics. In the pages that follow, some of the evidence of close parallelism will be presented, without an attempt to "prove" that Keats's creed was derivative. The probabilities strongly suggest that it was, to a considerable degree at least; but it seems wiser to let the illustrations speak for themselves. Perhaps they represent causative, perhaps only remarkably coincidental, forces. It would be pleasant, were that our privilege, to overhear some of the conversations between the two men during 1816–17, but these are forever irrecoverable.

One of the favorite "luxuries" of Hunt's poetry is a sentimental erotism. Not only is he fond of such warm, voluptuous languor as he poured into his *Story of Rimini* (1816), but whenever he turns to inanimate nature his delight comes not primarily from the trees and streams and clouds but from his ingrained habit of mythologizing these. Virtually everything is personified, and nearly every personification is feminine—and almost sure to be naked—seemingly existing only for the pleasure of poets. Of course Hunt is not the originator of this treatment of nature; Ovid and William Browne were much addicted to it. Hunt's distinction is that he gives a more exclusive attention to the females. At any rate, he often creates the impression that his enjoyment of nature is richly mingled with the erotic. In "The Nymphs," for example—a poem which we know that Keats read[35]—he leads

---

[35] The poem was included in *Foliage* (1818), a collection with which Keats was familiar. In his letters Keats makes at least three references specifically to "The Nymphs," references which prove that he had read this poem, in whole or in part, before he wrote Letter 31. See the index to the Letters, under "The Nymphs."

one to believe that a poet could have no higher aspiration than to bathe with panting desire in the streams where the naiads voluptuously swim and float. In the same way, Part II depicts the clouds as nepheliads, strewn in every sort of sybaritic nudity like odalisques in a seraglio. As they prepared to leave the ecstatic poet,

> every lady bowed
> A little from its [her cloud's] side without a word:
> And swept my lips with breathless lips serene. (II, 226-28)

Hunt's interest in the erotic does not stop with the voluptuous pleasures that a femininely mythologized nature offers him; he speculates about the future fate of the poets who give themselves up to the adoration of love. In "The Nymphs" he implores these creatures to carry him to some sylvan scene. They do as he requests, and he addresses them in this wise:

> Etherial human shapes, *perhaps the souls*
> *Of poets and poetic women,* staying
> To have their fill of pipes and leafy playing,
> *Ere they drink heavenly change* from nectar bowls.
> You finer people of the earth,
> Nymphs of all names . . .   (I, 33-38)

Thus on their way to final immortality and bliss, poets may be pleased to inhabit the lovely bodies, and to enjoy the sensuous pleasures, of these nymphs. And there is another point worth noticing, rendered more obvious in some writings presently to be considered, but also implicit in "The Nymphs": Hunt likes to think of heaven as a series of gently graduated heavens, making no abrupt transition from the joys and values of mortality.

These ideas, it may be thought, are mere wanton play of the fancy; but we shall see them again, in prose as well as in poetry. Consider the verses which bring Part I of "The Nymphs" to a close:

> I have not told
> *Your perfect loves,* ye Nymphs! Those are among
> The perfect virtues only to be sung
> By *your own glorious lovers,* who have passed
> Death and all drear mistake, and sit at last
> In the clear thrill of *their hoped age of gold.*

It might be Campbell speaking if he were an amorist. It might be Keats. For one word says as much as the entire context: "their *hoped* age of gold." What the imagination hopes to have, that it shall one day supremely enjoy. Physical love is the prime pleasure on earth; therefore it will be the highest meed of heaven.

This attitude finds expression even in critical prose. What, for example, is the finest part of Milton?

Allusions to romance and to Greek mythology, which he never could prevail on himself to give up, are the most refreshing things in his Paradise Lost and Regained, *next to the bridal happiness of poor Adam and Eve.* (Preface to *Foliage,* p. 26, in the 1818 edition)

With such a precedent, it is not strange that Keats's first *Endymion* aimed to "tell but one wonder of thy [Cynthia's] *bridal night"* (1. 210), and that Letter 31 selected Adam's love-dream as an analogue of the beauty that is "truth."

Love and the poetry of love are not, however, as Hunt implies elsewhere, the only guides to the Golden Age. Poetry on other subjects, if it stirs the heart, lifts one to superior worlds, and the imagination in such moments "teaches us that we have something within us more than mortal."[36] Music is, or may be for those who respond with rapture, not "mere suggestions of our human feeling," but the sign of "infinite things," the voice of Heaven without the words," a language luring "well-tuned hearts" to that "blest air" where they shall be finally able to understand it.[37] In another poem, music is "like winds in Eden's tree-tops," and should be heard only when lovers' hands are joined:

> For only so such *dreams* should end,
> Or *wake in Paradise.* (*Song,* p. 332)

Dancing, too, can be a kind of replica of the Golden Age:

They [the French] spend their afternoons in dancing under the trees or indoors, or attending the theatres, where they see *imitations of the Golden Age* in dances *more poetical.* (Preface to *Foliage,* 1818, p. 17.)

Art in all its forms, or at least in its genial forms—for Hunt deprecates Greek tragedy—exists as a mirror or foreshadowing of that supreme felicity which all men hope some day to enjoy. The aim of poets, then, ought to be to create happiness in their poems, and to assist in restoring the Golden Age. As he says in a "Sonnet to Shelley on the Degrading Notions of Deity," it is deplorable that there are poets who prefer to "seat a phantom, swelled into grim size,"

> in the midst of the all-beauteous skies,
> And all this lovely world, that should engage
> Their mutual search for *the old golden age.* (p. 242)

---

[36] "Comedy," *Critical Essays on the Performers of the London Theatre . . .* (London: John Hunt, 1807).

[37] "A Thought on Music," ll. 17–45. The Oxford edition is assumed in all quotations from the poems.

Like Shelley, whom he so deeply admired, Hunt hoped that art might be the adumbration of the new age. His hopes were less transcendental, and interrupted by fewer periods of dejection. He proclaimed them less often and less phrenetically, but one long poem, *The Descent of Liberty* (1815)—a copy of which was in Keats's library—shows the utopian prospect clearly and sustainedly. In this symbolic drama in blank verse, several of the patterns of thought most characteristic of the young Keats are found. For example, the following lines, spoken by a woman, show the imagination in its now familiar operation of adumbrating a beatific future:

> you've heard me, Sir,
> In my young fancy picture out a world,
> Such as our present-timed, unfinal eyes,
> Knowing but what they see,—and not even that,—
> *Might gather from the best of what's before them,*
> Leaving out evil as a vexing thorn. (III, 143–48)

The voices of Campbell and Rogers and Shelley and Keats can all be heard in this desireful thinking. But even before the woman speaks, the world—physically, politically, seasonally, psychologically—has begun to change, so that her words, culled from her own former prevision and hope, now actually fit the world about her:

> Spring and Summer
> Married, and Winter dead to be no more. (III, 153–54)

Like Adam's and Endymion's dreams, her fancy has prefigured this paradisal, elysian earth.

Another passage from *The Descent of Liberty* corroborates the graduated conception of the poets' heaven already seen in "The Nymphs." When the climax of the drama is reached, the goddess Liberty descends from the sky, followed successively by Peace, Music, Painting, and Poetry. Poetry, not Liberty, speaks the most revealing words as she narrates her history and that of deceased poets:

> From the isles that streak the mellowing west
> And echoing bowers of rest . . .
> Hither with a thought am I
> At call of Peace and Liberty.
> *There I left on rosy beds*
> *The poets* with their laurelled heads,
> Who when on earth gave happy voice
> To Truth and Right, and *now rejoice*
> *Each with her he loved the best,*
> Pleasure-eyed, in perfect rest. (III, 464–75)

From this airy elysium, she says, the poets look down with satisfaction on the praise given to their works by humankind, and (her story continues):

> Then before me they appear,
> *Each with his divinest dear,*
> And in friendly zeal contend,
> Which of all, to some great end
> Of good and just, can raise to sight
> *Happiest visions of delight,*
> By themselves perhaps to be
> *After made reality.*   (III, 487–94)

"A shadow of reality to come" (Letter 31) was Keats's phrase for the veracity of the poetic imagination, and in "Lamia" he declared:

> Real are the dreams of gods, and smoothly pass
> Their pleasures in a long immortal dream.   (I, 127–28)

In Rogers and in Campbell, similar as they are to Keats in many respects, there is no resemblance so close, none so naïvely sensuous and erotic as Hunt's picture of the poets' heaven. In heaven as on earth, Hunt and Keats agree, imagination's function and privilege are to prefigure an ever happier existence, which will automatically come into being to answer the prefiguration.

No man in his saner moments, it may be thought, would make such bold guesses as Keats's and Hunt's about postmortal existence. Nevertheless, Hunt has left an essay in prose, where his passions ought not to have run away with him, that explains his faith in some detail. "An Earth upon Heaven" is the title of the essay—not heaven upon earth, but a postmortal heaven constructed of what has been superlatively happy on earth. As Keats said, "happiness on earth repeated in a finer tone." At some later time, Hunt says, the Christian heaven may be a possibility, but it would be too painful a transition to enter immediately a region so unlike earth.

It is a pity that none of the great geniuses, to whose lot it has fallen to describe a future state, has given us his own notions of heaven. Their accounts are all modified by the national theology. . . . Dante's shining lights are poor. Milton's heaven, with the armed youth exercising themselves in military games, is worse. His best Paradise was on earth, and a very pretty heaven he made of it. For our parts, admitting and venerating as we do the notion of a heaven surpassing all human conception, we trust that it is no presumption to hope, that the state mentioned by the Apostle is the *final* heaven; and that we can ascend and gradually accustom ourselves to the intensity of it, by others of a less superhuman nature. . . . We could wish to take gently to it; to be loosed not entirely at once. Our song desires to be a "song of degrees."

At this point the theme begins to kindle his imagination; his yearning and his desire to persuade grow stronger:

Earth and its capabilities—are these nothing? And are they to come to nothing? Is there no beautiful realization of the fleeting type that is shown us? No body to this shadow? No quenching to this taut and continued thirst? No arrival at these natural homes and resting-places, which are so heavenly to our imaginations, even though they be built of clay, and are situated in the fields of our infancy? We are becoming graver than we intended; but to return to our proper style.

Again Keats's words come to mind: "a shadow of reality to come," "imagination and its empyreal reflection," "the prototype must be here after." But the reins of Hunt's straining fancy were pulled in; does this mean that he is only playing with fancies, that he is not really serious about the matter? It does not, as the next sentences demonstrate:

Nothing shall persuade us, for the present, *that Paradise Mount*, in any pretty village in England, *has not another Paradise Mount to correspond, in some less perishing region*; that is to say, *provided anybody has set his heart upon it* [italics mine] :—and that we shall not all be dining, and drinking tea, and complaining of the weather (we mean, for its not being perfectly blissful) three hundreds years hence, in some snug interlunar spot, or perhaps in the moon itself.

It appears to us, that for a certain term of centuries, Heaven *must* consist of something of this kind. In a word, we cannot but persuade ourselves, that to realize everything that we have justly desired on earth, will *be* heaven;—we mean, for that period: and that afterwards, if we behave ourself in a proper pre-angelical manner, we shall go to another heaven, still better, where we shall realize all that we desired in our first. Of this latter we can as yet have no conception; but of the former, we think some of the items may be as follows . . .

Any Paradise Mount on earth, it seems, has its prototype "in some less perishing region," provided the heart wills it. That is a bold statement, but it is perfectly matched by Keats's letter: "the prototype [of the singer's beautiful face] must be here after" because of "the holiness of the heart's affections." Likewise Hunt's italicized "must" betrays the wishfulness in his faith, even as Keats's "must" betrayed his wishfulness. In both his prose and his verse, we see, Hunt is consistent in his depiction of a heaven constructed of "everything that we have justly desired on earth," and in the different gradations of heaven itself or, should it be said, in the hierarchy of heavens. The latter conception is perhaps less explicit, but clearly inferable, in the passages previously quoted from "The Nymphs" and *The Descent of Liberty*.

As Hunt goes on to describe the constituents of his heaven, he confesses that its three most essential properties will be the pleasures of friendship, love, and books. There will be many lesser friends, but one above all others, "the best friend we have had upon earth": a mistress, not a wife. For there are no marriages in heaven:

Item, then, a mistress: beautiful, of course,—angelical expression,—A Peri, or Houri, or whatever shape of perfection you choose to imagine her, and *yet retaining the likeness of the woman you loved best on earth* [italics mine] : in fact, she herself, but completed; all her good qualities made perfect, and her defects taken away[38] (with exception of one or two charming peccadilloes, which she can only get rid of in a post-future state): good-tempered, laughing, serious, fond of everything about her without detriment to her special fondness for yourself, a great roamer in Elysian fields and forests, but not alone (they go in pairs there, as the jays and turtle-doves do with us): but above all things, true . . .

And how will they spend their time?

Between writing some divine poem, and meeting our friends of an evening, we should walk with her, or fly (for we should have wings, of course) like a couple of human bees or doves, extracting delight from every flower, and with delight filling every shade. There is something too good in this to dwell upon; so we spare the fears and hopes of the prudish. We would lay her head upon our heart, and look more pleasure into her eyes, than the prudish or the profligate ever so much as fancied.[39]

Her head upon our heart, or our head upon her breast—Keats and Hunt have the same idea of the beatitude of eternity.

To complete the delights of friendship and love, Shakespeare and Spenser and others will be in the same heaven, and they will write new books. Poetry, friendship, and love—of such is the kingdom of Hunt's heaven. How like, it need scarcely be said, to Keats's "pleasure thermometer" and "favorite speculation," and also to his "third chamber of life": "a lucky and a gentle one—stored with the wine of love—and the bread of friendship."[40]

Before taking leave of Hunt's happy vision of heaven, a word is pertinent concerning the tone of his essay. Now and then the tone is light, to be sure; at some points the writer almost appears to be amusing his fancy; at others, again, the current of strong feeling pushes through. Were there no other indications in his writings that the naïve heaven here described was part of his belief, it would be proper to dismiss the essay as polite, genial fancy. But the other indications have been exhibited already, in sufficient numbers and earnestness to be convincing. Consequently the light tone in portions of the essay can plausibly be explained as a device of expression rather than an evidence of disbelief. The writer is no longer young and passionate; the autumn of his life has come and he is content to muse on the fair dreams of his youth, unwilling to abandon his hope for their ultimate realization, and too wise in

---

[38] Again compare Keats: "Do you not remember forming to yourself the singer's face more beautiful than it was possible . . . the prototype must be here after—that delicious face you will see."

[39] This essay appeared in *The Companion* in 1828 and was several times reprinted. That Keats did not read the essay is no argument against his susceptibility to the ideas which it contains, ideas which, as we have seen, appeared earlier in poems which we know Keats to have read.

[40] Letter 64, p. 145.

the ways of the world to raise his voice. If this is not so, why did his definition of poetry, in a famous essay, contain such sentences as these:

When we go to heaven, we may idealize in a superhuman mode, and have altogether different notions of the beautiful; but till then, we must be content with the loveliest capabilities of earth.[41]

. . . next to Love and Beauty, which are its parents, [Poetry] is the greatest *proof* to man of the pleasure to be found in all things, and of *the probable riches of infinitude.*[42]

The last words are found on the first and most important page in the essay, "What is Poetry?"—an essay which goes on to declare that "beauty and truth become identical in poetry."[43]

Let it especially be noted that Hunt does not merely say poetry is a source of hope or an invitation to believe. He says it is the "greatest *proof* to man of . . . the probable riches of infinitude." Was not Keats's argument the same when he insisted that Adam's dream was "a *conviction* that imagination and its empyreal reflection is the same as human life and its spiritual repetition"?

Probably Hunt did not always believe this. But there were times when he did believe it—that is unquestionable. Keats's flux was the same.[44]

---

[41] "What is Poetry?" See *Imagination and Fancy* (London: Smith, Elder and Company, 1891), p. 18. The phrase, "the loveliest capabilities of earth," evidently carries the same meaning as "earth's capabilities" in the essay, "An Earth Upon Heaven."

[42] *Ibid.*, p. 1. The italics are mine.

[43] *Ibid.*, p. 6.

[44] It is fair to say that the essay, "What is Poetry?" was not published till 1844. Yet there is little reason to doubt that Hunt held the same or similar ideas in the days when he was Keats's friend. We have given examples from "The Nymphs," which Keats had read before he wrote Letter 31, and from *The Descent of Liberty* (1815), which was among the books in his library. We have found similar ideas in other poems and passages of prose by Hunt which were published during Keats's lifetime. "An Earth Upon Heaven" (1828), when compared with *The Descent of Liberty* (1815) and "The Nymphs" (which Keats had read by 1817), shows that Hunt's views of the poets' heaven had not changed during at least thirteen years. Thus the sentences quoted from "What is Poetry?" (1844) may be regarded as a late expression of an attitude consistently held, and with which the young Keats could hardly fail to have been acquainted.

VI. THE PREFIGURATIVE THEME IN THE POEMS AND LETTERS OF 1818

There is a survival of fitness in poetry as well as in biology. In Keats, fitness was swiftly and amply attested; he grew rapidly in self-knowledge after the "young minded" *Endymion* was put aside. The record of this rapid mental growth has been frequently traced and need not be repeated here. For we are interested in the survival, not of the fittest, but of one of the most compulsive and ardent of Keats's traits of mind. *Endymion* is, of course, the principal incarnation of this compulsive and ardent trait, but it reappears later from time to time on the crest of rapture. "The elevation of the moment" is commonly the key to its emergence. As time passes and youthful optimism fades away into the light of common day, these rare and splendid moments cannot always be trusted to unlock the elysian future or the heavenly present. Doubt mingles with credence, as happened at times even in *Endymion*. In other words, maturity and wisdom are coming to Keats, and hope and daring begin to feel their mortal chains, until in "Lamia" and "The Fall of Hyperion" the revolution is almost complete, and "the dreamer tribe" is sent down to death and darkness. To this grave climax our story must also come, but in the meantime we shall be following mainly the high road, or rather the high, looping flights of ecstasy. The order will be approximately chronological.

In a fervent effusion on Milton, evoked by the sight of "a real authenticated lock of Milton's hair,"[1] Keats asks: "O where are thy dominions?" then swears by "thy mortal lips," "thine earthly love," and "Beauty, in things on earth, and things above," that he will dedicate his life to the honoring of Milton in verse. The implication seems to be that Milton now dwells in some immortal realm, and can perhaps hear Keats's impassioned words. After the first flush of excitement Keats admits that he is not yet sufficiently the artist to honor Milton properly, and cannot hope to be such until he grows "mad with glimpses of futurity!" Does he mean that he must see more of heaven than he has yet been privileged to behold?

Whatever his meaning, he looks forward eagerly to this state of "madness" (ecstasy?), and concludes his poem by confessing that his forehead is "hot and flush'd," and that he was so "startled" by the sight of Milton's lock of hair that:

> I thought I had beheld it from the flood.

This apparent annihilation of time during a moment of rapture is not an un-

---

[1] Letter 40, pp. 85 ff.

common human experience, but such *moments éterne₄₅* were rather frequent with Keats. Witness his first view of Lake Windermere, the "Ode to a Nightingale," "Ode on a Grecian Urn," and the "Bright star" sonnet. Add wish and fervor to such moments and they become prefigurative, a kind of forestate of heaven. One thinks again of Browning's lover who wishfully defines heaven as "the instant made eternity."

In a sonnet to J. H. Reynolds, Keats expressed much the same wish as Browning's lover:

> O that a week could be an age, . . .
> Then one poor year a thousands years would be, . . .
> So time itself would be annihilate . . .
> O to arrive each Monday morn from Ind!
> To land each Tuesday from the rich Levant!
> In little time a host of joys to bind,
> And keep *our souls in one eternal pant!*   (ll. 1–12)

A set of verses addressed to Apollo describes a state of "madness" similar to that aroused, or anticipated, by the sight of Milton's hair: "To thee my soul is flown," Keats declares to Apollo,

> And my body is earthward press'd.
> It is an awful mission,
> A terrible division;
> And leaves a gulph austere
> To be fill'd with worldly fear.
> Aye, when the soul is fled
> To high above our head,
> Affrighted do we gaze . . .
> And is not this the cause
> Of madness?—God of Song,
> Thou bearest me along
> Through sights I scarce can bear:[2]

Perhaps Keats speaks in metaphor, but often, as in *Endymion*, the image appears to represent literal reality to him—the straining of the soul to leave "its bodily tenement," to "dodge/Conception to the very bourne of heaven," and to cross "the fragile bar / That keeps us from our homes ethereal." (*Endymion*, I, 325, 294–95, 360–61).

The "Lines on the Mermaid Tavern" probably strike most readers as an amusing play of fancy, but to one familiar with the prefigurative, elysian bent of Keats's imagination, it seems doubtful that he was merely playing with a convention to which he attached no credence. At all events, the "Souls of

---

[2] "God of the Meridian" is the first line of this poem without a title.

Poets dead and gone" enjoy "fruits of Paradise" and "beverage divine" so exactly modeled on the best of earthly pleasures that one can scarcely fail to recall the "favorite speculation" of Letter 31 or the paradisal anticipations of Leigh Hunt.

"What a happy thing it would be," wrote Keats to a friend in March 1818,

if we could settle our thoughts, make our minds up on any matter in five minutes and remain content—that is to build a sort of mental cottage of feelings quiet and pleasant— to have a sort of Philosophical Back Garden, and cheerful holiday-keeping front one— but Alas! this never can be: for as the material cottager knows there are such places as France and Italy and the Andes and the Burning Mountains—so the spiritual Cottager has knowledge of the terra semi incognita of things unearthly; and cannot for his life, keep in the check rein—[3]

The "terra semi incognita"—Keats is here "more careful of his fruits" than in Letter 31, but it is still the "terra . . . unearthly" to which his Pegasus snatches him aloft willy-nilly.

Endymion the shepherd-prince had been dragged under earth and sea and ultimately into heaven to prove that happy dreams are true. There were whispers of skepticism along the way, however, and in 1818 they began to trouble the poet. Before this time there had been scarcely any allusion to the possible unpleasantness of dreams. Surely, one reflects, it could give Keats no joy to proclaim the veracity of a nightmare. In a verse-letter to his friend Reynolds, who was ill, he wrestled with this problem.[4] Beginning with a hotchpotch of dream-images designed to make his friend smile, he suddenly realized that the *victim* of such dreams could not be happy, and that "Few are there who escape these visitings" (1. 13). The few who escape, however, enjoy such dreams as *"Titian colors touch'd into real life"* (1. 19). Keats does not declare that these fortunate dreams come true for the waking consciousness, but during sleep a lesser miracle occurs: as Eve to Adam and Cynthia to Endymion (and the statue to Pygmalion!), Titian's paintings come alive for the dreamer; they live and move and breathe.

The happier aspect of dreams is thenceforth sustained through a considerable section of the poem as Keats verbally depicts Claude's Enchanted Castle. But this mood cannot continue; its ironic unreality breaks through, and the poet wishfully exclaims:

> *O that our dreamings all of sleep or wake*
> *Would all their colours from the Sunset take:*
> From something of material sublime,
> Rather than shadow our own Soul's daytime
> In the dark void of Night.   (11. 67–71)

---

[3] Letter 57, p. 122.

[4] Letter 58, p. 125 (appearing in editions of the poems as "To J. H. Reynolds, Esq.").

But he dares not "philosophize" yet, he says, even though

> Things cannot to the will
> Be settled, but they tease us out of thought.
> Or is it that Imagination brought
> *Beyond its proper bound,* yet still confined,—
> Lost in a sort of Purgatory blind,
> Cannot refer to any standard law
> Of either earth or heaven? It is a flaw
> In happiness to see beyond our bourn—   (ll. 76–85)

These are the words of one who is discovering illusion in the very temple of his faith. Endymion and the shepherds had hoped to cross "the fragile bar," but even Endymion, in a despairing moment, accused the immortal world of being only "cloudy phantasms" (IV, 651), and taxed himself for making "truth" out of a dream:

> Against his proper glory
> Has my own soul conspired . . .
> There never lived a mortal man, who bent
> His appetite *beyond his natural sphere,*
> But starv'd and died.   (IV, 643–48)

Pregnant words, these, and significantly echoed in the verses to a sick friend. In his own experience Keats knows that the imagination, "deceiving elf," has often lured him into communion, or illusory communion, with a transmundane, elysian realm, only to dash him again to earth when the transport was over. To have trusted the imagination too far, then, to have risen too high on "the elevation of the moment," may have been his error. After all, can the mortal imagination really bridge the abyss between earth and heaven? Something like this seems to be his meaning in those verses to Reynolds which depict the imagination in dubious station between heaven and earth (ll. 78–85). Like Purgatory which is stationed halfway between heaven and hell, his imagination has stranded him midway between earth and heaven, promising to bridge the chasm yet inherently unable.

Nearly all students of Keats have felt that one of the major records of his progress toward "philosophy" is the simile which he evolved between human life and a "mansion of many apartments."[5] Three such apartments were all that he described, and he gave most space to the first two. But the third, which criticism usually passes over, is quite as important, showing the survival of Endymion's "pleasure thermometer": "Your third chamber of life shall be a lucky and a gentle one—stored with the wine of love—and the bread of friendship."[6]

---

[5] Letter 64, pp. 143–45.
[6] *Ibid.,* p. 145.

In June, Keats set forth on a walking tour through northern England. In a letter to his brother Tom he described his first impression of Lake Windermere:

> June 26—I merely put *pro forma*, for there is no such thing as time and space, which by the way came forcibly upon me on seeing for the first hour the lake and mountains of Winander—I cannot describe them—they surpass my expectation—. . . . the two views we have had of it are of the most noble tenderness—they can never fade away—they make one forget the divisions of life; age, youth, poverty and riches; and refine one's sensual vision into a sort of north star which can never cease to be open lidded and stedfast over the wonders of the great power.[7]

In these rapt words Keats does not affirm that his vision is a prevision of the hereafter, but it plainly comes to him in the likeness of heaven and eternity. When he wrote the "Bright star" sonnet some months later, repeating some of the language and tone of the description of Windermere, he was again stirred by the thought of eternity. The bliss of love made him yearn for "an immortality of passion" even though he did not yield to the illusion that such an immortality was possible.

Slightly more than a month after he first stared with eagle eyes on Lake Windermere, he had reached Burns's country, and writing to his friend Bailey, concluded with a poem which contains perhaps the most intimate and striking delineation in all his writings of his perfervid imagination in action. Yet for some reason the verses have gone almost unnoticed by critics.[8] Beginning with a list of pleasures available to those who enjoy scenery while walking, the poem passes at once to the supreme pleasure of walking through Burns's country:

> There is a deeper joy than all, more solemn in the heart,
> More parching to the tongue than all, of more divine a smart
> When weary feet forget themselves upon a pleasant turf,
> Upon hot sand, or flinty road, or Sea shore iron scurf,
> Toward the Castle or the Cot where long ago was born
> One who was great through mortal days and died of fame unshorn. . . .
> At such a time *the Soul's a Child*, in childhood is the brain
> Forgotten is the worldly heart—alone, it beats in vain—
> *Aye if a madman* could have leave to pass a healthful day,
> To tell his forehead's swoon and faint when first began decay,
> He might make tremble many a man whose spirit had gone forth
> To find a bard's low cradle place about the silent north.
> Scanty the hour and few the steps *beyond the bourn of care*,
> *Beyond the sweet and bitter world*—beyond it unaware;

---

[7] Letter 71, pp. 154–55.

[8] An exception should be made for James R. Caldwell, who in his recent book gives considerable space to the poem, but finds in it a more psychoanalytic meaning than I shall venture to suggest. See *John Keats' Fancy*, pp. 38 ff.

Scanty the hour and few the steps because a longer stay
Would bar return and make a man *forget his mortal way.*
O horrible! to lose the sight of well remember'd face,
Of brother's eyes, of sister's brow . . .
No, no, that horror cannot be—for at the cable's length
Man feels the gentle anchor pull and gladdens in its strength—
One hour half idiot he stands by mossy waterfall,
But in the very next he reads his Soul's memorial . . .
Yet be the anchor e'er so fast, room is there for a prayer
That man may never lose his mind on mountains bleak and bare;
That he may stray league after league some great birthplace to find
And keep his vision clear from speck, his inward sight unblind—[9]

Imaginative ecstasy seems to carry the poet "beyond the bourn" (cf. "beyond our bourn" in the "Epistle to Reynolds"), almost making him "forget his mortal way." And the extraordinarily intense, perfervid nature of this ecstasy moves close to what Keats can only call madness or semi-idiotism, just as in the verses to Apollo he wondered if ecstasy were not "the cause of madness." Evidently aesthetic transport sometimes overflows the bounds of joy and moves near to pain. When this happens, the mind is carried into a kind of no man's land, "lost in a sort of Purgatory blind" ("Epistle to Reynolds"). But anchored to earth as he is by "the heart's affections," the poet rejoices that the madness of ecstasy never quite reaches insanity, and that after every wild imaginative voyage he can return to his earthly moorings.

The poem is a strange and almost disturbing document. Exactly how to interpret it we shall probably never know, and it is likely that Keats himself could not have told us. All that we can be sure of is that "the elevation of the moment" repeatedly carries this poet "beyond the bourn," that in moods of optimism and amid fortunate circumstances he feels he enters into (or envisions) heaven, while in moods of skepticism or amid unfavorable cirsumstances, he lands in the "Purgatory blind" and wonders whether ecstasy is heaven cr idiotism. This is the *furor poeticus* with a vengeance.

It is in quite another mood that Keats wrote his poem describing the poets' elysium, "Bards of Passion and of Mirth," from which some verses were quoted in chapter ii to illustrate the "essential beauty" (the postmortal, concrete "things of beauty") which the imagination creates. As with the "Lines on the Mermaid Tavern," this second picture of elysium (of "happiness on earth repeated in a finer tone") is no proof in itself that Keats looked forward to joining his fellow poets there. But the prefigurative compulsion of his imagination was so strong, and left so many unequivocal confessions of its "favorite speculation," that one is inclined to take his word for it when he declares that his poem is "on the *double* immortality of poets."[10]

---

[9] Letter 79, pp. 195–97. Italics mine.   [10] Letter 98, p. 265.

"Hyperion" is not concerned with the poets' elysium or with the immortalizing of "this earthly love." As *Endymion* took happiness for its subject, "Hyperion" takes sorrow, and is thus a more realistic and mature representation of the human drama. Nevertheless it is interesting to observe the carry-over of Keats's "favorite speculation," and to see how he adapted it to the scene of Titanic woe which he chose to represent.

As was pointed out in the study of the song "O Sorrow" in Book IV of *Endymion*, there are indications that the truth-in-beauty of this song was an embryonic form of the "eternal truth" proclaimed by Oceanus in the Titan epic. The "truth" of the song consisted in an imaginative vision of a law of aesthetic compensation: the world of nature increased in beauty proportionally as lovers suffered from sorrow.

"Hyperion" opens with a graphic depiction of the "realmless" Saturn attended by the sympathetic Thea. Thea then reluctantly describes Saturn's deposition and present impotence, which she calls "the monstrous truth" (I, 65). There is nothing comforting in this tragic and undeniable truth of fact; it has no beauty and brings no solace; it is not prefigurative. Yet Keats appears to insist on this unoptimistic species of truth, here and later, even while the familiar prefigurative "truth" is introduced as compensation.

The next portion of the poem has its scene in heaven, where the splendid figure of Hyperion anxiously ponders his destined dethronement. Keats has purposely contrasted Hyperion's heavenly palace with the dreary sadness of the deposed, now mortal Saturn. Hyperion and his dwelling are resplendent, and for this resplendence there is a reason, a prefigurative beauty-truth soon to be disclosed. Meanwhile, Coelus, primeval father of the Titans, gives the first intimation of this beauty-truth:

> O brightest of my children dear, earth-born
> And sky-engendered, Son of Mysteries
> All unrevealed even to the powers
> Which met at thy creating; at whose joys
> And palpitations sweet, and pleasures soft,
> I, Coelus, wonder, how they came and whence;
> And at the fruits thereof what shapes they be,
> Distinct, and visible; symbols divine,
> Manifestations of that beauteous life
> Diffus'd unseen throughout eternal space:
> Of these new-form'd art thou, oh brightest child!
> (I, 309–19)

Coelus' words are mysterious because his understanding of the teleology involved is imperfect. The best he can do is to report that at Hyperion's birth his parents were filled with strange joys that seemed to be prophetic. Though the syntax of the passage is troublesome, and though the "visible" shapes may appear to contradict the "unseen" beauteous life, the general meaning can be paraphrased thus: Hyperion's present splendor and power, though fated soon to end, are the fruit of earlier, prefigurative "joys / And palpitations sweet." Though Coelus does not perceive that these prefigurations are a manifestation of a cosmic evolution-in-beauty, his words are the first hint to the reader of the evolutionary "eternal law" which Oceanus is soon to describe. This eternal law has come to Oceanus in an unequivocal prefigurative vision.

Book II delineates, with almost unrelieved gloom, the torture and misery of the vanquished Titans. Oceanus' speech is the one light in this gloom, unless we count a brief allusion to Asia. Scarcely noticed by critics and unexplained by Keats, Asia is the only one of the Titans (Oceanus excepted) who is not a victim of sorrow:

> More thought than woe was in her dusky face,
> For she was prophesying of her glory;
> And in her wide imagination stood
> Palm-shaded temples, and high rival fanes,
> By Oxus or in Ganges' sacred isles.
> Even as Hope upon her anchor leans,
> So leant she . . .   (II, 56-62)

Without attempting to explain the mythological authority for this—Keats's sources are inextricably mixed and confused—we can recognize that Asia's happiness is the product of a prefigurative imagination. She is the very figure of Hope, strikingly contrasted with the dejection and misery surrounding her.

After the Titans have been depicted in their misery, Saturn speaks to them of their fallen state, the cause of which he cannot comprehend. But as he surveys their faces, he notices with surprise that Oceanus appears unaffected by the general misery:

> "Thou, Oceanus,
> Ponderest high and deep; and in thy face
> I see, astonied, that severe content
> Which comes of thought and musing: give us help!"
> (II, 163-66)

Though the ancient myths related that Oceanus did not take part in the Titanic insurrection, they did not distinguish him as a contemplative man. Keats added the latter characteristic and thus prepared him to be the fittest mouthpiece of the "truth" which was to be the center of the poem. Likewise in *Endymion*, it was the "contemplative" elder shepherds who discoursed upon "our homes ethereal" and who were

> vieing to rehearse
> Each one his own anticipated bliss   (I, 372-73)

It would be unreasonable to expect a repetition of this naïve conception of heaven in the later poem, but the message that Oceanus brings is born of the same "heart-certain" imagination. Nothing but his prefigurative vision, unshared by his comrades though now narrated to them, could have brought that "severe content" to his face:

> Yet listen, ye who will, whilst I bring proof
> How ye, perforce, must be content to stoop:
> And in the proof much comfort will I give,
> If ye will take that comfort *in its truth.*
> We fall by course of Nature's law, not force
> Of thunder, or of Jove. Great Saturn, thou
> Hast sifted well the atom-universe;
> But for this reason, that thou art the King,
> And only blind from sheer supremacy,
> One avenue was shaded from thine eyes,
> Through which I wandered to *eternal truth.* . . .
> Thou art not the beginning nor the end.
> From chaos and parental Darkness came
> Light, the first fruits of that intestine broil,
> That sullen ferment, which for wondrous ends
> Was ripening in itself. The ripe hour came . . .
> Upon that very hour, our parentage,
> The Heavens and the Earth, were manifest:
> Then thou first born, and we the giant race,
> Found ourselves ruling new and beauteous realms.
> Now comes the *pain of truth*, to whom 'tis pain;
> O folly! for to bear *all naked truths,*
> And to envisage circumstance, all calm,
> That is the top of sovereignty. Mark well!
> As Heaven and Earth are fairer, fairer far
> Than Chaos and blank Darkness, though once chiefs;
> And as we show beyond that Heaven and Earth
> In form and shape compact and beautiful,
> In will, in action free, companionship,
> And thousand other signs of purer life;
> So on our heels a fresh perfection treads,
> A power more strong in beauty, born of us
> And fated to excel us, as we pass
> In glory that old Darkness. . . .
> > for 'tis the eternal law
> *That first in beauty should be first in might:*
> > (II, 177–215, 228–29)

(The varying usage, or double aspect, of "truth" I have italicized.) Oceanus goes on to declare that Neptune, who is destined to supplant him, is surpassingly beautiful, thus proving the "eternal law." He himself has come among them, he adds,

> to see how dolorous fate
> Had wrought upon ye; and how I might best
> Give consolation in this woe extreme.
> Receive *the truth*, and let it be your balm.   (II, 240–44)

It can hardly be doubted that Keats intended Oceanus' speech as the exposition of his cardinal theme, very much as the "pleasure-thermometer" in *Endymion* explained and upheld the cardinal theme of prefigurative love-dreams. In the third and fragmentary book of "Hyperion" the description of Apollo's "loveliness new born" (III, 79), of his "immortal fairness" (III, 125), and of his deification (the latter takes place just before Keats abandoned his poem) are the first extended and dramatic proofs of the veracity of Oceanus' imagination.

We have still to notice, however, the several usages of "truth" in Oceanus' speech: "in its truth" (l. 180), "eternal truth" (l. 187), "the pain of truth" (l. 202), "all naked truths" (l. 203), "Receive the truth" (l. 243). There is a sense in which each of these phrases has the same referent, namely, "the eternal law" of l. 228. But let us not fail to see the two opposed aspects of this referent: its consolation and its pain. From these opposed aspects spring the antithetical usages of "truth." "The pain of truth" and "all naked truths," like the "monstrous truth" referred to by Thea (I, 65), denote the extreme suffering of the Titans. These truths, these grievous corollaries of the consolatory "eternal truth" of beauty, are not prefigurative "truth." They are present, torturing reality; their essence is pain and ugliness. They may be said to represent humankind's present destiny, which, according to Oceanus' prefigurative vision, the future will gradually transform into a kind of Golden Age. Ultimately the pain-truths of the present will cease to exist, giving place to the beauty-truths of the millennial future.

To face "all naked truths" bravely and unflinchingly, Oceanus insists, is "the top of sovereignty." This is quite a different ethic from the "sovereign power of love" in *Endymion*, with its insistence on happiness. If Oceanus is not happy as Endymion was happy, if there is no delirium in his veins, he is vouchsafed a "severe content"—the reward of his simultaneous resignation to present suffering and the long-term aesthetic compensation for such suffering.

Though this long-term aesthetic teleology may look new and strange, at least two germs of the idea had existed previously: (1) The song "O Sorrow" in *Endymion*, one of the illustrations offered by Keats of his "favorite speculation," envisioned a progressive beautification of the physical universe as a compensation for the sorrows of lovers. True, it was not promised that the entire universe would be thus transformed, but the idea of universal aesthetic compensation for personal sorrow is analogous to the compensation that Oceanus envisions for the Titans' misery. (2) In Letter 31 Keats described the progressive refinement of imaginative experience (using the recollected singer's face as an illustration), and posited a postmortal elysium consisting of "what we called happiness on earth repeated in a *finer* tone." We cannot, of course, be sure that he envisioned this refinement of the mortal imagination as a continuous process linked to the ultimate supernal refinement. But the evolutionary law of "Hyperion," seized by the imagination and made operative throughout the physical universe, may have been suggested to him by what he had observed of the imagination's interior world.

That he had some further notion to this effect is evident from a letter written early in 1818, wherein he conjectured that an imaginative musing upon "a page full of poesy or distilled prose" serves as "a starting post towards all 'the two and thirty Palaces' " [the thirty-two "places of delight" of the Buddhist doctrine, according to the note by M. B. Forman], and might even produce a community of minds throughout the human race:

Minds would leave each other in contrary directions, traverse each other in numberless points, and at last greet each other at the journey's end. An old man and a child would talk together and the old man be led on his path and the child left thinking. Man should not dispute or assert but whisper results to his neighbour and thus by every germ of spirit sucking the sap from mould ethereal every human might become great, and humanity instead of being a wide heath of furze, would become a grand democracy of forest trees![11]

Thus Keats conjectured that the aesthetic impulse, if diffused widely enough and overcoming the disputatious tendency in men, might meliorate the lot of the human race. That such a gradually attained Golden Age would not be limited merely to poets is clear, and this reminds us of other statements: that "Sancho will invent a journey heavenward as well as any body,"[12] and that savages, religionists, and poets are alike in their "guesses at Heaven."[13] Meanwhile, the earthly scene itself and the human lot may actually be meliorating: at least there is a progressive evolution of knowledge if not expressly of beauty—"a grand march of intellect" as Keats declares elsewhere, after comparing Milton and Wordsworth.[14]

But to return to "Hyperion." It is not an improbable conjecture that Keats's conception of Apollo, fragmentarily described in the unfinished third book, represents symbolically the birth of imagination and poetry into the world—man's awareness of and devotion to beauty. It is evident, as Oceanus

---

[11] Letter 48, pp. 103–4.
[12] Letter 44, p. 96.
[13] "The Fall of Hyperion," I, 4.
[14] Letter 64, p. 144.

tells the Titans, that Saturn and his ruined brethren understand only one law in the universe—the law of might. With so limited an understanding, Saturn is puzzled to explain his overthrow by "untremendous might" (II, 155), and even the radiant Hyperion is baffled to explain why "that *infant* thunderer, rebel Jove" (I, 249) should succeed him. In the same way, the arch rebel of them all, the passionate and irreconcilable Enceladus, exhorts the Titans to wrathful revenge, using only physical power and courage to overcome "that *puny* essence," Jove (II, 331). There is no suggestion that the Titans in any way understood, or were capable of understanding, Oceanus' "eternal truth." Oceanus is thus a kind of inchoate poet among them, the first recognizer of the power of beauty in the world, and also of the prefigurative veracity—and possible creativity—of the imagination. No wonder, then, that the muscular Titans, the apostles of Might, could not be reconciled either by Oceanus' vision or by the graceful, almost stripling Apollo who was fated to overcome the last of their race.

In what way did Keats plan to complete his poem? The question cannot be answered with certainty, but one might plausibly conjecture that his first intention (possibly altered or abandoned later) was to incarnate, or at least partially to fulfill, Oceanus' prefigurative vision, even as Endymion's dreams had been fulfilled. It is a fact that the equivalent of a prefigurative vision of the joyous Apollo is given to Clymene, though she only partially comprehends it, at the close of Book II (ll. 244–99), and that Mnemosyne in Book III confirms Apollo's prophetic dreams of her and of the musical bliss which he is destined to pour out upon the world (III, 59 ff.). Though the deification that Apollo undergoes is a far cry from Endymion's naïve "immortality of passion" (Apollo "die[s] into life"—vicariously submits to tragedy and death, that is), Keats had more or less committed himself to the fulfillment of Oceanus' prefigurative vision, and had therefore to find some plausible way of incarnating that vision. Perhaps, had he gone on with the poem, he would have vouchsafed the depiction of this incarnation to Apollo the "fore-seeing god," as he described him in one of his letters.[15] For such a depiction of a universal evolution via the prefigurative imagination he had ample precedent outside *Endymion* and Letter 31, such as Hunt's *Descent of Liberty*, Shelley's millennial poems, and even the last two books of *Paradise Lost*.

We can thus see how both "Hyperion" and *Endymion* are in a very real sense symbolic of Keats's effort to justify his, or for that matter anyone's, devotion to poetry. The creed of *Endymion* held that poets should devote themselves to the depiction of love, because love begets happiness, destining faithful lovers for elysium and bringing a new Golden Age to earth. The

---

[15] Letter 38, p. 83.

creed of "Hyperion" suggests that the spirit of poetry progressively beauti-fies the world, molding it gradually to an ultimate perfection. Each creed was a "truth" to the poet, a "truth" seized by the imagination through its beauty.

Did Keats, *qua* Keats, actually hold such beliefs? The question was earlier asked with reference to *Endymion* and Letter 31. The answer given then seems valid now: the beauty-truth of "Hyperion" was a "favorite specu-lation," the heart's desire of a favorite self of John Keats. Chastened by the unflinching contemplation of sorrow and misery, he was not returning to the naïve optimism of *Endymion,* but his fervent and hopeful imagination still sought consolation for the world's woe, and found it in his favorite way: a vision of beauty that "must be truth."

VII. THE PREFIGURATIVE THEME IN
THE POEMS OF 1819

Having traced the prefigurative theme and its variations in Keats's imagination during 1818, we come now to the poems of 1819, his most splendid and mature creations. As might be expected, the prefigurative spell was losing some of its power. This does not mean that Keats had lost his yearning for eternity or that his imagination was less fervid. It means that he was wiser now and more on his guard, more convinced than ever of the essential tragicality of human existence. This is the year in which his early addiction to happy dreams and their elysian counterpart grows more and more suspect, until, almost with a sense of having been betrayed, he turns upon himself mercilessly and scourges the dream-poet that he once had been. There were, nonetheless, a few rapturous moments in store for him, moments that would exalt him to a mood not unlike that of Letter 31, though more fragile and more ephemeral.

"The Eve of St. Agnes," composed in January or February of the new year, is often described as Keats's sublimation of his love for Fanny Brawne, to whom he had become engaged on December 25, 1818. There is no reason to question this description, but it may be interesting to trace the relationship between the love story and the prefigurative bent of the poet's imagination. It is not quite by accident that "St. Agnes" retains, or repeats, some of the salient themes of *Endymion*, though Keats did not know Fanny Brawne when he wrote the earlier poem : such themes as the incomparable excellence of young love, the verification of love dreams, and the affinity between sleep and bliss.

That Keats should suddenly have become so passionately attached to Fanny Brawne is hardly surprising. Such an attachment could have been predicted at least as early as 1816 or 1817 when he wrote "I stood tip-toe" and *Endymion*, for both poems contained rhapsodic encomiums of the "sovereign power of love," and there were sundry confessions in other early poems of the spell that woman's beauty could cast upon him :

For that to love, so long, I've dormant lain . . .

Light feet, dark violet eyes, and parted hair ;
Soft dimpled hands, white neck, and creamy breast,
Are things on which the dazzled senses rest
Till the fond, fixed eyes forget they stare.

> God! she is like a milk-white lamb that bleats
> For man's protection. . . .
>   In truth there is no freeing
> One's thoughts from such a beauty . . .[1]
>
> Fill for me a brimming bowl . . .
> To banish women from my mind . . .
> In vain! away I cannot chace
> The melting softness of that face, . . .
> That breast—earth's only Paradise.
>   ("Fill for me . . . ," ll. 1–4, 13–16—dated 1814)

One is reminded also of the candid, sportive amorousness of "O blush not so!" and "Dawlish Fair," and of the delightful prose-fragment written in the lecture room at St. Thomas' Hospital:

> The authoure was goyinge onne withouten descrybynge ye ladye's breste, whenne lo, a genyus appearyd —"Cuthberte," sayeth he, "an thou canst not descrybe ye ladye's breste, and fynde a simile thereunto, I forbyde thee to proceed yn thy romaunt." Thys, I kennd fulle welle, far surpassyd my feble powres, and forthwythe I was fayne to droppe my quille.[2]

For a comic treatment of libido we could call to witness "Ben Nevis, A Dialogue"; here Keats dramatizes the mountain's amusingly lecherous assault upon a woman mountain climber.

The diction and tone of Keats's earliest erotica are unusually adolescent and namby-pamby, but the sentiments are not materially different from the erotica of 1817 or 1819. "The Eve of St. Agnes" is an idealization of throbbing young love, passionate and corporeal. Keats put this beyond doubt when he insisted to the shocked Woodhouse that Porphyro's "melting" into Madeline's dream, "solution sweet" (stanza xxxvi) signified the full—and premarital—sexual consummation of the lovers.[3] Though matters do not visibly come to such a pass in the "Bright star" sonnet, the love there described is frankly physical. One may be reminded of the concluding passage in "Fancy" (together with the telltale rejected lines) where Keats deftly undresses Hebe before the Olympians (while "Jove grew languid") even as he undresses Madeline before Porphyro. We should remember, too, Keats's honest report upon what happened one night after he read the Paolo-Francesca episode in Dante. Rather than chastening him, as Dante intended, the

---

[1] These excerpts are from three conjoined sonnets in *Poems 1817*: "Woman! when I behold thee . . . ," "Light feet, dark violet eyes . . . ," "Ah! who can e'er forget . . ."

[2] See M. B. Forman, *The Poetical Works . . .* , V, 322.

[3] See Woodhouse's vivid account of his conversation with Keats, in Finney, *The Evolution of Keats's Poetry*, II, 690 ff.

infernal punishment of the lovers lost all moral significance and was transformed into a luxurious sex-dream:

> The dream was one of the most delightful enjoyments I ever had in my life—I floated
> about the whirling atmosphere . . . with a beautiful figure to whose lips mine were
> joined as it seem'd for an age . . .[4]

Next day he "tried a sonnet upon it—there are fourteen lines but nothing of
what I felt in it—O that I could dream it every night—"[5] Keats does not
expect such a rosy fate, of course; he is no longer an Adonis enjoying six-
month-long love dreams, or a Latmian shepherd dreaming of a goddess'
embraces. But the old yearning for "an immortality of passion" is still with
him.

Let us remember that Keats was from the beginning a lover-poet. Then
"St. Agnes" will seem less novel in its theme than in its evocative medieval
setting and its superlative imagery and music. The heart's affections, Keats
still believes, suffer no loss of "holiness" merely because their objects are
corporeal and mundane rather than Platonic and transmundane.

We may now turn to the text. Carefully observing the rites prescribed
for maids on the eve of St. Agnes, Madeline retires to her chamber and seeks
her bed. When she has fallen asleep, Keats describes her as

> Blissfully haven'd both from joy and pain. (xxvii, 6)

As in *Endymion*, sleep is accepted—and particularly love's sleep—as a realm
of bliss where pain and ugliness visit not. This tendency to associate unmiti-
gated happiness with sleep is evidently the source of Porphyro's subsequent
desire for a "drowsy Morphean amulet" (xxix, 5). Similarly he desires to
"drowse beside thee," that is, Madeline (xxxi, 9), not because he wishes to
extinguish sensation but because ecstasy insensibly draws him toward the
analogous bliss of sleep.

When Madeline does not awaken, he muses a while in a kind of trance,
then "awakening up" takes her lute and plays

> an ancient ditty, long since mute,
> In Provence call'd, "La belle dame sans mercy." (xxxiii, 3-4)

Disturbed, she moans softly, then:

> Her eyes were open, but she still beheld,
> Now wide awake, the vision of her sleep:
> There was a painful change, that nigh expell'd
> The blisses of her dream so pure and deep

---

[4] Letter 123, p. 326.
[5] *Loc. cit.* The sonnet: "As Hermes once . . ."

At which fair Madeline began to weep,
And moan forth witless words with many a sigh;
. . . .

"Ah, Porphyro!" said she, "but even now
"Thy voice was at sweet tremble in mine ear,
"Made tuneable with every sweetest vow;
"And those sad eyes were spiritual and clear:
"How chang'd thou art! how pallid, chill, and drear!
"Give me that voice again, my Porphyro,
"*Those looks immortal*, those complainings dear!
"Oh leave me not in this eternal woe,
"For if thou diest, my Love, I know not where to go."

Beyond a mortal man impassion'd far
At these voluptuous accents, he arose,
Ethereal, flush'd, and like a throbbing star
Seen mid the sapphire heaven's deep repose
Into her dream he melted, as the rose
Blendeth its odour with the violet,—
Solution sweet: meantime the frost-wind blows
Like Love's alarum pattering the sharp sleet
Against the window-panes; St. Agnes' moon hath set. (xxxiv—xxxvi)

Like Adam's and Endymion's, Madeline's dream has come true. Once again Keats has chosen to employ a prefigurative vision, though this time he has relied on reality rather than celestial thaumaturgy to substantiate the dream. He is not asserting, as he did in *Endymion* and Letter 31, that dreams and imagination are necessarily true, but he is recurring, without assertion or denial, to his early and "favorite speculation."

There are other points to notice. The song which awoke Madeline was "La belle dame sans mercy." Everyone knows Keats's later poem on the same subject, where a lover's "fond imagination" betrays and cheats him, even as Endymion in despairing moments believed that his imagination was deceiving him. The poem called "La Belle Dame" is thus the very palinode to the idea that the imagination is veraciously prefigurative. But in "The Eve of St. Agnes," the ditty known as "La belle dame sans mercy," played softly in Madeline's bedchamber, awakens her to the "truth" of her dream.

Consider now the "painful change" (xxxiv) which results from the fracture of Madeline's dream. This change must be ephemeral, since it derives not so much from the loss of her dream as from the unexpected and incredulous substantiation of it. While the ephemeral pain lasts, Madeline sees Porphyro in the guise of mortality—"pallid, chill, and drear"—and fears that he may die. This is why she is at first alarmed, for her dream showed him under the light of immortality, with "spiritual" eyes and "looks immortal." Here is the now familiar usage of "spiritual" as synonymous with "immortal," and here is Keats's well-established association between the ecstasy of imagination and immortality.

When Madeline, being afraid that her perfect dream, suddenly substantialized, might "die," begs to be reassured by her kneeling lover, his reaction is thoroughly Keatsian :

> *Beyond a mortal man* impassion'd far
> At these voluptuous accents, he arose . . .

Porphyro is not dreaming, but love, passionate love, carries him in rapture beyond "the fragile bar" separating mortality from immortality; he enters momentarily into heaven. As Endymion had long before declared :

> this earthly love has power to make
> Men's being mortal, immortal.

While the two lovers blissfully enact their love-dream, the sleet patters ominously on the windowpanes and the moon goes down. Like an enchanted island is their love in a malevolent, hostile world. Reality wars against dream. Nevertheless, the dream is destined to prevail. In response to Madeline's fears, Porphyro begs "for aye" to be her vassal blest, and assures her that they are "sav'd by miracle" (xxxviii). As the dead lovers in *Endymion* were saved by a resurrective miracle, so Porphyro and Madeline will successfully escape from their surrounding foes, and live "for aye" in bliss :

> Hark! 'tis an elfin-storm from faery land,
> Of haggard seeming, but a boon indeed. (xxxix, 1–2)

The gods, or the elements, or those that rule the land of faery, have conspired to aid these lovers by miracle. The storm will permit their escape, undetected, over the moors. Nature's laws alter when lovers are in danger. The land of faery moves into the land of fact, rendering the latter powerless. So also when the nightingale sang, charming "magic casements . . . in faery lands forlorn." Except that the forlornness of faery was not at all suggested to Porphyro and Madeline, and so their dream was flawless.

> They glide, like phantoms, into the wide hall;
> Like phantoms, to the iron porch, they glide;
> . . . .
> And they are gone: ay, ages long ago
> These lovers fled away into the storm.
> That night the Baron dreamt of many a woe,
> And all his warrior-guests, with shade and form
> Of witch, and demon, and large coffin-worm,
> Were long be-nightmar'd. . . .   (xli—xlii)

Ever since, we may guess, they have dwelt, immortal "phantoms," in the elysian land of faery. In the very temple of imagination is the realm of faery born, and into faery again return the imagination's more than mortal creatures. Is it possible to say, while one is reading their story, while Keats the transported poet is creating it for them, that outside his mind it has no veritable existence?

Something like this is the impression that his breathless story and his magic words create. Something like this must have been his feeling as he wrote, hovering with creative wings in that almost palpable faery land. The dreams of his lovers, which were also dreams of his own, became waking and everlasting beatitude—while the dreams of the Baron, foe of heaven-entering love, were disfigured with the ugly images of the coffin, unresurrective neighbor to the worm.

Among the poems written in Keats's most remarkable creative period, the spring of 1819, the "Ode on Melancholy" is distinguished for serenity, objectivity, and balance. It rises to no such pitch of ecstasy as the "Nightingale" and the "Grecian Urn," and consequently implies nothing about the "truth" of beauty. Wisely and soberly, the poem limits itself to the "Beauty that must die." For in this world no thing lasts forever. Beauty and joy are fleeting in proportion as the palate is "fine" (sensitive) and the tongue is "strenuous" (eager).

In this poem Keats does not strain after an "immortality of passion" as he did in Endymion, he does not yearn "to see beyond the bourn" or to cross "the fragile bar/That keeps us from our homes ethereal"; he is not "beyond a mortal man impassioned far" as was Porphyro, and he does not wing his way into the immortal land of faery where the Nightingale sings everlastingly and whither Porphyro and Madeline fly in deathless love. Nor is he entranced with the "eternal Now" of a Greek vase. However regretful he may be that "Beauty must die," he faces the fact unflinchingly, and encloses it in a structure of such poetic beauty that the axiom loses all its terror and almost ceases to dismay.

Furthermore, it can hardly be accidental that the several beauties enumerated in the Ode (roses, sea-rainbows, peonies, a mistress' eyes) are entities of the external world rather than of the imagination. The significance of this distinction between the objective and the imaginary worlds is pressed home in the poem called "Fancy," where the superior and uncloying, "ever new" pleasures of imagination (l. 71) are contrasted with the "cloying," "fading" pleasures of direct perception (ll. 12, 15). Thus the "Ode on Melancholy" eschews any flight into imaginative realms, keeping its focus steadily on the real and mutable world of objects.

In the "Ode to a Nightingale" the story is different. Keats perhaps began the poem while seated in the garden listening to a real nightingale, as his friend Charles Brown reported, but it is clear from the beginning that he yearns for release from the actual world and for identification with the bird—all because he is "too happy in thine [the nightingale's] happiness." He longs to "leave the world unseen" and with the nightingale "fade away into the forest dim," where he can

> dissolve, and quite forget
> What thou among the leaves hast never known,
> The weariness, the fever, and the fret
> Here, where men sit and hear each other groan;

His most "strenuous" wish, then, is not to burst on his tongue (or in his ear, to be exact) the ineffable happiness of the nightingale's song, but to flee with this song to an eternal temple of delight where the "cloying" and "fading," the "fever and fret" of the mortal world shall be forever extinguished.

Now this desire to be "beyond a mortal man impassioned far" and at the same time to preserve and prolong the splendid ecstasy can only be achieved by imagination. Hence Keats appeals to the "wings of Poesy," having first sought aid of wine to carry him Lethe-wards. The wine might have created a partial oblivion by acting in the manner of an opiate, but poetry and "the fine spell of imagination" could alone carry him away into the forest dim and allow him to dissolve into the otherworld whence the supernally happy song of the nightingale seemed to come.

Naturally the identification of the poet and the bird could not be entirely successful; Keats was not a Latmian shepherd deifiable by a goddess. Yet the union of poet-mind and singing bird came very near to his utmost wish: the bird singing in the garden in bright daylight imperceptibly changed to a nocturnal bird caroling beneath "the Queen-Moon" and "all her starry Fays"; that is, she changed from a perceived to an imagined bird. Thus released from the objective world, she assumed her place in the supernal otherworld which only the imagination could create.

Meanwhile, the poet's imagination luxuriates amid the flowers which he "cannot see"; then almost automatically he falls "half in love with easeful Death":

> Now more than ever seems it rich to die,
> To cease upon the midnight with no pain,
> While thou art pouring forth thy soul abroad
> In such an ecstasy!

So more than mortal is the happiness which he shares with the rapturous bird that death itself seems "rich" and "easeful," and is called "soft names" like a lover. The psychology is simple: so keen is the poet's ecstasy that he seems to have reached the limits of conscious felicity; the next step, naturally and inevitably, is unconsciousness. For another reason, too, death beckons: the interruption or cessation of ecstasy would be too painful to endure; he has so completely forgotten the everyday world that he prefers unconsciousness to "the journey homeward to habitual self." "And so [may I] live ever—or else swoon to death," he prayed in another, and like, situation. Make the moment of bliss eternal, or give me death!

Then as he contemplates the image of his own body "become a sod" while the nightingale sings his "requiem," he feels for a second time the need of asserting the bird's immortality:

> Thou wast not born for death, immortal Bird!

Imaginatively ranging through the wide realms ruled by this immortal Bird, he passes in review emperors and clowns, Ruth amid the alien corn, and, finally and wondrously, the "magic casements . . . in faery lands forlorn." For a moment, we may suppose, the faery lands seemed "a present palpable reality,"[6] part and portion of the real world, not less so than emperors and clowns, not less real than the "elfin-storm from faery land" which blew across the moors to "save by miracle" Porphyro and Madeline.

But then, as the melodious word "forlorn" begins to toll upon the ear, the irony of its meaning reaches the mind, and the magic spell is ended. The happy song of the bird becomes a "plaintive anthem," as the poet imaginatively transfers his regret to it. Gradually the song fades into the distance like a dream, and the poet asks himself:

> Was it a vision, or a waking dream?
> Fled is that music:—Do I wake or sleep?

So intense and precious has been his experience, and so seeming-real, so truly is he persuaded that he has visited the otherworld, that like Madeline on waking from her love-dream and Endymion on waking from his, he is not quite sure whether the so-called real world may not, after all, be an "unsubstantial pageant," and faery the only true existence.

A few lines previously he had regretfully protested the loss of his "dream";

> Adieu! the fancy cannot cheat so well
> As she is fam'd to do, deceiving elf.

The illusion was dissolving and he was helplessly returning to the world of fact and "habitual self." But "clouds of glory," as it were, hovered still about him, and it was difficult to believe, though honesty compelled the ad-

---

6 Letter 76, p. 178.

mission, that the ineffable beauty seized by his imagination was not truth. "The fancy cannot cheat," he told himself, but even in saying this he was admitting that the fancy *had* cheated for a moment, and that he needed to remind himself of the impossibility of a prolonged cheating. Had the same experience been vouchsafed to Endymion or to his "young minded" poet, or had the musical word "forlorn" not begun to toll ominously, fracturing the magic spell, the "immortal Bird" might have registered the same triumphant message as the Grecian Urn, also immortal, raptly whispered to the poet.

A word should be added on the well-known issue of the nightingale's immortality. The mystery, and the apparent illogicality, which some readers have felt in Keats's addressing the imagined nightingale as "immortal Bird," may be a consequence of reading the poem with too severe an attention to rational, not poetic, logic, and of not yielding oneself willingly to the flight on "wings of Poesy" into the enchanted otherworld which only imagination can visit. No wonder that for Keats the nightingale seemed to dwell in such a world rather than in the everyday world of fever and fret! From the first stanza, even the first line when read anticipatively, he insists that he is "too happy in thine [the nightingale's] happiness."

What authority has Keats for assuming that the nightingale has never known weariness or fever? None whatever, except that she makes him "too happy" for mortality, and sings so seeming-happily herself that she *must* be no earthly creature! In like manner he had reasoned concerning the recollected singer's face in Letter 31 ("more beautiful than it was possible and yet with the elevation of the moment you did not think so . . . the prototype must be here after . . .").

A single assertion (in stanza iii) of the nightingale's immortal felicity seemed not enough to Keats, and therefore he repeated it, more tellingly, in stanza vii:

> Thou wast not born for death, immortal Bird!
> No hungry generations tread thee down;

It is impossible, during "the elevation of the moment" at least, to conceive of such undescribable happiness in the mortal sphere, where pain and death are ceaselessly operative. The bird *must* be a visitant from faery or elysium, or the poet himself must be visiting these realms. We have only to turn back to a poem considered previously to discover the heaven where this immortal nightingale dwells:

> Bards of Passion and of Mirth,
> Ye have left your souls on earth!
> Have ye souls in heaven too,
> Double-lived in regions new?

> Yes, and those of heaven commune
> With the spheres of sun and moon . . .
> And one another, in soft ease
> Seated on Elysian lawns
> Brows'd by none but Dian's fawns
> Underneath large blue-bells tented,
> Where the daisies are rose-scented,
> And the rose herself has got
> Perfume which on earth is not;
> *Where the nightingale doth sing*
> Not a senseless, tranced thing.
> But *divine melodious truth* . . .

To the poets in their postmortal elysium the beautiful song of the nightingale has become "truth," uncloying and everlasting. Or to look at it another way, since even this elysian nightingale is mirrored in a poet's imagination, Keats the mortal poet has often listened in rapture to earthly nightingales, which to his prefigurative imagination have become the type and presage of their heavenly species.

From this point of view it becomes unnecessary to censure Keats's logic, as Bridges and others have done,[7] or to defend it by turning the attention to the bird's song rather than the song bird, or to the species rather than the individual, or to the mythological deathlessness of dryads, as Colvin,[8] Amy Lowell,[9] and Garrod,[10] respectively, have suggested. There have been other solutions proposed: Bradley, for example, regards the bird as a symbol of "the absolute and eternal beauty,"[11] and Stoll sees her as part of the world of "appearances" which make up the medium of poetry.[12] The suggestions of Stoll and Colvin seem on the whole the most nearly satisfactory, but neither of them fully accounts for Keats's insistence on the ineffable happiness of the bird and for the two assertions that the weariness and hunger, the fever and fret of mortality are totally unknown to her.

Perhaps we should turn to another poet, rather than to the critics, for a corroboration of Keats's happiness-logic. Shelley's "To a Skylark" will serve. Though Shelley tends at times to deprive his bird of physical existence, likening it to an "unbodied joy," every stanza of his rhapsody insists on the

---

[7] Robert Bridges, "A Critical Introduction to Keats," *Collected Essays Papers &c.* (London: Oxford University Press, 1929), IV, 130.

[8] Colvin, *John Keats* . . . , p. 419. De Sélincourt follows this interpretation, *The Poems of John Keats*, p. 475.

[9] Amy Lowell, *John Keats*, II, 252.

[10] H. W. Garrod, *Keats*, pp. 114–15.

[11] A. C. Bradley, "Keats and 'Philosophy'," *A Miscellany*, p. 206.

[12] E. E. Stoll, "The Validity of the Poetic Vision: Keats and Spenser," *Modern Language Review*, XL (1945), 1–7.

supreme delight and happiness of the bird's song, until like Keats's nightingale
his lark loses every mortal attribute:

> I have never heard
> Praise of love or wine
> That panted forth a flood of rapture so divine. . . .

> With thy clear keen joyance
> Languor cannot be:
> Shadow of annoyance
> Never came near thee:
> Thou lovest; but ne'er knew love's sad satiety.

> Waking or asleep,
> Thou of death must deem
> Things more true and deep
> Than we mortals dream,
> Or how could thy notes flow in such a crystal stream? (ll. 76–85)

"Thou of death *must* deem . . ." "Beauty *must* be truth." Happiness, more-
than-mortal happiness, is the proof, the only proof needed, of this skylark's
prescience of life beyond death, and of her perfect "ignorance of pain" (l. 75).
Were this not so, Shelley reasons, were the skylark merely mortal like human
beings, and not in touch with some immortal and immitigable happiness, her
song would lose its joyous rapture.[13] Keats's nightingale was close of kin.

A fact not always remembered in discussions of the "Ode on a Grecian
Urn" is that Keats was not describing a particular urn standing before his
eyes. Scholars have demonstrated that the scenes depicted in his poem came
from several sources, including actual vases, drawings of vases, paintings,
and the frieze of the Parthenon. We are not concerned to enumerate these
sources, but to make it clear that when he wrote the poem Keats was depict-

---

[13] This "happiness-logic" is not quite the exclusive property of the Romantic poets.
Cf. Michael Bruce's "To the Cuckoo" ("Thou hast no sorrow in thy song, / No winter
in thy year!"); Izaak Walton's *The Compleat Angler* (the music of the nightingale's
voice "might make mankind think miracles are not ceased," and one who hears her at
midnight "might well be lifted above earth, and say, 'Lord, what music hast thou provided for the saints in heaven, when thou affordest men such music on earth!' "—chapter
i); and Chaucer's *Romaunt of the Rose* (the birds in the garden where Mirth and Idleness dwell, sing "as angels don espirituel," and "never yitt sich melodye / Was herd of
man that myghte dye."—Fragment A, ll. 670–76). Probably the best parody of this
logic of rapture is the description of resurrected dickeybirds by Horace Walpole: they
will "sing eternally the self-same tune, / From everlasting night to everlasting noon."
See "Epitaph of Two Piping Bullfinches of Lady Ossory's"; H. N. Fairchild quotes
several verses from the poem in *Religious Trends in English Poetry* (New York:
Columbia University Press, 1939), II, 18.

ing an *imagined* urn. This is important, because the "Ode on a Grecian Urn" and the "Ode to a Nightingale" both treat beauty that is at once imagined and "immortal," while the "Ode on Melancholy" treats beauty directly perceived, insisting on its mutation and decay.

Bearing in mind the purely imaginative character of the "Grecian Urn," we can examine some of its details in this light. The first stanza begins quietly with an apostrophe to the urn, but ends with a series of short, breathless questions. Keats has been caught up by the excitement of the scenes depicted: he wonders whether the human figures are "deities or mortals, . . . men or gods," and whether the scene is "Tempe or the dales of Arcady." There are also maidens madly pursued, and pipes and timbrels, bringing the stanza to a climax with a final question: "What wild ecstasy?" The scene has come alive for the poet, and he responds almost breathlessly to the excitement and ecstasy, automatically associating these with Tempe or Arcadia, symbols of flawlessly happy earthly existence. Has his deep-seated elysium-yearning already taken hold of him?

The second stanza begins quietly on the subject of heard and unheard melodies, preferring the latter which sound

> Not to the sensual ear, but, more endear'd,
> Pipe to the spirit ditties of no tone.

When Keats contrasts "the sensual ear" with "the spirit," he contrasts sensory perception not with the soul or intellect, but with imagination. Imaginatively heard music is "more endear'd" because its delights do not "cloy" or "fade" and are "ever new" (cf. "Fancy"). In the second half of the stanza Keats turns to the lovers:

> Fair youth, beneath the trees, thou canst not leave
> Thy song, nor ever can those trees be bare;
> Bold Lover, never, never canst thou kiss,
> Though winning near the goal—yet, do not grieve;
> She cannot fade, though thou hast not thy bliss,
> For ever wilt thou love, and she be fair!

The first reaction of Keats the lover-poet is to pity the imagined lover's inability to kiss his mistress, but this mood passes quickly. Instead of regret for the changelessness and the "frozen" quality of this love experience, Keats now feels something akin to exultation. For the love of these two is eternal, like their beauty. And the scene preserves forever the piquant delight of anticipation, catching the lovers just before their consummation. In other words, the "being," the immutability of this scene co-exists with a semblance of "becoming," a "becoming" eminently desirable. And we must not fail to notice that Keats's chief interest is not in an abstract distinction between a lower or "sensual" and a higher or "spiritual" value in the representation, but in its simultaneous beauty and eternality. "She cannot fade," he reassures the lover (almost as if the latter could hear the poet's voice!). We may instructively recall the beauty of the "Ode on Melancholy," "beauty that must die," and the rapturous voice of the nightingale, whose "plaintive anthem *fades*" as soon as the illusion of immortality and heavenly felicity dissolves. Only the imagination can perform the miracle of arresting change and dissolution; and often, as with the transmuted nightingale, the imagination itself fails. Let us watch Keats carefully in the remainder of the poem to see whether the imagination can hold steadfastly to its vision of eternity.

The third stanza rings over and over the theme of unfading happiness:

> Ah, happy, happy boughs! that cannot shed
> Your leaves, nor ever bid the Spring adieu;
> And, happy melodist, unwearied,
> For ever piping songs for ever new;
> More happy love! more happy, happy love!
> For ever warm and still to be enjoy'd,
> For ever panting, and for ever young;
> All breathing human passion far above,
> That leaves a heart high-sorrowful and cloy'd,
> A burning forehead, and a parching tongue.

If there were any doubt in the previous stanza of the desirability of a perennial springtime, or any fear that the lovers would be unhappy because they could not, like Endymion and Cynthia, embrace, there is assuredly neither doubt nor fear in this stanza. The melodist's songs are "for ever new," and love is "for ever young" and never "cloy'd." Moreover—and this is a striking example of empathy, and proof that Keats's imaginative vision had passed far beyond the lifelessness of marble—the love is "for ever *panting*" and "for ever *warm*."[14] A less empathic poet would have remembered the irony implicit in his theme: eternity belongs to lifeless representations, fixed and cold, rather than to living, breathing beings. In the "Bright star" sonnet Keats faces this irony, though yearning to escape from it, but in stanza iii of the "Ode" he rapturously proclaims the simultaneous eternality and warm, panting passion of the lovers. They seem to his ardent imagination to embody the uncloying "immortality of passion" which Endymion and Cynthia, Porphyro and Madeline, and Keats and Fanny Brawne (in the "Bright star" sonnet) so yearningly desired.

---

[14] The empathy here consists in the poet's so completely projecting his consciousness into the marble figures of the lovers that he endows them with vitality and sensation not proper to their medium. He lives inside them, as it were, ceasing to be merely a spectator of marble figures and scene. This could the more easily happen since the urn existed only as an object of imagination, not as an object of perception.

Recalling Letter 31, we may plausibly ask: What indeed are these "for ever young" lovers but "a vision in the form of youth" whose "prototype must be here after"? To Keats's ecstatic imagination it must have seemed that "immortal bowers" had been revealed to his "mortal sense." In rapt microcosmic vision he had crossed "the fragile bar" and reached the courts of heaven.

Such is the import of the first three stanzas of the poem, an import repeated and boldly formulated in the final stanza. In the penultimate stanza, however, the poet's thought takes an unexpected turn. Describing a priest conducting an antique sacrifice before a group of people, he reflects that some mountain village where these people lived is now empty, and the thought of this saddens him. Colvin acutely observed that here the poet's imagination "shifted its ground," choosing "to view the arrest of life as though it were an infliction in the sphere of reality."[15] This is true, but does Colvin quite touch the quick of the matter? Is not the secret of this shift to be found, as was seen in the "warm" and "panting" lovers of the preceding stanza, in the extraordinary intensity and empathy of Keats's imagination? Has not the "deceiving elf" of the fancy persuaded him again, for the moment, of the *extensional* reality of an image, just as happened with the "immortal" nightingale and her faery land?

When we come to the final stanza we observe the first, and sole, break in the imaginative vision ("Cold Pastoral! . . ."). Yet it is scarcely a break, only a momentary allusion to the objective world. Perhaps this passing glance at the outer world was motivated by the poet's mourning sympathy for the sacrificial throng, seemingly so alive and extensional to him. Whatever the motivation, the reminder of mortality is brief and unobtrusive, and is overwhelmed in the jubilant close:

> Thou shalt remain, in midst of other woe
> Than ours, a friend to man, to whom thou say'st,
> Beauty is truth, truth beauty,—that is all
> Ye know on earth, and all ye need to know.

Though men are mortal, though age and death are inevitable, yet hope and gladness, through the heaven-imaging creations of art, are their rightful heritage. For the beauty and happiness depicted on the urn, so vibrantly alive to Keats's aroused imagination, "*must* be truth." "The prototype must be here after."

It can hardly be accidental that the "Ode" is the happiest of Keats's poems. Even the empathic penultimate stanza confirms the intensity of the joy in other parts of the poem. And no mere verbal device, but unrestrained joy

---

15 Colvin, *John Keats* . . . , p. 418.

makes a kind of reiterant descant of the adjective "happy," which comes tumbling forth again and again, as if the emotion were not obvious enough without this added label, or as if in sheer exuberance this word, like the experience it signified, could not be curbed.

This surging happiness, together with the beauty-truth equation, impels one to question the adequacy of the interpretation often put forward, in one form or another: that Keats's theme was primarily "the permanent character of the beautiful in art as opposed to its mortality and change in nature and humanity."[16] If this is true, why does the beauty-truth equation not occur in Keats's other poems, especially in the poems treating works of fine or literary art? And why is the equation not equally applicable to a tragic work of art, to the depiction of age and misery in *King Lear*, say, or in Keats's own "Hyperion"? Why did the equation have to wait for a superlatively happy poem about perennial youth and love, to call it forth? The answer seems to be that the durability and frozen movement of works of art were not the principal inspiration of Keats's "Ode." It is a fairly trite observation that men are mortal and art isn't. Keats's rapture can hardly be accounted for merely by the "eternity" that results from freezing motion and change; any picture or sculpture does this.

If we turn for a moment to Byron's poetic comments on the sculptures that he saw in Italy, we come to a similar conclusion. In the Venus de' Medici, the Apollo Belvedere, the Dying Gaul (or Gladiator), and the Laocoön, he recognized the eternity that results from "freezing" motion. But no ecstasy, and no illusion of heaven, were excited by the "ever-dying Gladiator's air"[17] or by the Laocoön's "eternal throes."[18] Yet when he beheld the Venus he was "dazzled and drunk with beauty,"[19] and "the veil / Of heaven [was] half undrawn."[20] Likewise the Apollo Belvedere seemed to him "a heavenly guest— / A ray of immortality," and "not of human thought"—except in so far as it fulfilled perfectly the

> dream of Love
> Shaped by some solitary nymph, whose breast
> Long'd for a deathless lover from above . . .[21]

While all four of these sculptures shared the "eternity" common to their marble medium, only the happy and voluptuous subjects (the Venus and the Apollo) struck Byron as simulacra of heaven.

---

[16] The statement is by de Sélincourt, *The Poems of John Keats*, p. 476. Cf. Robert Bridges: "the supremacy of ideal art over nature, because of its unchanging expression of perfection"—*op. cit.*, pp. 131–32.

[17] *Don Juan*, IV, lxi.   [18] *Ibid.*

[19] *Childe Harold*, IV, stanza 1.

[20] *Ibid.*, IV, xlix.   [21] *Ibid.*, IV, clxii–clxiii.

To come back now to Keats's "Ode." Whether it was an accident of mood or of imagined marble medium, or of associations with the timeless "Greek spirit," or of a subject excluding age and unhappiness, or of some happy conjunction of these and other elements, his poem is an almost continuous paean to happiness, happiness that is fadeless. The feverish and fluctuating quality of ecstasy in the "Ode to a Nightingale," and the reconciled acceptance of "Beauty that must die" in the "Ode on Melancholy," are nowhere hinted. The note of confidence and high hope, of triumph and rejoicing, is continuously sounded.

So perfectly has the mood of happiness been sustained, and so triumphant is the climactic message born of this, that Keats automatically places the Urn in the same heaven whence the "immortal Bird" sang to him:

> Beauty is truth, truth beauty,—that is all
> Ye know *on earth*, and all ye need to know.

To my knowledge no discussion of the "Ode" has drawn attention to the modest phrase, "on earth." Is it there by accident only? To Keats's rapt imagination the Urn must have seemed an empyreal visitor, a foreshadowing of heaven in the likeness of marble, yet no mere product of mortal hands. It had come to him in a vision, as angels to Christians and nightingales to poets, to promise heaven. When in the elysian hereafter this visioned Urn, depicting an everlasting spring and lovers never satiated, would have become life itself, not a mere image of life, then its beauty would be truth and its truth beauty.

Let a word be added for the skeptical—they who decline to be carried away by "the elevation of the moment"! I freely admit that alternative interpretations attenuating, or even ruling out, the 1817 meaning of the beauty-truth equation are possible and plausible. The equation may conceivably have acquired a new meaning, or even have carried very little meaning at all outside a glad exclamation. Supposing the prefigurative element to be wholly absent from Keats's mind, one might surmise that the eternity which teased him out of thought was, despite indications to the contrary, the relative imperishableness, changelessness, and high value of any work of art. If this view is preferred, or any other view denying the prefigurative bent of the poem, one has still to take account of the rejoicing, triumphant tone of the conclusion, and can accordingly explain the beauty-truth equation as a natural recurrence of a language long familiar to the poet, and indissolubly associated with imaginative ecstasy.

If the afflatus of the moment sometimes betrayed Keats into the acceptance of his imaginative visions as previsions or "truth," in his sober moments he was seldom subject to the illusion. For example, in March 1819, while writing a letter to his brother George in America, he discerned that poetry and "truth" were distinct, not equal, that "truth" belonged to "philosophy," whereas "erroneousness" and "grace" belonged to poetry.[22] If we substitute "beauty" for "grace" (the passage suggests the synonym), it is clear that in a reflective moment Keats perceived a disparity between beauty and "truth," a disparity which his imagination had often encouraged him to overlook. Yet the imagination was to have its way with him at least twice after this, for the "Nightingale" and the "Grecian Urn" were both composed subsequent to (probably in May) the discriminating passage in the letter.

Everyone knows "La Belle Dame sans Merci," so that summary is superfluous. Of course it should be read primarily as a poem, a story in ballad form, but one can hardly avoid seeing a symbolic meaning as well. For the first time Keats was writing a poem about the "cheating" imagination; he caused his dreaming lover to be deluded, not rewarded. The full significance of this change is brought home when we compare the deluded lover's dream with the dreams of Endymion and of Madeline. Madeline was, in fact, awakened to the "truth" of her love-dream by Porphyro's playing the very melody, "La belle dame sans mercy." But the ailing lover of the ballad discovered only the falsity of his love-dreams. All day long he walked beside his lady, "a faery's child," who assured him of her love. And in the evening they came to her elfin grot, where

> she lulled me asleep,
> And there I dream'd—Ah! woe betide! . . .

Instead of Madeline's delicious prefigurative dream, this lover is visited with a dream prefiguring desertion and woe. The land of faery is no longer the perfect realm where happy dreams take on the semblance of truth, but a mirage of the imagination, a cruel betrayal. Thus indirectly Keats seems to be unsaying his "favorite speculation."

The tide that turned with "La Belle Dame" swept higher with "Lamia," and rolled mercilessly across the land of dreams and its "young minded" denizens in "The Fall of Hyperion." The story of Keats's recantation of "the dreamer tribe" has been narrated by other writers and need not be repeated here. But a few observations on "Lamia," especially in its relation to the prefigurative imagination, may be in order.

First of all, of course, "Lamia" is a tale. But it appears to be symbolic

---

[22] Letter 123, pp. 315–18. To this passage we shall return for more detailed study in the chapter on non-prefigurative truth.

also. It is a kind of expanded "La Belle Dame" in which the penalty for trusting a wishful dream is not mere loss of the dream but death itself. Or it can be looked upon as an inverted *Endymion*; at times Keats appears almost to be proclaiming the fact. The theme of both poems is the love of a mortal for an immortal, combined with a trust in prefigurative dreams; but the issue of one is bliss and apotheosis whereas the issue of the other is pain and death. The earlier poem affirmed that happy love-dreams are veraciously prefigurative; but though "Lamia" opens with a description of two such prefigurative love-dreams, both of which come true, the dreams are enjoyed by gods, not by men, and Keats pointedly declares, upon the happy verification of Hermes' dream:

> It was no dream; or say a dream it was,
> Real are the dreams of gods, and smoothly pass
> Their pleasures in a long immortal dream. (I, 126–28)

Though Keats has planned his poem to demonstrate the very obverse of Endymion's happy creed and to punish Lycius, a kind of Endymion *redivivus*, for trusting in dreams, he still allows the *gods* to enjoy blissful prefigurative dreams. He is thus transferring his "favorite speculation" to a realm where the skepticism of mortals can have no force. And at the same time he is indirectly warning his readers of the fate that awaits any mortal (Lycius specifically, and John Keats symbolically) who trusts to wishful dreams.

In another respect, too, Keats takes pains to warn his readers, and even Lycius himself, of the disaster that awaits him if he repeats Endymion's naïveté. Endymion had declared, and his adventures had gone on to prove, that

> earthly love has power to make
> Men's being mortal, immortal.

But Lamia, herself an immortal, calls Lycius' attention to the unbridgeable gulf between mortals and immortals:

> Thou canst not ask me with thee here to roam
> Over these hills and vales, where no joy is,—
> Empty of immortality and bliss!
> Thou art a scholar, Lycius, and must know
> That finer spirits cannot breathe below
> In human climes, and live . . .   (I, 276–81)

Were Lycius wise, he would see the corollary of Lamia's words: that just as immortals cannot be happy in the mortal sphere, so mortals cannot, without apotheosis (cf. *Endymion*), share the happiness of immortals. Keats makes this plain to the reader, if not to the "young minded" Lycius; for he has resolved to show that hope and wish and dream are not truth but illusion, that they lead not to heaven but to death. At the climax of his poem Lycius will be slain for the same reason that Endymion was deified.

Though commentators have rather neglected Lamia's revelatory words (that mortals cannot successfully be joined to immortals), Keats's poem lays stress on the point. His friend Woodhouse was aware of this; after Keats read the poem aloud to him, he wrote out a synopsis for Keats's publisher, in which he explained that when Lycius desired to marry Lamia, "this would be a forfeiture of her immortality & she refuses; at length (for says K——— 'women love to be forced to do a thing, by a fine fellow . . .') she consents."[23]

The love-smitten Lycius is not, of course, able to bear the pain of Lamia's revelation, and accordingly falls into a swoon in the old Endymion manner. From this he awakes to a "trance" of love (I, 286), in which he allows the astute Lamia to persuade him that she is not a "goddess" but a mortal woman :[24]

> Thus gentle Lamia judg'd, and judg'd aright,
> That Lycius could not love in half a fright,
> So threw the goddess off, and won his heart
> More pleasantly by playing woman's part . . . (I, 334–37)

Now that he can regard Lamia as mortal like himself, Lycius can forget her warning about the gulf that lies between mortals and immortals. Overjoyed, he bursts forth in extravagant eulogy of "a real woman" (I, 332), superior, he avers, to "Fairies, Peris, Goddesses" (I, 329). Keats makes it clear that Lycius is merely deluding himself by thus converting his wish into reality.

The lovers are happy for a time, living in their magic world of illusion, but the populace of Corinth moves to and fro about their invisible palace, and bald old Apollonius, repellently described, keeps an ominous eye on his former pupil. The lovers are doomed, of course, from the beginning; mortal and immortal can be only illusorily wedded so long as there is no miracle of apotheosis.

Book II opens with an almost cynical deprecation of "faery land" and "love in a palace." The world is too fond of believing in these illusions, Keats implies. Surely he has in mind not the world only, but the author of *Endymion* and his species? As the story is resumed, the world of everyday fact begins to encroach upon the dreamworld of the lovers, and swiftly the climax

---

[23] See Finney, *The Evolution of Keats's Poetry*, II, 693.

[24] The ending of the poem, in which Lamia breathes "death breath" under the stern eye of Apollonius, probably does not contradict Keats's original characterization of her. For Lamia's "death breath" is not, one surmises, the illogical death of an immortal, but rather the detection and dissolution of her mortal impersonation. As Apollonius avers, she is a serpent as well as a "goddess," and doubtless she returns to this form. Woodhouse reports simply that she "vanishes away." See Finney, *loc. cit.*

approaches in which the populace of Corinth is invited to a wedding feast in the magic palace. The "gossip rout," "the herd" with "common eyes," Keats calls the guests (II, 146, 149–50), delineating them in the same unpleasant light as he does Apollonius, who is, of course, one of the guests. It looks as if "the herd" is a symbolic equivalent of the world of commonplace reality which has so often interfered with the poet's "eternal moments," those ecstasies which carried him on the wings of the deceiving fancy into an elysian otherworld. At least it is clear that his sympathy lies wholly with the lovers, and that he is taking a kind of moody revenge for their imminent death by making both the guests and Apollonius repulsive.

But why, then, did Keats kill Lycius? It was in his power to save him and to discomfit the bald-headed, cold-eyed philosopher. Evidently he had determined to strike at the root, however painful to himself, of the imaginative illusion of which he had so frequently been the victim. Lamia, with her power of dreaming "of all she list" (I, 204) and of raising magic structures invisible to the populace, is rather pointedly intended, it would appear, as a symbol of the dreaming, creative, but nonextensional, illusory imagination. And Lycius her lover, whose happiness hangs upon her magic powers, who falls in love with her and, regarding her first as an immortal, is deceived into accepting her as "a real woman"—Lycius who is doomed to die when his illusion is fractured, must represent the dream-poet, prone to accept beauty as truth, illusion as reality. No wonder, then, that Keats sides with the lovers and protests violently when the aged, skeptic, cold-blooded philosopher, blind to "the holiness of the heart's affections" and insensible to the heart's desire of ardent youth, lays bare the illusion in Lycius' love, and mercilessly slays both the lovers: Lamia the illusion and Lycius the lover of illusion. Cold, feelingless, skeptic "philosophy" thus trespasses on the faery lands of imagination and tramples them to fragments.

But Keats allowed it to happen, in spite of his violent protest and obvious sympathy with the victims. In terms of symbolic mental biography, he was bravely, determinedly scourging the dream-poet within him, slaying a long-cherished, favorite self, author of a "young minded," dreamful, "favorite speculation."

"What the imagination seizes as beauty must be truth," he had once maintained. Now he knew that such beauty, however entrancing and highly to be treasured, is only "airy nothing." "No substance but mere illusion," as Burton said of Lamia. A poet who aspires to be great dares not feed exclusively upon illusion; he had better, as Keats told himself, strive like Shakespeare to be "a miserable and mighty poet of the human heart."[25]

---

[25] Letter 128, p. 347.

So far had Keats come in two years. We need not follow him through the painful trial and judgment of "The Fall of Hyperion," where he conducted a kind of living inquest—this time on himself directly, not on Lycius. The "dreamer tribe" was condemned without reprieve, but John Keats, who was greater than the sum of dreams within him, was privileged to survive:

> Thou hast felt
> What 'tis to die and live again before
> Thy fated hour. That thou hadst power to do so
> Is thy own safety; thou hast dated on
> Thy doom.   (I, 141–45)

Let us not forget that even this austere judgment was delivered to the poet in a vision. The voice was Keats's own voice projected into the imagined Moneta. Truth, sober, undelusive truth, still reached this poet via imaginative vision. Nor was this truth entirely divorced from beauty; in the hereafter, perhaps, it had no prototype, and it could not be called prefigurative in any naïve sense, but in the here and now its beauty was awful and sublime.

Rather than leave Keats poised at this melancholy extreme, we may wisely go back a few months to look at the "Bright star" sonnet, a poem which symbolizes in brief compass the whole of his poetic life, admirably balancing the opposing tendencies within him.

There are critics who, admitting the excellence of the octet of the sonnet, frown upon its sestet.[26] They prefer not to have a woman's breast juxtaposed with a star. Perhaps they have been too much in love with the dry light of reason to observe that Keats's sonnet, like the closing sentence of a letter in which he addressed Fanny Brawne as his "fair Star," is a prayer.[27] Probably the prayer carries no expectation of fulfillment, but it is no less devout for that. To Keats the heart's affections were not base but holy. They were worthy of recognition by the powers of the universe.

Somewhere out in the cosmic void is the steadfastness of a star; inside a specific mental cosmos is the desire for that steadfastness. The star has splendor but is solitary. The mind of the poet loves beauty but shuns loneness. The star is cold and inhuman, at once naturalistic and Christian ("nature's . . . Eremite"); the breast of a loved one is warm and intimate,

---

[26] See Garrod, for example: ". . . upon whatever page of Keats' poetry there falls the shadow of a living woman, it falls calamitously like an eclipse. The so-called *Last Sonnet* is, no doubt, all that it has been felt to be by lovers of Keats' poetry; and it seems wanton to say the whole truth about it. Yet the oftener I read it, the more does the contrast force itself upon my attention, between the lofty, the almost heroic, gravity of its opening lines, and the inferior effects in which it closes."—*Keats*, p. 59.

[27] See Letter 139, pp. 362–63.

at once profane and devout. The star is a symbol of light while it exists in the midst of darkness. There are light and darkness in the mental cosmos of a man; there are love and death.

Though Keats addresses his orison to the star, the star is not the Venus to whom he prayed like a heathen in closing his letter to Fanny Brawne ("I will imagine you Venus tonight and pray, pray, pray to your star like a heathen").[28] He was there identifying Fanny with, and in the sonnet he is distinguishing her from, a star. The star of the poem is an Eremite, ascetically remote, except in its beauty, from Venus the "amorous glow-worm of the sky" ("Ode to Psyche," l. 27), and similarly remote from the impassioned "throbbing star" to which Porphyro is likened in "The Eve of St. Agnes" (xxxvi).

In the splendid image of the star shining upon the moving waters "round earth's human shores," Keats seems to pass imperceptibly from an earthbound propitiator of the star to a star-placed spectator of the earth. From this astral altitude he then looks down upon a distant planetary body, distinguished from other cosmic bodies by the moving waters upon its surface and—a second thought, as it were—by its human inhabitants. "The moving waters . . . round earth's *human* shores": the adjective serves as the link between the loci in space and the consciousness which connects them. The star, the night, the earth, the waters, and John Keats are all associated because there is, amid all their immeasurable desolation, a human mind to join them. It is only this mind which, by a conscious fiction, enables the nonhuman universe to suspend its eternal indifference and momentarily to look with interest on the human drama.

The human earth which is purified by the absolving waters is further cleansed by the white covering of snow. And with a subtlety characteristic of the poet, the qualifying "soft" which makes a compound of the participle "fallen" not only evokes the image of the white mantle of snow over the earth, but creates the vision of snow as it falls, binding earth and sky, remote distance and lone human consciousness. And further, the "soft fall and swell" of Fanny's breast echoes the "soft-fallen snow," so that the rhythms of moving waters, of stars in their courses, of the seasonal fall of snow, and of the pulse and respiration of a human life are magically brought into a single intimate relationship. The imaginative whole, nevertheless, is built upon a duality, a duality which is forever impossible of dissolution. There is no ecstatic nightingale's song or visionary Arcadian urn to dissolve the poet's awareness of this duality. His deepest intention is to present the irony, forever irreconcilable, of desire illimitable, and reachless object of desire.

---

28 See Letter 139, pp. 362–63.

The same dichotomy of mortal desire seeking immortal fulfillment we know to have been twice the experience of Endymion and his poet, the language as well as the experience being adumbrative of the sonnet (*Endymion*, II, 739–45; III, 190–94). And the sonnet recalls other occasions when Keats's desire for immortality was strongly stimulated by aesthetic delight, especially the passage describing his first view of Lake Windermere,[29] so similar in thought and imagery. Yet there is no hint of a longing for death in the letter on Windermere; the view of the lake is like a glimpse of heaven: it "make[s] one forget the divisions of life," and convinces one that "there is no such thing as time and space." Of course there *is* time and there *is* space, empirically speaking; they were the ceaseless source of unhappiness between Keats and his love and, more fundamentally, between the two selves inside Keats. But moments of supreme happiness, when vouchsafed to one whose desire is insatiable and whose imagination is vivid, seem to be timeless. This seeming was sometimes *being* to a rapt poet.

The two passages in *Endymion* which anticipate the sonnet are like the description of Windermere in that they include no expressed wish for death. But perhaps the wish is intimated to the wary reader, who discovers, only a short distance beyond these apogees of ecstasy when the object of desire is flown and the mood of despair has recurred, that Endymion also longs for death. If he cannot "*lull* himself to immortality" he will wish, like the poet in his sonnet, to "*swoon* to death." The verbs are not accidentally parallel.

Sequentially if not simultaneously, then, though perhaps not very prominently, *Endymion* implies the duality which makes up the very essence of the "Bright star" sonnet. What is superior in the later poem is the exemplary lucidity and candor, the brave facing of irony, the conspicuous and conscious balance achieved, and the splendid finality of phrase.

Keats's dilemma, as he clearly saw, was unresolvable: when delight achieves permanence it loses sensation and human identity, like the star, and is therefore no longer delight—only a haunting, delusive image, a futile wish given spatial form. Mortality, immortality—the poignant contrast of existence limited to the one, with thought and feeling permitted to speculate on and yearn for the other! Surely it is the supreme irony, an irony of which Keats was fully conscious, that his sonnet, while it imaginatively Christianizes the physical universe, takes the form of a futile prayer to the fancied mercy of the indifferent cosmos.

All through life this poet was tantalized by the idea of eternity, the realm beyond "the fragile bar" that "tease[s] us out of thought." His nerves longed for it, and "the elevation of the moment" carried him at times "beyond

---

[29] Letter 71, pp. 154–55.

the bourn"; but his reason told him that it was not to be possessed, not really, perhaps, to be comprehended. There it was in man's mythical creations of heaven, Elysium, and the Golden Age, and in the perennial youth of the Greek spirit; in the agelessness of medieval romance and the "spiritual" pleasure of Shakespeare's verse; in the voice of the nightingale and in the marble drama of the "Grecian Urn." Always it hovered before his rapt imagination and always it eluded his grasp.

Yet in the "Bright star" sonnet his vision was clear. He suffered no illusions about the fulfillment of his astral prayer. He was, as he now realized, a kind of Tantalus reaching for the apples of the Hesperides.

VIII. NON-PREFIGURATIVE TRUTH
IN KEATS'S WRITINGS

If the days of Keats's life were totaled and multiplied by the hours and minutes in them, the minutes dedicated to the prefigurative attitude would seem few in proportion. Measured by fervor and intensity, the Hesperidean or elysian strain is vivid and cardinal, but measured by duration, it yields in significance to other characteristics of Keats's mental life.

His more normal and everyday condition of mind, as it is revealed through his usage of "truth," will be explored in this concluding chapter. More space is not given to it because there are few difficulties in interpretation and because the sober, mature, and undeluded side of Keats is already well known. Since a thorough collation and study of his usage of "truth" has never been made, we shall scan every remaining occurrence of "truth" in the letters, following a chronological sequence.[1] All significant examples of "truth" in the verse (for which the Concordance is of course available) have been noticed in previous chapters.

In an early letter Keats criticized Wordsworth for his poem, "Gipsies," declaring that:

if Wordsworth had thought a little deeper at that moment he would not have written the poem at all—I should judge it to have been written in one of the most comfortable moods of his life—it is a kind of sketchy intellectual landscape—not a search after *truth*—[2]

Without adducing the all too obvious evidence of the poem (in which Wordsworth complacently rebukes a group of gipsies for their "torpid life . . . which the very stars reprove"—ll. 22–23), and without consulting Hazlitt's blunt, impatient condemnation of the poem,[3] we can see at once Keats's general import. The "truth" not found in Wordsworth's poem is simply the poet's fidelity to his subject, his submission to its inmost essence rather than to a superficial, obtrusive, "imported" homily.

In Letter 31, where the word "truth" is used in several senses, its first

---

[1] To conserve space, the full context of the various statements will not always be reproduced. Appendix A contains a concordance of all occurrences of "truth" in Keats's writings, making it easy to turn to the designated page in M. B. Forman's edition of the letters and thus have the complete context at hand. Expressions such as "in truth" and "truth is" are negligible and are not recorded.

[2] Letter 26, p. 56.

[3] In a note to the essay "On Manner" in *The Round Table*.

occurrence comes just four sentences prior to the famous proposition that "beauty must be truth":

In passing however I must say of one thing that has pressed upon me lately and increased my humility and capability of submission and that is this *truth*—men of genius are great as certain ethereal chemicals operating on the mass of neutral intellect—but they have not any individuality, any determined character—I would call the top and head of those who have a proper self men of power—[4]

This "truth" is a judgment, a comparative judgment empirically conceived. Characteristically it flashes upon Keats as images rather than as abstractions, and "proves" itself by feeling, not by reason. It has "pressed upon" him, showing the criterion often revealed elsewhere, as when he insists that "axioms in philosophy are not axioms until they are *proved upon our pulses.*"[5]

The other usages of non-prefigurative truth in Letter 31 were discussed in chapter ii. They are two in number, and they both have the same referent: the product of "consecutive reasoning," such truth as Bailey's ratiocinative mind could presumably attain, but which Keats's emotional, imaginative mind could not understand.

The word "truth" next appears a month later in a judgment of a painting, which leads Keats to a generalization:

The excellence of every art is its intensity, capable of making all disagreeables evaporate, from their being in close relationship with beauty and *truth*.[6]

Notice that the words "beauty" and "truth" are coupled, not equated. The context leaves no question as to the non-prefigurative nature of this "truth," but any attempt to define its meaning precisely is likely to end in either arbitrary assumptions or sheer perplexity. Do "beauty and truth" consist in "women one feels mad to kiss" (cf. the context), in faces "swelling into reality," in the evaporation of "disagreeables," or in a "momentous depth of speculation"? The safest conclusion is that the aesthetic truth which Keats had in mind was related to "intensity" and was embodied in *King Lear* though absent from Benjamin West's painting, "Death on the Pale Horse." But this is far from a definition.

Later in the same letter Keats left cloudy verbiage behind and wrote a lucid and admirable essay on "negative capability":

I had not a dispute but a disquisition, with Dilke on various subjects; several things dove-tailed in my mind, and at once it struck me what quality went to form a man of achievement, especially in literature, and which Shakespeare possessed so enormously—I

---

[4] Letter 31, p. 67.
[5] Letter 64, p. 142. Cf. also "convincing one's nerves," p. 144, and "a proverb is no proverb to you till your life has illustrated it," Letter 123, p. 318.
[6] Letter 32, p. 71.

mean *negative capability*, that is, when a man is capable of being in uncertainties, mysteries, doubts, without any irritable reaching after fact and reason—Coleridge, for instance, would let go by a fine isolated *verisimilitude* caught from the penetralium [for penetralia] of mystery, from being incapable of remaining content with half-knowledge. This pursued through volumes would perhaps take us no further than this, that with a great poet the sense of beauty overcomes every other consideration, or rather obliterates all consideration.[7]

The word "truth" does not occur in the passage, but "verisimilitude" looks like an approximate synonym. What quantities of exegetical ink might have been saved if Keats had regularly used this word instead of "truth"! Yet this is its sole appearance in his writings. A "verisimilitude" is a fitting name for the kind of perception attractive to the poet's "sense of beauty." With "irritable" fact or reason such a perception is only secondarily, perhaps not at all, concerned, being a product of beauty and "*half*-knowledge." In this temperate and perspicuous statement Keats was not carried away by "the elevation of the moment"; he was "careful of his fruits." One might surmise, indeed, that the "fine [= beautiful?] isolated verisimilitude" is a synonym, conceived in a sober and calm-judging mood, not only for non-prefigurative beauty-truths, but even, perhaps, for such "favorite speculations" as that of Letter 31. If this is true, prefigurative and non-prefigurative truth become but two phases of the poet's "sense of beauty" and "half-knowledge"—phases dependent on the presence or absence of the credence-producing "elevation of the moment." We shall soon find further reason for entertaining this view.

When Keats asked his publisher to accept an emendation of the "pleasure thermometer" passage in *Endymion* (I, 777 ff.), he observed: "I assure you that when I wrote it it was a regular stepping of the imagination towards a *truth*."[8] Did he mean by the "when" clause that at the time he first wrote the passage it seemed more valid, more veracious, than it struck him many months later when he came to revise it? If so, he was aware to some extent of the necessary relativism of thought. We shall note presently that on occasion he was uncommonly aware of such relativism. But in any event the "pleasure thermometer" was, as we discovered in chapter i, a value judgment apprehended in the form of beautiful images. As such, would there be anything wrong in calling it a "verisimilitude" proceeding from the poet's "sense of beauty" and "half-knowledge"?

While studying the "eternal truth" of aesthetic evolution in "Hyperion," a brief quotation was given from Letter 48 to show Keats's conception of the possible melioration of the human race through a universal dissemination of the aesthetic impulse. There is hardly a doubt that while Keats was

---

[7] *Ibid.*, p. 72.
[8] Letter 42, p. 91.

evolving this conception, which came to him as usual in the form of images, he was convinced of its truth. But when he neared the end of his letter he paused to survey his "airy citadel," and began to look at it in a changed light:

I was led into these thoughts, my dear Reynolds [Keats confesses] by the beauty of the morning operating on a sense of idleness—I have not read any books—the morning said I was right—I had no idea but of the morning, and the thrush said I was right—seeming to say . . .

What the thrush said is given in some verses that follow, the central idea of which is the thrush's advice:

> O fret not after knowledge—I have none,
> And yet my song comes native with the warmth.

Then Keats adds:

Now I am sensible all this is a mere sophistication (however it may neighbour to any *truths*), to excuse my own indolence—so I will not deceive myself that man should be equal with Jove—but think himself very well off as a sort of scullion-Mercury, or even a humble bee. It is no matter whether I am right or wrong, either one way or another, if there is sufficient to lift a little time from your shoulders.[9]

"A mere sophistication"—that is, a sophistry or rationalization; not truth but neighbor to truth—such is his airy citadel. And it is only a pleasure dome (created in order "to lift a little time from your shoulders," or so it seems in retrospect), not truth's exacter palace. Furthermore, the whole structure owes its magic creation to "the beauty of the morning." We may well ask: could Keats have furnished a fitter illustration of "a fine isolated verisimilitude" born in beauty and not "fretting" after "irritable" knowledge?

The letter is also an excellent example of the conscious relativism of Keats's thinking. While the sun rises and the flowers open and his half-indolent mood spins forth its enchanting airy citadel, inviting all men likewise to spin theirs and then meet in heaven or nigh heaven—while the spinning process goes on and the poet's "sense of beauty overcomes every other consideration," the airy citadel *seems* to be truth. When at last the thrush's voice has been transmuted to verse and the poet realizes that his letter must come to a close, the light tension of his enchanted palace relaxes, and he moves off, as it were, to view his work and judge the architecture. Then, and not till then, he clear-sightedly evaluates his creation, confident still of its appropriateness to the situation, the time, and the mood, yet able to see its limitations also, and its unfitness for other times and other situations—in short its *semi*verity.

Scarcely a month later Keats fell into the theme of relativism again, ex-

---

9 Letter 48, pp. 104–5.

panding it far beyond the self-judgment of Letter 48 to generalizations that include the whole of human experience, with emphasis on the inner realm of value and the outer realm of objective existence. This perceptive passage, so little regarded by writers on Keats, deserves to be better known:

Give me a long brown plain for my morning so I may meet with some of Edmund Ironside's descendants. Give me a barren mould so I may meet with some shadowing of Alfred in the shape of a gipsey, a huntsman or a shepherd. Scenery is fine—but human nature is finer. The sward is richer for the tread of a real, nervous, English foot—the eagle's nest is finer for the mountaineer has look'd into it—Are these facts or prejudices? Whatever they are, for them I shall never be able to relish entirely any Devonshire scenery—[10]

The reason for this disrelish, Keats implies, is that no heroic associations dignify the country, and only "dwindled Englishmen" dwell there. "Are these *truths* or prejudices?" he might have asked, instead of "Are these facts or prejudices?" But he did not stop to decide, for the "fineness" (the beauty?) of his surmise was what attracted him, not its objective accuracy. His "sense of beauty" was content with half-knowledge.

The letter goes on to disparage, with infectious mock grandeur, the "dwindled Englishmen" and "passable" women of Devonshire. Then there is a transition to the subject of religion, probably suggested to Keats by his reflections on the relation of facts to prejudices:

You know my ideas about religion. I do not think myself more in the right than other people, and that nothing in this world is provable. I wish I could enter into all your feelings on the subject merely for one short 10 minutes and give you a page or two to your liking. I am sometimes so very sceptical as to think poetry itself a mere jack-a-lantern to amuse whoever may chance to be struck with its brilliance. As tradesmen say every thing is worth what it will fetch, so probably every mental pursuit takes its reality and worth from the ardour of the pursuer—being in itself a nothing—Ethereal things may at least be thus real, divided under three heads—Things real—things semi-real—and no things. Things real—such as existences of moon & stars and passages of Shakespeare. Things semireal such as love, the cloud &c which require a greeting of the spirit to make them wholly exist—and nothings which are made great and dignified by an ardent pursuit—which by the by stamps the burgundy mark on the bottles of our minds, insomuch as they are able to *"consecrate whate'er they look upon."*[11]

"Nothing in this world is provable"—this is the first step in his thought, growing out of the allusion to religion, and partly deriving, perhaps, from his unwillingness to offend the theological Bailey by disagreeing with any of his opinions. But Keats was not merely deferential; for what he says about the "jack-a-lantern" of poetry and about "facts or prejudices" indicates that he was describing his own state of mind.

---

[10] Letter 53, p. 111.
[11] *Ibid.*, pp. 111–12.

It is well to remind ourselves of the consistency of this attitude with his general disapproval of opinionatedness both in poetry and in man. Shakespeare's supreme excellence, as Keats saw it, consisted in this very freedom and detachment of mental outlook; he was "capable of being in uncertainties, mysteries, doubts, without any irritable reaching after fact and opinion."[12]

Thus the transition from religion to poetry in Keats's letter is natural enough. If the validity of religion cannot be ascertained in the world that we live in, by the same law the value of poetry must be debatable. Perhaps the world of poetry, however vivid and "real" to a poet, is "no substance but mere illusion," as Burton described Lamia. Perhaps poetry is no more than a deceptive "jack-a-lantern," a "deceiving elf" ("Ode to a Nightingale") destined to lead ardent poets astray. Had not Endymion, yearning lover-poet, accused his pursuit of dreams, at times when the skeptic mood was on him, of being

> A mad-pursuing of the fog-born elf,
> Whose flitting lantern, through rude nettle-briar,
> Cheats us into a swamp . . .   (II, 278–80)

In the letter Keats sanely recognizes the relative, unprovable value of the religious and poetic idols that men serve on earth. His classifications are somewhat capricious, but his main point is driven home. He is even glad, and a little excited, at the imaginal analogies that float into his ken: religionists and poets are like tradesmen, sermons and poems are like bottles of wine, their "reality and worth," indeed the reality and worth of "every mental pursuit," borrowed "from the ardour of the pursuer—being in itself a nothing."

Is it possible that Keats had in mind his "favorite speculation" when he wrote these telltale words? There is no way of knowing, though the words describe perfectly the psychology ("the ardour of the pursuer") behind the beauty that "*must* be truth." We can be sure, however, that some of his speculations, former ones as well as present ones, passed through his memory, for he closes his letter with a confession that he cannot vouch for the truth of any of his speculations:

. . . it is an old maxim of mine and of course must be well known that every point of thought is the centre of an intellectual world—the two uppermost thoughts in a man's

---

[12] For other statements disapproving of opinionatedness, see the definition of "men of genius" (Letter 31), the account of "negative capability" (Letter 32), a criticism of Wordsworth's didacticism (Letter 44), an extended delineation of "the poetical character" ("a poet has no identity . . . not one word I ever utter can be taken as an opinion growing out of my identical nature . . ."—Letter 93), the praise of "disinterestedness" (Letter 123, pp. 316–18), and the disparagement of Dilke for his tenacity of opinion (Letter 156, p. 426).

mind are the two poles of his world, he revolves on them and every thing is southward or northward to him through their means. We take but three steps from feathers to iron. Now my dear fellow I must once for all tell you I have not one idea of the *truth* of any of my speculations—I shall never be a reasoner because I care not to be in the right, when retired from bickering and in a proper philosophical temper.[13]

With splendid consistency—such as he does not always show—Keats doubts his doubts, or rather, doubts his analysis of the unreality of reality. And yet this is the same man who, during moments of transport, could believe in prefigurative truth!

The whole fabric of his letter (and the nature of his thinking in general), says Keats, amounts merely to a "speculation," or series of "speculations," each of which is, for the time being, "the centre of an intellectual world." Later moments may bring other thoughts "uppermost," and then new intellectual worlds with new centers will replace the present one, each of them containing some element of truth, the exact degree of which the poet cannot calculate, and scarcely wishes to calculate. For it is the essence of mentality, Keats now sees clearly, to be constantly shifting its center of reference ("from feathers to iron," for example), and therefore always changing its perspective. Under such circumstances any continuous or complete vision of truth is impossible, and perhaps it is impossible ever to have the same vision twice. What Keats is saying, in short, is that all perception—or his, at least—is relative.

Perhaps rational minds can reduce this relativism, he seems to intimate, but such minds as his constantly shift their perspectives; for he is not a "reasoner" and cares "not to be in the right." Is this not the equivalent of "negative capability," which is "capable of being in uncertainties, mysteries, doubts, without any irritable reaching after fact and reason"? Is not the "philosophical temper," as Keats conceives it, just such a state of unopinionative "half-knowledge," building its speculative "airy citadels" that do not pretend to be truth but nevertheless "neighbour" on truth? And are not these speculative airy citadels but another name, another metaphor, for the "fine isolated verisimilitudes" which issue from "the penetralia of mystery"? In short, are not the "truths," "speculations," and "verisimilitudes," all of them coexisting with "half-knowledge" and "seized" *qua* images (in their beauty, that is), simply variant names for approximately the same mind-event?[14] Do not these "truths," "speculations," and "verisimilitudes" all

---

[13] Letter 53, pp. 112–13.

[14] All occurrences of the term "speculation(s)" are registered in Appendix A. J. M. Murry's definition of Keats's use of "speculation" may be accepted for the three occurrences of the word in the verse, but it is wholly inapplicable to the twenty-two occurrences in the letters and marginalia. See Murry, *Studies in Keats, New and Old* (London: Oxford University Press, 1939), pp. 93–97.

aim more or less at truth, while they allow the imaginal embodiment, the "sense of beauty" to "overcome every other consideration"? Half-truths they might be called. Though this term is not used by Keats, he justifies it with such expressions as "semi-speculations,"[15] "favorite speculation," "verisimilitude," "half-knowledge," "half-seeing,"[16] "however it may neighbour to any truths," "I have not one idea of the truth of any of my speculations," and so on.

To my knowledge, only two writers have attached much importance to the conscious relativism of Keats's thinking: Veronika Orend-Schmidt, in a book rarely mentioned by Keats's critics,[17] and H. N. Fairchild.[18] In a chapter on Keats's *Weltanschauung*, Miss Orend-Schmidt declares that the *"Prinzip der Relativität"* was the invariable criterion of Keats's thinking.[19] Although evidence does not warrant so sweeping a conclusion, there is unquestionably much in Keats that can appropriately be described as conscious relativism. In Appendix B, I have given page references to evidence not cited by Miss Orend-Schmidt.

In his essay on Keats in *The Romantic Quest*, Fairchild devotes a few pages to what he calls the poet's "scepticism," though he does not relate this to his usage of "truth." A somewhat wrong impression, I feel, is given by the word "scepticism," which implies too strong a habit of *dis*belief on Keats's part. As we have seen, belief was likely to be ardent with him at times; at other times he did not so much disbelieve as question, and the question itself was not strong enough to erase his feeling that his speculations "neighboured" on truths.

Such was the temper of the Keatsian mind when it was not carried away by credence-producing moments of rapture. During the calmer, unrapturous intervals when his fervid faith subsided and his relative mood resumed, did Keats look on even his favorite prefigurative visions as only verisimilar speculations? We cannot know for certain. But the inference is not unreasonable.

There remain three occurrences of "truth" to be studied. In December 1818 the words beauty and "truth" gravitated into something like equivalence:

I never can feel certain of any *truth* but from a clear perception of its beauty—and I find myself very young minded even in that perceptive power—which I hope will increase.[20]

---

[15] Marginal note on *Paradise Lost*. See M. B. Forman, *The Poetical Works . . .* , V, 294.   [16] Letter 44, p. 96.

[17] V. Orend-Schmidt, *John Keats' Schönheitsideal und Weltanschauung* (Marburg: G. Braun, 1929).   [18] H. N. Fairchild, *The Romantic Quest*.

[19] Orend-Schmidt, *op. cit.*, pp. 92–93.   [20] Letter 98, p. 259.

To rational minds such a confession must look like either naïveté or wanton misuse of words. But obviously Keats was describing the habitual operation of his mind, its manner of "seizing" its perceptions *qua* images. And he was evidently referring to a judgment of some sort ("*any* truth"), not to a pre-figurative vision. Unfortunately the context offers no positive referent or illustration of such a "truth," though there are indications that he had in mind some recent perception of the different qualities, or values, of Raphael's and Guido's paintings. If this was his referent, the "truth" (a comparative judgment) must have flashed into his mind in the form of images (of "beauty," that is), in much the same way as the earlier truth discriminating men of genius from men of power (Letter 31, p. 67). Whether the poet regarded his truth as relative and verisimilar, only time and changing perspective (a new "center of an intellectual world") could determine.

Early in 1819 the "young minded" identification of "beauty" and "truth" gave way to a perception of their inevitable disparity:

May there not be superior beings amused with any graceful, though instinctive attitude my mind may fall into, as I am entertained with the alertness of a stoat or the anxiety of a deer? Though a quarrel in the streets is a thing to be hated, the energies displayed in it are fine; the commonest man shows a grace in his quarrel—by a superior being our reasonings may take the same tone—though erroneous they may be fine—this is the very thing in which consists poetry; and if so it is not so fine a thing as philosophy—for the same reason that an eagle is not so fine a thing as a *truth*—give me this credit—do you not think I strive—to know myself?[21]

One willingly grants the credit, and gratefully observes that now at last, or again (if the consciously relativistic Keats is kept in mind), he clearly sees that beauty (= "grace" and "fineness"), "instinctiveness," and "erroneous reasonings" (="speculations," "verisimilitudes"?) belong to poetry, whereas truth, disinterestedness (discussed earlier in the passage), and accuracy belong to philosophy. There remain some difficulties, such as the nature of the "truth" and the "philosophy" thus discriminated. Was he here referring, contrary to his habit, to a nonpoetical philosophy, or, according to his habit, to a superior, profounder, more disinterested type of "philosophical" poetry?[22] The question can hardly be answered, even though the main distinction between the "erroneous reasonings" of poetry and the (errorless?) truth of "philosophy" is clear enough. One wonders why, after thus perceiving the fundamental disparity of poetry and philosophy, of beauty and truth, Keats could write two months later: "Beauty is truth, truth beauty . . ." The "elevation of the moment" must have betrayed him.

---

[21] Letter 123, p. 317.

[22] For a definition of Keats's use of the word "philosophy," see A. C. Bradley, "Keats and 'Philosophy,'" *A Miscellany*, pp. 191 ff.

The last instance of "truth" in the letters belongs, fittingly enough, to the relativistic species, and, as if sensible of climax, serves as a kind of recapitulation of earlier statements on relativism:

I wrote Brown a comment . . . wherein I explained what I thought of Dilke's character. Which resolved itself into this conclusion. That Dilke was a man who cannot feel he has a personal identity unless he has made up his mind about every thing. The only means of strengthening one's intellect is to make up one's mind about nothing—to let the mind be a thoroughfare for all thoughts. Not a select party. The genus is not scarce in population. All the stubborn arguers you meet with are of the same brood. They never begin upon a subject they have not p'eresolved on. They want to hammer their nail into you and if you turn the point, still they think you wrong. Dilke will never come at a *truth* as long as he lives; because he is always trying at it.[23]

Dilke's fault, in Keats's eyes, was his opinionativeness. And seemingly he regarded his opinions as truths, for Keats declares pointedly that Dilke's opinions can never be truths, *because* he is fixedly attached to them! The logic is unorthodox, but it harmonizes perfectly with what Keats has said on many other occasions. It is no accident, for instance, that he ascribes Dilke's opinionativeness to his need to "feel he has a personal identity." The poetic mind, as Keats more than once declared, "has no identity,"[24] and Keats himself has "no opinion growing out of my identical nature."[25] Of the same species was Shakespeare, whose pre-eminent quality, as Keats saw it, was his capability "of being in uncertainties, mysteries, doubts, without any irritable reaching after fact and reason."[26]

To strengthen one's mind, Keats holds, fact and reason are not essential, or at least not primary, and "truth" is not begotten of them alone or mainly. "Truth" is to be discovered by the "disinterested," "speculative" mind, by the imaginative, undidactic, unopinionative mind of a poet. Dilke is plainly not a "disinterested" man; he is too interested in a single view of things. Therefore Keats feels that truth, the nature of which is multiform and fluctuating, requiring innumerable perspectives for its total apprehension, will never be captured by Dilke and his fellow reasoners. One should not be content with a single point of view, but should take his station successively at many "centers" of "intellectual worlds." For the nature of reality, or at least the means of apprehending it—here Keats would probably agree with William James—may "be so complex as to consist of many interpenetrating spheres of reality, which we can thus approach in alternation by using dif-

---

23 Letter 156, p. 426.
24 Letter 93, p. 228.
25 *Ibid.*
26 Letter 32, p. 72.

ferent conceptions and assuming different attitudes . . ."[27] If "every point of thought is the center of an intellectual world," as Keats declared, truth can be approached ("neighboured" upon) only by the mind which allows itself to a "a thoroughfare for all thoughts," inhabiting successively as many "intellectual worlds" as possible.

Probably it is a mistake to think of Keats primarily as a truth-seeker. His "sense of beauty" was ever his guide, even when he yielded to his instinctive love for imaginative "speculation." For the poet, the "chameleon poet," "lives in gusto," and relishes "the dark side of things" as much as "the bright one, because they both end in speculation." The chameleon poet goes among the fields observing the ways of animals, and through city streets observing the ways of men, comparing and classifying and conjecturing, always tentatively and never dogmatically. All the while his imagination is busy building its speculative, verisimilar "airy citadels" that "neighbour" on truth. What impels the chameleon poet to do this is the "relish," the "gusto," of being "everything and nothing"[28] by imaginative sympathy; the dry worship of truth has in itself little attraction for him. Instinctively responding to the varying quality of human experience, following his "sense of beauty" wherever it leads him, and relishing the imaginative activity set in play— "this it is that makes the amusement of life—to a speculative mind."[29]

Consistent to the last, though sometimes puzzling in its language, Keats's view of non-prefigurative truth leans toward the relativistic. "A proverb is no proverb to you till your life has illustrated it."[30] He might as easily have written: "A truth is no truth to you, a speculation is no speculation, a verisimilitude is no verisimilitude, till your life has illustrated it." And once having illustrated it, life goes on, he would say, to modify it by innumerable other truths thronging the mind, passing through its thoroughfare, pausing sometimes until motion seems arrested and belief appears fixed, yet destined always to resume their onward movement, molding and remolding the mind-mirror of the poet, shaping and reshaping his view of the world, but never really halting their motion, never limiting their flux, never immobilizing their image. The life of the universe would pass through such a mind, as it did through Shakespeare's. And along with the life, the judgments and attitudes, the innumerable "truths" possible to men in such a world, in all situations and times, from Socrates and Jesus to Cortez and Napoleon, from Achilles and Troilus to Juliet and Iago, from the "speculations of Satan in

---

[27] William James, *The Varieties of Religious Experience* (Modern Library ed.), p. 120.

[28] Letter 93, pp. 227–28.   [29] Letter 123, p. 316.

[30] *Ibid.*, p. 318.

the serpent prison"[31] to the hopes, the dejections, and "favorite speculations" of Endymion, of Oceanus, Saturn, Porphyro, Lycius, and Moneta. Such was Keats's ideal, such was his conception of the poet who would become a "philosopher."

At times, under the spell of an ardent and credent imagination, he had hypostatized a wish and called it "truth," prefigurative truth. But the illusion never persisted for long. The world of immediate reality flowed in again, and with it the relativistic attitude to experience and judgment, in which the illusion of prefigurative truth was seen, perhaps not certainly as an illusion, but as "a *favorite* speculation," a verisimilitude coexisting with "half-knowledge." Never could mortal man attain to absolute knowledge; but he could, Keats learned as he grew in wisdom, increase his knowledge and experience, enlarge the disinterestedness of his mind, deepen his comprehension of the human scene, and thus diminish gradually the "erroneousness"of his perceptions, making them more worthy to be called "truths" and "philosophy."

---

[31] Marginal note on *Paradise Lost*. See M. B. Forman, *The Poetical Works* . . . , V, 305.

APPENDIX

A. LISTINGS OF KEY WORDS

Here are tabulated all occurrences of the following words in Keats's prose writings: truth, verisimilitude, ethereal, empyreal, sensation(s), spiritual, speculation(s), abstract (and its derivatives), imagination, fancy. The Concordance can be consulted for the same words when they occur in the poetry. References to the letters are uniformly to the edition by M. B. Forman, *The Letters of John Keats* (New York: Oxford University Press, 1935); citations from essays and marginalia may be found in M. B. Foreman (ed.), *The Poetical Works and Other Writings of John Keats* (New York: Charles Scribner's Sons, 1938–39), 8 vols.

TRUTH[1]

. . . a kind of sketchy intellectual landscape—not a search after truth . . . (Letter 26, p. 56)

. . . one thing that has pressed upon me lately . . . and that is this truth . . . (Letter 31, p. 67)

. . . the holiness of the heart's affections and the truth of imagination—What the imagination seizes as beauty must be truth . . . (Letter 31, p. 67)

The imagination may be compared to Adam's dream—he awoke and found it truth. (Letter 31, p. 68)

And yet such a fate can only befall those who delight in sensation rather than hunger as you do after truth. (Letter 31, p. 68)

. . . from their being in close relationship with beauty and truth. (Letter 32, p. 71)

. . . a fine isolated verisimilitude . . . (Letter 32, p. 72)

. . . a regular stepping of the imagination towards a truth. (Letter 42, p. 91)

. . . a mere sophistication (however it may neighbour to any truths) . . . (Letter 48, p. 105)

. . . I have not one idea of the truth of any of my speculations . . . (Letter 53, p. 112)

. . . I never can feel certain of any truth but from a clear perception of its beauty . . . (Letter 98, p. 259)

. . . For the same reason that an eagle is not so fine a thing as a truth . . . (Letter 123, p. 317)

Dilke will never come at a truth as long as he lives; because he is always trying at it. (Letter 156, p. 426)

ETHEREAL

. . . ethereal things . . . (Letter 15, p. 31)

. . . ethereal chemicals . . . (Letter 31, p. 67)

. . . our most ethereal musings on earth . . . (Letter 31, p. 69)

. . . a sort of ethereal pigs . . . (Letter 44, p. 94)

. . . ethereal finger-pointings . . . (Letter 48, p. 103)

---

[1] Expressions such as "truth is" and "in truth" are negligible and are not recorded.

. . . sucking sap from mould ethereal (Letter 48, p. 104)

Ethereal things . . . (Letter 53, p. 112)

. . . the nettles and thorns etherealized . . . Letter 57, p. 122)

. . . touching the spring delicately and ethereally . . . (Letter 64, p. 142)

. . . ethereal and authentically divine . . . (Letter 64, p. 144)

. . . ethereal existence . . . (Letter 71, p. 157)

I thought them ethereal above men . . . (Letter 79, p. 192)

. . . the unearthly, spiritual and ethereal (Letter 94, p. 233)

. . . the more ethereal part of it mounts into the brain . . . (Letter 123, p. 302)

EMPYREAL

. . . imagination and its empyreal reflection . . . (Letter 31, p. 68)

. . . a tapestry empyrean . . . (Letter 48, p. 103)

SENSATIONS

. . . the idea of your sensations. (Letter 21, p. 42)

. . . a heart always open to such sensations . . . (Letter 26, p. 55)

. . . undepraved sensations . . . (Letter 28, p. 60)

. . . O for a life of sensations rather than of thoughts! (Letter 31, p. 68)

. . . high sensations . . . (Letter 64, p. 140)

. . . a history of her life and sensations. (Letter 75, p. 174)

. . . sensation and watchfulness . . . (Letter 90, p. 223)

. . . one has no sensations . . . (Letter 94, p. 233)

No sensation is created by greatness . . . (Letter 94, p. 234)

. . . he could not get rid of the sensation . . . (Letter 98, p. 258)

With what sensation do you read Fielding? . . . (Letter 98, p. 258)

. . . without any change in my sensations . . . (Letter 115, p. 285)

. . . a delightful sensation . . . (Letter 123, p. 315)

. . . on poetical sensation . . . (Letter 123, p. 324)

. . . suppose a rose to have sensation . . . (Letter 123, p. 335)

. . . a too lax sensation of life . . . (Letter 144, p. 372)

. . . a history of sensations . . . (Letter 145, p. 374)

. . . the shock of extreme thought and sensation . . . (Letter 145, p. 374)

I wish to give myself up to other sensations. (Letter 151, p. 384)

I had another strange sensation . . . (Letter 156, p. 400)

. . . pleasant or unpleasant sensation. (Letter 156, p. 402)

. . . a sensation of some sort. (Letter 156, p. 402)

I think it will give you the sensation . . . (Letter 156, p. 414)

. . . I wish to devote myself to another sensation—(Letter 156, p. 425)

I have a sensation at the present moment as though I was dissolving . . . (Letter 160, p. 436)

. . . if I turned to versify that acerbated the poison of either sensation. (Letter 183, p. 465)

. . . with the sensation of marching up against a battery. (Letter 228, p. 508)

. . . if I could with any bearable sensation . . . (Letter 233, p. 514)

I should have delighted in setting off for London for the sensation merely . . . (Letter 238, p. 520)

. . . my sensations with respect to Miss Brawne . . . (*Ibid.*)

. . . those depraved sensations which the want of any education excites in many. (*Letters*, p. 521 n., quoting a conversation of Keats with Severn, as reported by the latter to Lord Houghton)

SPIRITUAL

. . . to be self spiritualized into a kind of sublime misery . . . (Letter 26, p. 56)

. . . human life and its spiritual repetition. (Letter 31, p. 68)

. . . the tip-top of any spiritual honors . . . (Letter 37, p. 80)

. . . a kind of spiritual yeast in their frames . . . (Letter 40, p. 84)

. . . to feed upon spiritual mast and acorns . . . (Letter 44, p. 95)

. . . any one grand and spiritual passage . . . (Letter 48, p. 103)

. . . full of symbols for his spiritual eye, of softness for his spiritual touch . . . (*Ibid.*)

. . . the unearthly, spiritual, and ethereal . . . (Letter 94, p. 233)

A melodious passage in poetry is full of pleasures both sensual and spiritual. The spiritual is felt when the very letters and points of charactered language show like . . . the mysterious signs of an immortal freemasonry! ("On Edmund Kean as a Shakesperian·Actor." See M. B. Forman, *The Poetical Works and Other Writings* . . . , V, 229.)

SPECULATION(S)

. . . I would advise you, as a good speculation, to study Hebrew . . . (Letter 21, p. 41)

A question is the best beacon towards a little speculation . . . (Letter 26, p. 57)

In a word, you may know my favorite speculation . . . (Letter 31, p. 67)

. . . it has come as auxiliary to another favorite speculation of mine . . . (Letter 31, p. 68)

. . . momentous depth of speculation excited . . . (Letter 32, p. 71)

. . . you were at the moment estranged from speculation . . . (Letter 40, p. 84)

Every man has his speculations . . . (Letter 44, p. 96)

. . . I have not one idea of the truth of any of my speculations . . . (Letter 53, p. 112)

. . . I never have any speculations without associating you in them . . . (Letter 54, p. 115)

An extensive knowledge . . . helps, by widening speculation, to ease the burden of the mystery . . . (Letter 64, p. 140)

. . . they both end in speculation. (Letter 93, p. 228)

. . . if I ever am free from speculating on creations of my own brain . . . (Letter 93, p. 228)

. . . fill'd with speculations even of an unpleasant colour . . . (Letter 123, p. 314)

This it is that makes the amusement of life—to a speculative mind. (Letter 123, p. 316)

. . . speculation of the differences of human character . . . (Letter 128, p. 346)

. . . home speculations every day continue to make me more iron. (Letter 145, p. 374)

. . . exerting myself against vexing speculations . . . (Letter 156, p. 421)

. . . mercantile speculations . . . (Letter 161, p. 437)

. . . you must not suffer such speculations to molest you any more . . . (Letter 197, pp. 476–77)

One of the most mysterious of semi-speculations . . . (Marginal note—M. B. Forman, *The Poetical Works* . . . , V, 294)

. . . the possible speculations of Satan in the serpent prison . . . (Marginal note—*Ibid.*, V, 305)

ABSTRACT

. . . not to put it to the account of heartlessness but abstraction . . . (Letter 31, p. 69)

. . . the abstract idea I had of an heroic painting . . . (Letter 59, p. 129)

. . . running one's rigs on the score of abstracted benefit . . . (Letter 64, pp. 140–41)

. . . the abstract endeavor of being able to add a mite to that mass of beauty . . . (Letter 71, pp. 156–57)

. . . in the most abstracted pleasure there is no lasting happiness . . . (Letter 75, p. 173)

. . . I am obliged to write, and plunge into abstract images . . . (Letter 86, p. 216)

. . . I have relapsed into those abstractions which are my only life . . . (Letter 87, p. 217)

. . . love of beauty in the abstract . . . (Letter 90, p. 222)

. . . that sort of abstract careless and restless life . . . (Letter 94, p. 229)

The mighty abstract idea I have of beauty in all things . . . (Letter 94, pp. 240–41)

. . . in the heathen mythologies abstractions are personified . . . (Letter 123, p. 337)

. . . a very abstract poem . . . (Letter 139, p. 361)

. . . an abstract exertion of mind. (Letter 155, p. 397)

Right and wrong considered by each man abstractedly . . . (Letter 156, p. 407)

. . . a sort of delphic abstraction . . . (Marginal note. See M. B. Forman, *The Poetical Works* . . . , V, 295)

IMAGINATION

. . . a trial of my powers of imagination . . . (Letter 25, p. 52)

. . . as fancy is the sails, and imagination the rudder. (*Ibid.*, p. 53)

. . . talking about the imagination . . . (Letter 31, p. 67)

. . . the authenticity of the imagination. (*Ibid.*)

. . . the truth of imagination . . . (*Ibid.*)

What the imagination seizes as beauty . . . (*Ibid.*)

The imagination may be compared to Adam's dream . . . (*Ibid.*, p. 68)

. . . imagination and its empyreal reflection . . . (*Ibid.*)

. . . the simple imaginative mind . . . (*Ibid.*)

. . . on the wings of imagination so high . . . (*Ibid.*)

. . . a regular stepping of the imagination towards a truth. (Letter 42, p. 91)

. . . a few fine imaginative or domestic passages . . . (Letter 44, p. 96)

Women must want imagination . . . (Letter 69, p. 152)

. . . a luxurious imagination . . . (Letter 75, p. 173)

. . . you must allow for imagination. (Letter 79, p. 191)

. . . because they fall so far beneath my boyish imagination? (*Ibid.*, p. 192)

. . . as my imagination strengthens . . . (Letter 94, p. 241)

. . . you can imagine a Roman triumph . . . (Letter 98, p. 259)

. . . so much room for imagination. (Letter 98, p. 260)

What imagination I have I shall enjoy . . . (Letter 115, p. 285)

. . . we must temper the imagination . . . (Letter 123, p. 331)

. . . my troubles were all of the imagination . . . (Letter 127, p. 345)

. . . plunged so deeply into imaginary interests. (Letter 143, p. 369)

. . . the dull imaginations of my own brain. (*Ibid.*, p. 370)

Upon my soul 'twas imagination . . . (Letter 151, p. 385)

Imaginary grievances . . . (Letter 155, p. 397)

. . . I describe what I imagine. (Letter 156, p. 413)

. . . your imagination may not have time . . . (Letter 157, p. 431)

. . . I have imagined my illness more serious . . . (Letter 201, p. 480)

My imagination is a monastery . . . (Letter 227, p. 507)

. . . to employ your imagination . . . (Letter 234, p. 516)

FANCY

. . . as fancy is the sails, and imagination the rudder. (Letter 25, p. 53)

. . . a representation from the fancy . . . (Letter 31, p. 68)

. . . perplexed in a world of doubts and fancies . . . (Letter 37, p. 80)

Fancy is indeed less than a present palpable reality . . . (Letter 96, p. 178)

. . . my fancy was afraid of it . . . (Letter 135, p. 356)

. . . sweet again to my fancy . . . (Letter 143, p. 371)

. . . persuade myself to untether fancy . . . (Letter 166, p. 439)

. . . created them with a superhuman fancy. (Letter 183, p. 465)

. . . the fancy's creating a world of its own . . . (Marginal note. See M. B. Forman, *The Poetical Works* . . . , V, 298)

B. SUPPLEMENTARY EVIDENCE OF RELATIVISM

Passages showing Keats's consciousness of the relativism of his judgments may be found on the following pages of the Letters (same edition as cited in Appendix A) : pp. 69, 104–5, 141–45, 208, 227–29, 252, 259, 318, 393.

Passages revealing Keats's consciousness of the fluctuating, unsteady, and even capricious character of his mind may be found on the following pages of the Letters: pp. 39, 68, 142–43, 191, 329, 385.

INDEX